# THE RUSSIAN REVOLUTION

WITHDRAWN FROM HAVERING COLLEGES
SIXTH FORM LIBRARY

06460

*By the same author*

A HISTORY OF SOVIET RUSSIA
*in fourteen volumes*

1. THE BOLSHEVIK REVOLUTION, *Volume One*
2. THE BOLSHEVIK REVOLUTION, *Volume Two*
3. THE BOLSHEVIK REVOLUTION, *Volume Three*
4. THE INTERREGNUM
5. SOCIALISM IN ONE COUNTRY, *Volume One*
6. SOCIALISM IN ONE COUNTRY, *Volume Two*
7. SOCIALISM IN ONE COUNTRY, *Volume Three, Part I*
8. SOCIALISM IN ONE COUNTRY. *Volume Three, Part II*
9. *FOUNDATIONS OF A PLANNED ECONOMY, *Volume One, Part I*
10. *FOUNDATIONS OF A PLANNED ECONOMY, *Volume One, Part II*
11. FOUNDATIONS OF A PLANNED ECONOMY, *Volume Two*
12. FOUNDATIONS OF A PLANNED ECONOMY, *Volume Three, Part I*
13. FOUNDATIONS OF A PLANNED ECONOMY, *Volume Three, Part II*
14. FOUNDATIONS OF A PLANNED ECONOMY, *Volume Three, Part III*

MICHAEL BAKUNIN
INTERNATIONAL RELATIONS BETWEEN THE TWO WORLD
   WARS, 1919–1939
THE TWENTY YEARS' CRISIS, 1919–1939
NATIONALISM AND AFTER
THE NEW SOCIETY
1917: BEFORE AND AFTER
WHAT IS HISTORY?
FROM NAPOLEON TO STALIN
THE TWILIGHT OF COMINTERN, 1930–1935
THE COMINTERN AND THE SPANISH CIVIL WAR

* *with R. W. Davies*

947.084 (HIST)

# THE RUSSIAN REVOLUTION

## FROM LENIN TO STALIN (1917–1929)

Edward Hallett Carr
*Sometime Fellow of Trinity College*
*Cambridge*

HAVERING SIXTH FORM COLLEGE LIBRARY

**M**
PAPERMAC

© Edward Hallet Carr 1979

All rights reserved. No reproduction, copy or transmission of this
publication may be made without written permission. No
paragraph of this publication may be reproduced, copied or
transmitted save with written permission or in accordance with
the provisions of the Copyright Act 1956 (as amended). Any
person who does any unauthorised act in relation to this
publication may be liable to criminal prosecution and civil
claims for damages.

*First published 1979 by Macmillan Press Ltd*

*Reprinted 1983*

*First published in paperback 1980 by*
*PAPERMAC*
*A division of Pan Macmillan Publishers Ltd*
*18–21 Cavaye Place London SW10 9PG*
*and Basingstoke*
*Associated companies throughout the world*

*Reprinted 1981, 1983 (twice), 1985, 1987 (twice), 1989, 1990, 1991*

Printed in Hong Kong

---

British Library Cataloguing in Publication Data

Carr, Edward Hallett
  The Russian revolution
  I.Russia — History — 1917 —
  I. Title.
  947.084'1      DK265

  Hardcover ISBN 0-333-23342-5
  Papermac ISBN 0-333-29036-4

---

# Contents

|  |  |  |
|---|---|---|
| *Foreword* | | vii |
| *List of Abbreviations* | | ix |
| 1 | October 1917 | 1 |
| 2 | The Two Worlds | 9 |
| 3 | War Communism | 20 |
| 4 | The Breathing-Space of NEP | 30 |
| 5 | The New Soviet Order | 38 |
| 6 | The Scissors Crisis | 50 |
| 7 | Lenin's Last Days | 61 |
| 8 | The Rise of Stalin | 68 |
| 9 | The USSR and the West (1923–1927) | 84 |
| 10 | The USSR and the East (1923–1927) | 95 |
| 11 | The Beginnings of Planning | 106 |
| 12 | The Defeat of the Opposition | 115 |
| 13 | The Dilemma of Agriculture | 123 |
| 14 | Growing Pains of Industrialization | 131 |
| 15 | The First Five-Year Plan | 141 |
| 16 | The Collectivization of the Peasant | 153 |
| 17 | Patterns of Dictatorship | 163 |
| 18 | The USSR and the World (1927–1929) | 173 |
| 19 | The Revolution in Perspective | 185 |
| *Index* | | 193 |

# Foreword

The large *History of Soviet Russia* which has occupied me
for the past thirty years, and has just been completed in
four instalments, *The Bolshevik Revolution, 1917–1923, The Interregnum, 1923–1924, Socialism in One Country, 1924–1926,* and *Foundations of a Planned Economy, 1926–1929,* was based on much
detailed research and designed for specialists. It occurred
to me that some purpose might be served by distilling this
research into a short book of a quite different kind, without
the scholarly refinements of source references or footnotes,
designed for the general reader and for the student seeking
a first introduction to the subject. The result is the present
short history. The difference in scale and purpose means
that this is substantially a new composition. Scarcely a sentence
from the original work reappears unchanged in the new.

*The Russian Revolution: from Lenin to Stalin, 1917–1929* covers
the same period as the large history. This is a period for
which (in contrast with the later years) ample contemporary
Soviet sources are available. It is also a period which contained
in embryo much of the subsequent course of Soviet history;
an understanding of what happened then is needed to explain
what happened afterwards. To describe the nineteen-twenties
in terms of a transition from the Russian revolution of Lenin
to the Russian revolution of Stalin would, no doubt, be
an over-simplification. But it would personify an important
historical process, the conclusion of which still lies in the
unforeseeable future.

The many friends and colleagues whose names are cited in the prefaces to successive volumes of the large history also claim acknowledgment here as indirect contributors to the present work. To Professor R. W. Davies, who collaborated with me in the first volume of *Foundations of a Planned Economy, 1926–1929*, I am specially indebted for expert criticism of the chapters on industrialization and planning; and I have read with profit Professor Alec Nove's concise *Economic History of the USSR*. My warm thanks are once more due to Tamara Deutscher for her unfailing help in the preparation of this volume.

*November 7 1977*

E. H. CARR

# List of Abbreviations

| | |
|---|---|
| Arcos | All-Russian Cooperative Society |
| CCP | Chinese Communist Party |
| CER | Chinese Eastern Railway |
| Cheka | Extraordinary Commission |
| Comintern | Communist International |
| CPGB | Communist Party of Great Britain |
| Glavk(i) | Chief Committee(s) |
| Goelro | State Commission for the Electrification of Russia |
| Gosplan | State Planning Commission |
| GPU | State Political Administration |
| IFTU | International Federation of Trade Unions |
| IKKI | Executive Committee of the Communist International |
| Kadet | Constitutional-Democrat |
| Khozraschet | Commercial Accounting |
| Kolkhoz(y) | Collective Farm(s) |
| KPD | German Communist Party |
| MTS | Machine Tractor Station |
| Narkomfin | People's Commissariat of Finance |
| Narkomindel | People's Commissariat of Foreign Affairs |
| Narkomprod | People's Commissariat of Supply |
| Narkomtrud | People's Commissariat of Labour |
| Narkomzem | People's Commissariat of Agriculture |
| NEP | New Economic Policy |

| | |
|---|---|
| NMM | National Minority Movement |
| NUWM | National Unemployed Workers' Movement |
| OGPU | Unified State Political Administration |
| PCF | French Communist Party |
| PCI | Italian Communist Party |
| Profintern | Red International of Trade Unions (RILU) |
| RSFSR | Russian Socialist Federal Soviet Republic |
| Sovkhoz(y) | Soviet Farm(s) |
| Sovnarkhoz(y) | Council(s) of National Economy |
| Sovnarkom | Council of People's Commissars |
| SPD | German Social-Democratic Party |
| SR | Social-Revolutionary |
| TsIK | Central Executive Committee |
| USPD | German Independent Social-Democratic Party |
| USSR | Union of Soviet Socialist Republics |
| VAPP | All-Russian Association of Proletarian Writers |
| Vesenkha | Supreme Council of National Economy |
| VTsIK | All-Russian Central Executive Committee |

# 1 October 1917

THE Russian revolution of 1917 was a turning-point in history, and may well be assessed by future historians as the greatest event of the twentieth century. Like the French revolution, it will continue for a long time to polarize opinion, being hailed by some as a landmark in the emancipation of mankind from past oppression, and denounced by others as a crime and a disaster. It presented the first open challenge to the capitalist system, which had reached its peak in Europe at the end of the nineteenth century. Its occurrence at the height of the first world war, and partly as a result of that war, was more than a coincidence. The war had struck a deadly blow at the international capitalist order as it had existed before 1914, and revealed its inherent instability. The revolution may be thought of both as a consequence and as a cause of the decline of capitalism.

While, however, the revolution of 1917 had a world-wide significance, it was also rooted in specifically Russian conditions. The imposing façade of the Tsarist autocracy concealed a stagnant rural economy, which had made few substantial advances since the emancipation of the serfs, and a hungry and restive peasantry. Terrorist groups had been at work since the eighteen-sixties with recurrent outbreaks of violence and repression. This period saw the rise of the *narodnik* movement, later succeeded by the Social-Revolutionary Party, whose appeal was to the peasants. After 1890 industrialization began to make important inroads into the primitive Russian economy; and the rise of an increasingly influential and wealthy industrial and financial class, heavily dependent on foreign capital, encouraged the infiltration of some liberal western ideas, which found their fullest expression in the Kadet (Constitutional-De-

mocratic) Party. But this process was accompanied by the
growth of a proletariat of factory workers and by the early
symptoms of proletarian turbulence; the first strikes occurred
in the eighteen-nineties. These developments were reflected
in the foundation in 1898 of the Marxist Russian Social-Democratic Workers' Party, the party of Lenin, Martov and Plekhanov. Seething unrest was brought to the surface by the
frustrations and humiliations of the Russo-Japanese war.

The first Russian revolution of 1905 had a mixed character.
It was a revolt of bourgeois liberals and constitutionalists
against an arbitrary and antiquated autocracy. It was a revolt
of workers, sparked off by the atrocity of "Bloody Sunday",
and leading to the election of the first Petersburg Soviet
of Workers' Deputies. It was a widespread revolt of peasants,
spontaneous and uncoordinated, often extremely bitter and
violent. The three strands were never woven together, and
the revolution was easily put down at the cost of some largely
unreal constitutional concessions. The same factors inspired
the revolution of February 1917, but this time were reinforced
and dominated by war-weariness and universal discontent
with the conduct of the war. Nothing short of the Tsar's
abdication could stem the tide of revolt. Autocracy was replaced by the proclamation of a democratic Provisional Government based on the authority of the Duma. But the hybrid
character of the revolution was once more immediately apparent. Side by side with the Provisional Government, the Petrograd Soviet—the capital had changed its name in 1914—was
reconstituted on the model of 1905.

The revolution of February 1917 brought back to Petrograd,
from Siberia and from exile abroad, a host of formerly pro-
scribed revolutionaries. Most of these belonged to one of
the two wings—Bolshevik and Menshevik—of the Social-Democratic Workers' Party or to the Social-Revolutionary Party
(SRs), and found a ready-made platform in the Petrograd
Soviet. The Soviet was in one sense a rival of the Provisional
Government set up by the constitutional parties in the old
Duma; the phrase "dual power" was coined to describe an
ambiguous situation. But the initial attitude of the Soviet
was less clear-cut. Marx's historical scheme had postulated
two distinct and successive revolutions—bourgeois and socialist.
Members of the Soviet, with few exceptions, were content

DUAL POWER - PROVISIONAL GOVT + PETROGRAD
                                      SOVIET.

to recognize the events of February as the Russian bourgeois revolution which would establish a bourgeois-democratic régime on the western model, and relegated the socialist revolution to a still undetermined date in the future. Cooperation with the Provisional Government was the corollary of this view, which was shared by the first two leading Bolsheviks to return to Petrograd, Kamenev and Stalin.

Lenin's dramatic arrival in Petrograd at the beginning of April shattered this precarious compromise. Lenin, at first almost alone even among the Bolsheviks, attacked the assumption that the current upheaval in Russia was a bourgeois revolution and nothing more. The situation as it developed after the February revolution confirmed Lenin's view that it could not be confined within bourgeois limits. What followed the collapse of the autocracy was not so much a bifurcation of authority (the "dual power") as a total dispersal of authority. The mood of workers and peasants alike, of the vast majority of the population, was one of immense relief at the removal of a monstrous incubus, accompanied by a deep-seated desire to be left to run their own affairs in their own way, and by the conviction that this was somehow practicable and essential. It was a mass movement inspired by a wave of immense enthusiasm and by Utopian visions of the emancipation of mankind from the shackles of a remote and despotic power. It had no use for the western principles of parliamentary democracy and constitutional government proclaimed by the Provisional Government. The notion of centralized authority was tacitly rejected. Local Soviets of workers or peasants sprang up all over Russia. Some towns and districts declared themselves Soviet republics. Factory committees of workers claimed to exercise exclusive authority in their domain. The peasants seized land and divided it among themselves. And everything else was overshadowed by the demand for peace, for an end to the horrors of a bloody and senseless war. Soldiers' Committees were elected in military units, large and small, from brigades to companies, often demanding the election of officers and challenging their authority. The armies at the front cast off the harsh constraints of military discipline, and slowly began to disintegrate. This all-engulfing movement of revolt against authority seemed to most Bolsheviks a prelude to the fulfilment of their dreams of a new order of society; they had neither the will nor the means to check it.

When, therefore, Lenin set out to re-define the character of the revolution in his famous "April theses", his diagnosis was both perceptive and prescient. He described what had happened as a revolution in transition from a first stage, which had given power to the bourgeoisie, to a second stage, which would transfer power to the workers and the poor peasants. The Provisional Government and the Soviets were not allies but antagonists, representing different classes. The end in view was not a parliamentary republic, but "a republic of Soviets of Workers', Poor Peasants' and Peasants' Deputies all over the country, growing up from below". Socialism could not indeed be introduced immediately. But as a first step the Soviets should take control of "social production and distribution". Throughout the vicissitudes of the summer of 1917 Lenin gradually secured the adherence of his party followers to this programme. Progress in the Soviets was slower. When an All-Russian Congress of Soviets—the first attempt to create a central Soviet organization with a standing executive committee—met in June, out of more than 800 delegates, the SRs accounted for 285, the Mensheviks for 248, the Bolsheviks only for 105. It was on this occasion that Lenin, in response to a challenge, made the much-derided pronouncement that there was in the Soviet a party ready to take governmental power: the Bolsheviks. As the prestige and authority of the Provisional Government waned, the influence of the Bolsheviks in the factories and in the army grew rapidly; and in July the Provisional Government decided to proceed against them on a charge of conducting subversive propaganda in the army and acting as German agents. Several leaders were arrested. Lenin escaped to Finland, where he carried on a regular correspondence with the party central committee, now working underground in Petrograd.

It was during this forced withdrawal from the scene of action that Lenin penned one of the most famous, and the most Utopian, of his writings, *State and Revolution*, a study of Marx's theory of the state. Marx had not only preached the destruction of the bourgeois state by the proletarian revolution, but looked forward, after the victory of the revolution and a transitional period of the dictatorship of the proletariat, to the withering away and eventual extinction of the state. What the proletariat needed at the moment of its victory, Lenin observed, was "only a state in process of dying away, i.e. so constituted that it will at once begin to die away and cannot help dying away". The state was always an instrument of class domination and oppression. The classless society of communism and the existence of the state were incompatible. Lenin summed up in an aphorism of his own: "So long as the state exists, there is no freedom. When freedom exists, there will be no state." Lenin was not only a profound student of Marx, but had a sensitive ear for the revolutionary mood of workers and peasants whose enthusiasm was fired by the prospect of escaping from the shackles of a powerful and omnipresent state. *State and Revolution* was a remarkable synthesis of the teachings of Marx with the aspirations of the untutored masses. The party was scarcely mentioned in its pages.

By September, after an abortive attempt to seize power by a Right-wing general, Kornilov, the Bolsheviks had won a majority in the Petrograd and Moscow Soviets. Lenin, after some hesitation, revived the slogan "All power to the Soviets"—a direct challenge to the Provisional Government. In October he returned in disguise to Petrograd to attend a meeting of the party central committee. Under his persuasion the committee decided, with only two dissentients, Zinoviev and Kamenev, to prepare for an immediate seizure of power. The preparation was carried out mainly by a revolutionary military committee which had been set up by the executive committee of the Petrograd Soviet, and which was now firmly in Bolshevik hands. Trotsky, who had joined the Bolsheviks after his return to Petrograd in the summer, played a leading part in planning the operation. On October 25 (Old Style, equivalent to November 7 by the western calendar, which was introduced a few months later) the Red Guard, composed mainly of factory workers, occupied key positions in the city, and advanced on the Winter Palace. It was a bloodless *coup*. The Provisional Government collapsed without resistance. Some of the ministers were arrested. The Prime Minister, Kerensky, fled abroad.

The *coup* had been timed to coincide with the second All-Russian Congress of Soviets of Workers' and Soldiers'

Deputies, which opened on the following evening. The Bolsheviks now had a majority—399 out of a total of 649 delegates—and took charge of the proceedings. The congress pronounced the dissolution of the Provisional Government, and the transfer of authority to the Soviets, and unanimously adopted three major decrees, the first two being submitted to it by Lenin. The first was a proclamation, in the name of the "Workers' and Peasants' Government", proposing to all the belligerent peoples and governments to enter into negotiations for a "just and democratic peace" without annexations or indemnities, and appealing particularly to "the class-conscious workers of the three most advanced nations of mankind"—Britain, France and Germany—to help to bring the war to an end. The second was a decree on land, incorporating a text drawn up by the SRs, which responded to the petty bourgeois aspirations of the peasant rather than to long-term Bolshevik theories of a socialized agriculture. Landlords' ownership of land was abolished without compensation; only the land of "ordinary peasants and ordinary Cossacks" was exempt from confiscation. Private ownership of land was abolished for ever. The right of using land was accorded to "all citizens (without distinction of sex) of the Russian state desiring to cultivate it with their own labour". Mineral and other subsidiary rights were reserved to the state. The buying, selling and leasing of land, and the employment of hired labour, were prohibited. This was the charter of the small, independent peasant cultivating his plot of land with his own labour and that of his family, and serving primarily their needs. A final settlement of the land question was reserved for the future Constituent Assembly. The third decree, proposed by Kamenev, who presided at the session, set up a Council of People's Commissars (Sovnarkom) as a Provisional Workers' and Peasants' Government to govern the country under the authority of the All-Russian Congress of Soviets and of its executive committee till the meeting of the Constituent Assembly.

These pronouncements had several distinctive features. Lenin had ended his speech a few hours earlier in the Petrograd Soviet with the bold words: "In Russia we must concern ourselves with the building of the proletarian socialist state." In the more formal decrees of the Congress of Soviets, the concepts of "the state" and of "socialism" were kept in the background. In the enthusiasm of victory, when the old state with its attendant evils was being swept away, nobody was eager to face the problem of building a new state. The revolution was international, and took no account of national boundaries. The Workers' and Peasants' Government had no territorial definition or designation; the ultimate extension of its authority could not be foreseen. Socialism was an ideal of the future; Lenin observed, in introducing the decree on peace, that the victory of the workers would "pave the way to peace and socialism". But none of the decrees mentioned socialism as the aim or purpose of the revolution; its content, like its extent, was left to the future to decide.

Finally, the gesture of deference to the ultimate authority of the Constituent Assembly, which in retrospect seemed oddly illogical, was accepted without objection. Between February and October the Provisional Government and the Soviets had both demanded a constituent assembly—the traditional democratic procedure for the drafting of a new constitution; and the date of November 12 had been fixed for the elections. Lenin did not wish, or did not feel strong enough, to cancel them. As was to be expected in a predominantly rural electorate, the vote gave an absolute majority to the SRs—267 out of 520 deputies; the Bolsheviks had 161, the remainder being made up of a large number of splinter groups. When the deputies met in January 1918, the Workers' and Peasants' Government was firmly established in Petrograd, and was unlikely to abdicate in favour of a body which represented the confused moods of the countryside two months earlier. Bukharin spoke of "the watershed which at this moment divides this assembly into . . . two irreconcilable camps, camps of principle . . . for socialism or against socialism". The assembly listened to much inconclusive oratory. Late in the night it adjourned; and the government forcibly prevented it from re-assembling. It was a decisive moment. The revolution had turned its back on the conventions of bourgeois democracy.

The first consequence of the revolution to impinge on the western world, and to excite horror and indignation, was its withdrawal from the war and its desertion of the Allies at the desperate peak of their struggle with Germany. When this unforgivable betrayal was quickly followed by such measures as the repudiation of the debts of former Russian Governments and the expropriation of owners of land and factories, and when the revolution announced itself as the first stage in a revolution which was destined to sweep over Europe and the world, it was revealed as a fundamental assault on the whole of western capitalist society. But this threat was not taken very seriously. Few people in the west at first imagined that the revolutionary régime in Russia could survive for more than a few days or weeks. The Bolshevik leaders themselves did not believe that they could hold out indefinitely, unless the workers of the capitalist countries came to their aid by rising in revolt against their own governments.

This scepticism did not lack plausibility. The writ of the Workers' and Peasants' Government scarcely extended beyond Petrograd and a few other large cities. Even in the Soviets the Bolsheviks did not yet command unanimous support; and it was quite uncertain how far the All-Russian Congress of Soviets—the one sovereign central authority—would be recognized by the local Soviets which had sprung up all over the country, by the factory committees exercising "workers' control" in the factories, or by the millions of peasants now flocking back to their homes from the front. Bureaucrats, managers, and technical experts at all levels came out on strike, and refused to serve the new self-styled government. The armed forces at the disposal of the régime consisted of a nucleus of a few thousand Red Guards, and some loyal Lettish battalions surviving from the disintegration of the imperial armies which had fought in the war. Within a few weeks of the revolution, Cossack armies pledged to its overthrow were being organized in the regions of the Don, the Kuban, and the Urals. It had been easy for the Bolsheviks to topple the rickety Provisional Government. To substitute themselves for it, to establish effective control over the chaos which had overwhelmed the vast territory of the defunct Russian Empire, and to set up a new order of society geared to the aspirations of the masses of workers and peasants who had seen in the Bolsheviks their saviours and liberators, was a far more formidable and complex task.

# 2 The Two Worlds

THE first constitutional act which gave the Workers' and Peasants' Government a territorial name was the Declaration of Rights of the Toiling and Exploited People issued by the third All-Russian Congress of Soviets in January 1918—the Bolshevik counterpart of the Declaration of the Rights of Man and of the Citizen promulgated by the French revolution. This proclaimed Russia to be a Republic of Soviets of Workers', Soldiers' and Peasants' Deputies, adding that "the Russian Soviet Republic is founded on the basis of a free union of free nations, as a federation of Soviet national republics". The form of words preserved the international intentions of the revolutionary régime. Revolution was essentially international; it implied the substitution of class war for war between rival Powers. But the promotion of world revolution was also a prime necessity of the struggling Soviet régime. It was the only weapon available to the Bolsheviks when confronted with the embattled imperialist Powers; and without revolution, at any rate in the principal belligerent countries, the régime could hardly hope to survive. Nor could any distinction be drawn between the two belligerent camps; both were equally standard-bearers of the capitalist order, which the revolution sought to destroy. Hence any conception of foreign policy other than propaganda for revolution was at first alien to Bolshevik thinking. Trotsky, the first People's Commissar for Foreign Affairs, observed epigrammatically: "I will issue a few revolutionary proclamations to the peoples of the world, and then shut up shop."

External realities, however, soon dissipated this vision, and forced on the struggling Soviet republic the rôle of a national state in a world of national states. The appeal to the warring nations for peace negotiations had fallen on deaf ears. Something had to be done about relations with Germany, whose armies had penetrated deep into Russian territory, and were still conducting operations of war. One of the first acts of the new government was to conclude an armistice with the imperial German Government and to sue for peace. In February 1918 peace negotiations opened at Brest-Litovsk. Trotsky, who led the Soviet delegation, demonstratively abandoned the traditional practices of diplomacy, appealed to the belligerent peoples over the heads of their governments, openly carried on anti-war propaganda among the German troops, and embarrassed the German delegation by pressing the demand for "peace without annexations or indemnities", which Germany, in dealings with the western Allies, had purported to accept.

But German intransigence and the overwhelming superiority of German arms presented an inescapable dilemma. Trotsky could not reconcile it with his revolutionary principles to sign a humiliating treaty with an imperialist Power—a course which Lenin came to regard as inevitable. On the other hand, his sense of reality did not allow him to support the demands of Bukharin and other "Left communists" for a renewal of "revolutionary war". He devised the formula "No peace, no war". When, however, the Germans, not impressed by this undiplomatic eccentricity, resumed their advance, the same dilemma recurred in still starker form. Trotsky reluctantly cast his vote with Lenin for the acceptance of what Lenin himself called a "shameful" peace, involving the abandonment of the Ukraine, and of other large areas of former Russian territory, and resigned his post as People's Commissar for Foreign Affairs. The treaty was signed on March 3, 1918, and the German advance stayed. Simultaneously with the Brest-Litovsk negotiations, informal—and fruitless—approaches were made to British, French and American representatives in the hope of soliciting western aid against the Germans. These overtures to capitalist governments, no less than the signature of the Brest-Litovsk treaty, were bitterly resented, as a derogation from the international principles of the revolution, by a substantial minority of the party central committee, headed by Bukharin; and all Lenin's influence was required to secure approval for them.

The lessons of military impotence had now been borne in on the Bolshevik leaders. On February 23, 1918, even before the Brest-Litovsk treaty was signed, the Red Army, originally called "the Workers' and Peasants' Red Army" came into being; the date has since been celebrated annually as the birthday of the Red Army. Its name was intended to indicate its international revolutionary character and purpose. But the proclamation announcing its foundation was headed "The Socialist Fatherland in Danger", so that national as well as international consciousness presided over its birth. Trotsky was appointed People's Commissar for War with the task of organizing it. He was too much of a realist to suppose that an army could be built up out of raw untrained levies. His first response to the emergency was to recruit professional soldiers, former Tsarist officers, officially referred to as "military specialists", to train the new army. This expedient proved brilliantly successful. By the beginning of 1919 30,000 such officers had been enrolled. The Red Guard of 1917, which mustered barely 10,000 trained men, grew at the height of the civil war into a Red Army numbering five million. Trotsky himself displayed exceptional military talents. But he was also known for ruthlessness in his demand for unquestioning obedience and in punishing defaulters; and he had to extol virtues of military discipline which the revolution had set out to destroy. Desperate remedies were required in a desperate situation.

These expedients did not end the dangers besetting the régime, now transferred from Petrograd to its new capital, Moscow. Hostile "White" Russian military forces began to muster in different parts of the country. The German army remained, by agreement with a puppet national Ukrainian Government, in occupation of the Ukraine. The western governments, outraged by the revolution and by the Russian desertion of the Allies in the hour of their greatest need, decided to act. In March 1918 British, followed by French and American, forces occupied the northern port of Murmansk—ostensibly to protect the military stores accumulated there against a further German irruption. Meanwhile, the many thousand Czech prisoners of war in Russia, mainly deserters from the Austrian army, formed themselves into a Czech legion, and with the agreement of the Soviet Government set out for Vladivostok to embark there for the west. In Siberia the well-organized legionaries clashed with scattered and ineffective Soviet authorities, and—perhaps at first unwittingly—became a rallying-point for anti-Bolshevik forces. In April 1918 the Japanese Government, unwilling to be left out of the act, landed troops in Vladivostok, followed by British and American detachments two months later. In July British, French and American forces occupied Archangel. The survival of the Workers' and Peasants' Government in Moscow in the summer and autumn of 1918 seemed due not so much to its own strength as to the fact that the nations were linked in a life-and-death struggle on the western front, and had little thought for what happened elsewhere.

The collapse of Germany, and the armistice of November 11, 1918, gave a fresh turn to the screw. The incipient revolutionary situation in Berlin in the two months after the armistice, the successful revolutionary *coups* a few months later in Bavaria and in Hungary, as well as sporadic unrest in Britain, France and Italy, led the Bolshevik leaders to believe that the long-awaited European revolution was maturing. But events which offered hope and comfort to Moscow intensified the fear and hatred felt by the western governments for the revolutionary régime, and sharpened their determination to uproot it. The pretext that military operations in Russia were a subsidiary part of the war against Germany was perforce abandoned. Support was openly extended to Russian armies committed to the crusade against Bolshevism in Archangel, in Siberia, and in southern Russia. Now, however, a fresh complication occurred. The Allied troops, affected partly by war-weariness and partly by more or less outspoken sympathy for the workers' government in Moscow, were plainly unwilling to continue the fight. In April 1919 a mutiny in French naval vessels in Odessa forced the evacuation of the port. In Archangel and Murmansk the same end to the adventure was forestalled by the progressive withdrawal of the Allied troops. By the autumn of 1919 no Allied armed forces (except for Japanese and American contingents in Vladivostok) remained on Russian soil.

This set-back in no way modified the hostile intentions of the western Allies, who sought to compensate for the withdrawal of troops by an increased flow of military supplies, military missions, and verbal assurances to a number of would-be Russian "governments" arrayed against the Bolsheviks. The most promising of these was formed under the leadership of Kolchak, a former Tsarist admiral, who established some kind of authority over much of Siberia and began to move into European Russia; and in the summer of 1919 the Allied statesmen assembled in Paris for the peace conference entered into negotiations, which proved inconclusive, for the recognition of the Kolchak régime as the sole legitimate Russian Government. Denikin, a Tsarist general, enjoying strong Allied support, controlled southern Russia, overran the Ukraine, and in the autumn of 1919 reached a point 200 miles south of Moscow; and Yudenich, another general, mustered a White army in the Baltic for an assault on Petrograd. By this time, however, the Red Army had become an effective, though ill-equipped, fighting force. The various White armies were unable either to coordinate their efforts or to win the support of the populations in whose territories they operated. By the end of the year they were in headlong retreat. In January 1920 Kolchak was captured and executed by the Bolsheviks. By the spring of that year the White forces, except for a few isolated pockets of resistance, had been everywhere dispersed and destroyed.

The civil war hardened the stereotype, which had been shaping itself both in western and in Soviet thinking since October 1917, of two worlds confronting each other in irreconcilable contradiction—the capitalist world and the world of the revolution dedicated to overthrow it. After the collapse of German power in November 1918 Central Europe briefly became a bone of contention between the two worlds. The whiff of revolution in Berlin in January 1919 favoured the confident belief of the Bolsheviks that the death-knell of capitalism had sounded, and that the wave of revolution was in the process of spreading westward from Moscow. It was in this atmosphere that Lenin set out to realize an ambition nourished by him ever since the autumn of 1914—to replace the defunct Second or Social-Democratic International, which had split and destroyed itself on the outbreak of war through its abandonment of the principles of Marxism and internationalism, by a truly revolutionary Third or Communist International. It was the logical sequel of a decision taken by the party congress in March 1918 to replace the old party name Russian Social-Democratic Workers' Party, now sullied through its association with German social-democrats and Mensheviks, by the name Russian Communist Party (Bolsheviks).

Early in March 1919 more than 50 communists and sympathizers assembled in Moscow, of whom 35 held mandates from communist or near-communist parties or groups in 19 countries; many of these were small countries which had once formed part of the Russian Empire, and were now recognized as Soviet republics, including the Ukraine, Belorussia, the Baltic countries, Armenia and Georgia. The newly-founded German Communist Party sent a delegate with instructions to raise no objection of principle, but to seek a postponement of the creation of the International to a more propitious moment. Travel to Moscow from the west was virtually impossible. Groups in the United States, France, Switzerland, the Netherlands, Sweden and Hungary had given mandates to nationals resident in Moscow; the one British delegate had no mandate at all. The caution of the German delegate was overruled by the weight of enthusiasm. The arrival of a revolutionary Austrian delegate is said to have tipped the scale. The congress, constituting itself as the first congress of the Communist International (Comintern), voted a manifesto, drafted by Trotsky, tracing the decay of capitalism and the advance of communism since the *Communist Manifesto* of 1848; theses prepared by Lenin which denounced bourgeois democracy, proclaimed the dictatorship of the proletariat, and derided attempts to revive the discredited Second International; and finally a topical appeal to the workers of the world to bring pressure on their governments to end military intervention in Russia and recognize the Soviet régime. By way of providing the new-born International with an organization, the congress elected an executive committee (IKKI), and named Zinoviev as its president and Radek, now in a Berlin prison, as its secretary. A few days after the congress ended, the short-lived Hungarian Soviet republic was proclaimed in Budapest.

The fact of the foundation of a Communist International was more important than anything done at its first congress.

It was a dramatic announcement of the rift between the two worlds, and in particular of the rift which had declared itself within the international workers' movement. The founders of Comintern firmly believed that the workers of western countries who had lived through the fratricidal slaughter of the war—and especially the German workers, well-schooled in Marxism—would quickly abandon the national Social-Democratic and Labour Parties which had involved them in the holocaust, and rally to the cause of the international unity of the workers of the world proclaimed by Comintern. When this did not happen, and when the Second International even showed signs of revival, the set-back was attributed to corrupt and treacherous leaders who had betrayed their misguided followers. But the rift in western countries between a minority of committed communists and a majority of workers who remained faithful to "reformist" leaders perpetuated itself, and deepened as time went on.

The breach was aggravated by unforeseen developments within Comintern itself. The outlook of its founders was genuinely international; they looked forward to the day when its headquarters might move to Berlin or Paris. But what happened in Moscow in March 1919 was not a fusion of national communist parties into one international organization, but the harnessing of a number of weak, embryonic foreign groups to an essentially Russian organization, whose resources and main motive force came necessarily and inevitably from the Russian party and the Soviet Government. Nor was this illogical. The promotion of international revolution had two aspects, which reinforced one another. It was an obligation of all Marxists, but it was also an important defensive weapon in the armoury of the hard-pressed Soviet régime. So long as the overthrow of capitalist domination elsewhere was seen as a condition of the survival of the revolutionary régime in Russia, there could be no incompatibility between the two elements; they were different facets of a single coherent and integrated purpose. But this meant that the commitment of foreign communist parties to Comintern had less strong foundations than the commitment which seemed obligatory in Moscow.

The remainder of 1919 was a period of civil war, Allied intervention and Soviet isolation. A brief respite followed the collapse of the White armies in the winter of 1919–1920; and it was in this interval, in April 1920, in preparation for the second congress of Comintern, that Lenin wrote his famous and influential pamphlet, *The Infantile Disease of "Leftism" in Communism*. The target of attack was a so-called Left opposition in communist parties which resisted "compromises" in the name of "principles"; Lenin recalled, in particular, the opposition to Brest-Litovsk. Communists in western countries must participate actively in parliaments and trade unions, and not shrink from the compromises inherent in such participation. Mindful of hostile British intervention in the civil war, Lenin urged British communists to conclude "electoral agreements" with the Labour Party in order to "help the Hendersons and the Snowdens to defeat Lloyd George and Churchill". But this advice was tendered against a background of confidence in the early prospect of revolution. The tactical prescriptions of the pamphlet were deeply imbued with the need to enlighten the rank and file of workers' parties on the true character of their leaders, and to split the parties against the leaders. Henderson was to be supported "as the rope supports the man who is being hanged". It did not enter into Lenin's calculations that such tactics of compromise and manoeuvre might be continued, in default of international revolution, for years or decades.

At the end of April 1920 Pilsudski launched a Polish invasion of the Ukraine, occupying Kiev early in May; and the Soviet republic was plunged once more into a crisis as grave as that of the civil war. But this time the resistance was swifter and stronger. In June the Red Army counter-attacked. The defeat of the over-extended Polish forces became a rout, and at the beginning of August the Red Army entered Polish territory. These dramatic events coincided with the second congress of Comintern, which opened on July 19, 1920, with more than 200 delegates. These included, besides delegates of the small German Communist Party (KPD), delegates of the German Independent Social-Democratic Party (USPD), a war-time break-away from the German Social-Democratic Party (SPD), as well as of the French and Italian Socialist Parties; these three parties were divided among themselves on the question of adhesion to Comintern, and had come to the congress for enlightenment. Delegates also came from several British groups of the extreme Left, which decided to merge in a Communist Party of Great Britain (CPGB). The debates, against a background of victories of the Red Army, were full of confidence and excitement. The prescriptions of Lenin's pamphlet were not forgotten. Resolutions were passed urging communists to work in trade unions and bourgeois parliaments; and the British Communist Party was instructed—by a majority vote—to seek affiliation to the Labour Party. But the prevailing mood was now quite different. The congress appealed to the workers of the world not to tolerate "any kind of help to White Poland, any kind of intervention against Soviet Russia". World revolution was kept well in the picture.

> The Communist International [declared a manifesto of the congress] proclaims the cause of Soviet Russia as its own cause. The international proletariat will not sheath the sword till Soviet Russia becomes a link in a federation of Soviet republics of the world.

The "21 conditions" of admission to Comintern drawn up by the congress were designed to exclude waverers, and to make Comintern, not (like the Second International) a loose association of widely differing parties, but a single homogeneous, disciplined party of the international proletariat. Never had the prospect of world revolution seemed so bright and so near.

While the congress debated, the Soviet leaders had to take a vital decision. Was the Red Army to stand on the Polish frontier, and offer terms of peace to Pilsudski? Or was it to continue its now almost unopposed advance on Warsaw and other industrial centres of Poland? Lenin declared for the advance, dazzled by the prospect that the Polish workers would welcome the Red Army as their deliverers from the capitalist yoke, and that revolution in Poland would open the gate-way to Germany and western Europe. Trotsky and Radek came out against him; Stalin seems to have shared their doubts, but was absent at the front at the time of the critical decision. Tukhachevsky, the brilliant commander who had led the counter-offensive, was all for the advance, and wished to make the Red Army the army of Comintern.

Boldness and enthusiasm carried the day. By the middle
of August the Red Army was deployed before Warsaw. Here,
however, the major miscalculation in these proceedings was
quickly revealed. The Polish workers did not stir; and Pilsudski
successfully appealed for national resistance to the Russian
invader. In the next few weeks, the Red Army suffered the
humiliations of precipitate retreat which it had so recently
inflicted on its adversaries. The armies finally came to rest
at a point far to the east of the so-called "Curzon line",
which had been recognized by the Allied governments, as
well as by the Soviet Government, as the eastern frontier
of Poland. Here an armistice was signed on October 12,
1920. The Soviet republic had paid a heavy price for its
revolutionary optimism.

The prestige of the Red Army was partially retrieved by
the ease with which it repelled an attack by Wrangel, the
last of the White generals, in southern Russia in the autumn
of 1920. But the defeat in Poland had lasting repercussions
on Soviet relations with the western world. The campaign
had been based on a conviction that the Polish workers
would revolt against their rulers, and in conjunction with
the Russian forces instal a revolutionary government in Warsaw. The disappointment of that hope showed that the Polish
workers, like those of western Europe, were still too deeply
imbued with national loyalties to embrace the cause of international proletarian revolution. Elsewhere in Europe, while the
workers continued to demonstrate sympathy and enthusiasm
for the Russian revolution, they showed no alacrity to raise
the banner of revolution in their own countries. In October
the USPD decided by a narrow majority to merge with
the KPD, leaving the rump of its membership, together with
the largest German workers' party, the SPD, to nourish feelings
of bitterness and resentment against the KPD and against
Comintern. A little later the French Socialist Party transformed
itself into the French Communist Party (PCF), leaving behind
a substantial minority of dissidents; and a split in the Italian
Socialist Party led to the creation of a small Italian Communist
Party (PCI). These additions to the membership of Comintern
were hailed as triumphs in Moscow. But they hardened the
mistrust of Comintern now prevailing in many sections of
the workers' movement in the west. An attempted revolution-

ary *coup* in Germany in March 1921 (see p. 44 below) was a dismal failure. The post-war revolutionary wave in Europe was visibly receding.

Another lesson could also be drawn from the military defeat in Poland. The Russian peasant who supplied the manpower of the Red Army, while stoutly defending the revolutionary cause in his homeland, had no stomach for a fight to transport revolution to other countries. The peasant, now beginning to revolt against the miseries and the devastation which were the aftermath of the civil war, was recalcitrant to hardships sustained in the name of international revolution. In the hard winter of 1920–21 peasant disturbances in central Russia concentrated the anxious attention of the leaders on domestic problems, and began insensibly to re-shape Soviet thinking about the western world. Visions of international revolution had been encouraged—almost imposed—by the traumatic experience of the civil war. Once this was overcome, the aim of international revolution, though not disavowed, was allowed quietly to recede into a more distant future. Security and stability were the paramount needs of the moment. In this mood, steps were taken, simultaneously with the introduction of NEP, to regularize Soviet relations with the non-Soviet world.

# 3 War Communism

THE hostility of the outside world was only one of the hazards confronting the Bolsheviks after their assumption of power. The revolution in Petrograd had been bloodless; but sharp fighting occurred in Moscow between Bolshevik units and military cadets loyal to the Provisional Government. Dispossessed political parties began to organize against the authority of the Soviets. Communications were halted by a strike of railway workers, whose trade union was controlled by Mensheviks. Administrative services were disrupted; and hooligans took advantage of the anarchic conditions to riot and plunder. Six weeks after the revolution a governmental decree brought into being the All-Russian Extraordinary Commission (Cheka) for "combating counter-revolution and sabotage"; and local Soviets were invited to set up similar commissions. A few days later a revolutionary tribunal was set up to try "those who organize risings against the Workers' and Peasants' Government, who actively oppose or do not obey it, or who incite others to oppose or disobey it". It was not till June 1918 that the revolutionary tribunal pronounced its first death sentence. But indiscriminate killings both of Bolsheviks and of their adversaries occurred in many parts of the country; and the Cheka became increasingly busy rounding up active opponents of the régime. In April 1918 several hundred anarchists were arrested in Moscow; in July the Cheka was called on to suppress an attempted *coup* by SRs, who assassinated the German Ambassador—apparently in protest against the Brest-Litovsk treaty. During the summer of 1918 two prominent Bolshevik leaders were assassinated in Petrograd, and shots were fired at Lenin in Moscow. The ferocity with which the civil war was fought heightened the tension. Atrocities

on one side were matched by reprisals on the other. "Red
terror" and "White terror" both entered the political vocabulary.

These desperate conditions were reflected in the total disarray
of the economy. During the war, production had been crippled
and distorted by military needs, and by the absence of agricultural and industrial workers at the front. The revolution
itself, and the ravages of the civil war, completed the picture
of economic, social and financial disintegration; hunger and
cold overtook large sectors of the population. Initial Bolshevik
remedies for economic ills did not go beyond the proclamation
of such general principles as equal distribution, nationalization
of industry and of the land, and workers' control. In the
first months of the revolution many industrial enterprises were
taken over, sometimes by state organs responsible to the
Supreme Council of National Economy (Vesenkha), sometimes
by the workers themselves. For agriculture the Bolsheviks,
who still had little power in the countryside, had adopted
the programme of the SRs, and proclaimed the "socialization"
of the land and its equal distribution among those who tilled
it. What happened in fact was that the peasants seized,
and distributed among themselves, the estates, large and small,
of the land-owning nobility, and the holdings of well-to-do
peasants, commonly dubbed *kulaks*, who had been enabled
to accumulate land by the Stolypin reforms. None of these
measures arrested the decline of production. In finance, the
banks were nationalized and foreign debts repudiated. But
it was impossible to collect regular taxes or to frame a state
budget; current needs were met by resort to the printing-press.

For six months the régime lived from hand to mouth.
Then the gathering storms of the civil war and the economic
collapse drove the government in the summer of 1918 to
the more drastic policies later known by the ambiguous name
of "war communism". Food was the first priority. The workers
in towns and factories were hungry. In May the word went
out to organize "food detachments" to visit the countryside
and collect grain from *kulaks* and speculators—the "rural
bourgeoisie"—who were believed to be hoarding it. A decree
of June 11, 1918, provided for the creation in the villages
of "committees of poor peasants", which "under the general
direction of the People's Commissariat of Supply (Narkom-

prod)" were to supervise the collection, distribution and despatch to the towns of grain and other agricultural produce. Lenin hailed the constitution of these committees as "the October, i.e. proletarian, revolution" in the countryside, and thought that it signalized the transition from the bourgeois to the socialist revolution. But the experiment was short-lived. The decree, like others of the period, was easier to write than to enforce. The spontaneous action of the peasants in the first year of the revolution resulted in the division of the land among a multiplicity of small cultivators living at subsistence level—an increase in the number, and reduction in the size, of units of cultivation which contributed nothing either to the efficiency of agriculture or to the supply of food to the towns, since the small producer was more likely to consume what he produced for his own needs. Poor peasants were not easily organized; and rivalry sprung up between the committees and the village Soviets. Class stratification in the villages was real enough. But the criteria of classification of the peasantry as *kulaks*, middle and poor peasants, were uncertain and fluctuating, and were partly dictated by the political requirements of the moment. *Kulak*, in particular, became a term of abuse directed by party propaganda against peasants who incurred the wrath of the authorities through failure to comply with demands for the delivery of grain. Nor could the poor peasants be counted on, as party leaders in Moscow expected, to act as allies of the government against the *kulaks*. The poor peasant was conscious of the oppression which he suffered at the hands of the *kulak*. But his dread of the state and its minions was often greater; and he was apt to prefer the evil that he knew to the menace of a remote authority.

In December 1918 the committees of poor peasants were abolished, and the authorities switched their appeal to the so-called "middle peasants", who rose above the indigent level of the "poor peasants", but did not qualify for the label of "rich peasants" or "*kulaks*". But in the chaos of the civil war no expedient could stimulate agricultural production. The authorities from time to time invoked the cherished socialist goal of large-scale collective cultivation. A number of agricultural communes or "collective farms" (Kolkhozy) were founded by communist idealists, some of them foreigners,

on the basis of working and living in common. But they
scarcely contributed to the problem of feeding the cities.
"Soviet farms" (Sovkhozy) were set up by the Soviet Government, by provincial or local Soviets, or sometimes by industrial
enterprises under the control of Vesenkha, for the specific
purpose of providing food for famished urban and factory
workers; they employed wage-labour, and were sometimes
spoken of as "socialist grain factories". But they made little
headway against the resistance of the peasants, who saw in
the Sovkhozy a return to the large landed estates broken
up by the revolution, especially when, as often happened,
they were established on confiscated estates, and employed
the managers taken over from the old régime. Lenin on
one occasion repeated a saying alleged to have been current
among the peasants: "We are Bolsheviks, but not communists;
we are for the Bolsheviks because they drove out the landlords,
but we are not for the communists because they are against
individual holdings."

In industry, war communism may be said to have begun
with a decree of June 28, 1918, nationalizing every important
category of industry. This seems to have been inspired, partly
by the growing menace of the civil war, partly by the desire
to forestall spontaneous seizures of factories by workers without
the knowledge or authority of Vesenkha—what a writer of
the period called "elemental-chaotic proletarian nationalization
from below". But formal nationalization was of little account.
What mattered was to organize and administer what had
been taken over—a function which workers' control had proved
unable to exercise. This was the task of Vesenkha, which
set up a number of "centres" or "chief committees (glavki)"
to manage whole industries; some industrial undertakings were
administered by local authorities. Chaotic conditions called
urgently for centralized control, which may, however, sometimes have aggravated the chaos. Few of the qualifications
and skills required for industrial production were available
to the new régime. Industry at all levels continued to be
run in practice by those who had worked in it before the
revolution, and who now manned the "centres" and "glavki".
Party members were sometimes assigned to top positions, but
lacked the experience to make themselves effective. Senior
directors, managers and engineers, whose services were quickly

recognized as indispensable, were known as "specialists", and were rewarded with higher salaries and privileges. Industrial production was, however, increasingly dominated by the emergencies of the civil war. The demands of the Red Army were paramount. Effort had to be concentrated on a few essential industries at the expense of the rest. Small-scale enterprises employing only a handful of workers, and artisan industry both in the towns and in the countryside, were mainly immune from controls, but were frequently hampered by lack of materials. Manpower was mobilized for the front. Transport broke down. Supplies of raw materials were exhausted, and could not be replenished. Of the many statistics illustrating the catastrophic decline of industry perhaps the most revealing were those which recorded the depopulation of the big cities. In the three years after the revolution Moscow lost 44·5 per cent of its population, Petrograd, where the industrial concentration was heaviest, 57·5 per cent. The Red Army took its toll of the able-bodied; and masses of people drifted away to the countryside where, if anywhere, food might still be found.

The problems of distribution were no less recalcitrant. The aim announced in the party programme of replacing private trade by "a planned system of distribution of commodities on an all-state scale" was a remote ideal. A decree of April 1918 authorizing Narkomprod to acquire stocks of consumer goods for exchange against peasant stocks of grain remained a dead letter. Plans to enforce rationing and fixed prices in the towns broke down in face of the shortage of supplies and the absence of any efficient administration. Trade flowed, where it flowed at all, in illicit channels. Traders, sufficiently numerous to acquire the familiar nickname of "bagmen", travelled round the country with supplies of simple consumer goods which they exchanged with peasants for foodstuffs to be sold at exorbitant prices in the towns. "Bagmen" were frequently denounced by the authorities, and threatened with arrest or shooting, but continued to prosper. Some attempt was made to use the existing machinery of the cooperatives, and control was established, not without friction, over the central cooperative organs. Since money was rapidly losing its value, schemes were hatched for the barter of commodities between town and country; but the goods wanted by the peasant were also in short supply. In the critical year of the civil war, when the survival of the régime seemed to hang by a thread, and the territory even nominally controlled by it was being constantly contracted by inroads of the White armies, the method by which the essential needs of the Red Army, of the factories engaged in war production, and of the urban population were met was the crude method of requisitioning, dictated and justified by military necessity. To keep the Red Army supplied was the over-riding task of economic policy, and little attention could be spared for civilian needs or civilian susceptibilities. It was above all the widespread requisitioning of surpluses of grain which led the peasants, once the danger from the Whites was over, to rebel against the harshnesses of war communism.

War communism had important consequences for the organization of labour. The initial hope that, while compulsion would have to be applied to landlords and members of the bourgeoisie, the labour of the workers would be regulated by voluntary self-discipline was soon frustrated. "Workers' control" over production, exercised in every factory by an elected factory committee, which had been encouraged in the first flush of revolution, and had played a rôle in the take-over of power, soon became a recipe for anarchy. In the rapidly thickening crisis atmosphere of January 1918 Lenin significantly quoted the familiar, "He who does not work, neither shall he eat", as "the *practical* creed of socialism"; and the People's Commissar for Labour spoke of "sabotage" and necessary measures of compulsion. Lenin had a good word to say for piece-rates and for "Taylorism"—a fashionable American system for improving the efficiency of labour, which he himself had once denounced as "the enslavement of the man to the machine". Later he supported a campaign for the introduction of what was called "one-man management" in industry—the direct antithesis of "workers' control". The party congress of March 1918 which voted to ratify the Brest-Litovsk treaty also demanded "draconian measures to raise the self-discipline and discipline of workers and peasants". These proposals, like the Brest-Litovsk treaty itself, excited the indignation of the then Left opposition, in which Bukharin and Radek played leading parts.

The revolution had spot-lighted the ambiguous role of the

trade union in a workers' state. Relations between Soviets
of Workers' Deputies and trade unions, both purporting to
represent the interests of the workers, had been a crux since
the earliest days of the revolution, when the strongest unions
were dominated by the Mensheviks. When the first All-Russian
Congress of Trade Unions met in January 1918, the Bolsheviks
had secured a majority, though the Mensheviks and other
parties were also well represented. The congress had no
difficulty in calling the factory committees to order on the
ground that the particular interest of a small group of workers
must yield to the general interest of the proletariat as a
whole. Only a few anarchist delegates opposed the decision
to convert the committees into organs of the unions. Here
too the principle of the centralization of the authority dispersed
by the revolution was already at work.

The issue of the relation of the trade unions to the state
was far more stubbornly contested. Were the unions to be
an integral part of the apparatus of the workers' state like
other Soviet institutions? Or would they retain the function
of defending specific interests of the workers independently
of other elements of the workers' state? The Mensheviks,
and some Bolsheviks, arguing that, since the revolution had
not yet outlived its bourgeois-democratic stage, the unions
still had their traditional rôle to play, stood out for complete
independence of the unions from the state. But Zinoviev,
who presided, had no difficulty in securing a comfortable
majority for the official Bolshevik view that, in the process
of the revolution, the trade unions must "inevitably be transformed into organs of the socialist state", and in that capacity
must "undertake the chief burden of organizing production".
Declining production, and the needs of a desperate situation,
made this mandate vital. To raise labour productivity, to
improve labour discipline, to regulate wages and to prevent
strikes were responsibilities which the trade unions, in partner-
ship with Vesenkha and other state organs, were now required
to assume. The distinction between the functions of the trade
unions and those of the People's Commissariat of Labour
(Narkomtrud) became mainly formal; most of the principal
officials of Narkomtrud were henceforth trade union nominees.

The emergency of the civil war revived and kept alive
the mood of enthusiasm generated by the revolution itself,

and made strict measures of discipline acceptab
1919, with the civil war now at its height, general
for military service was ordered; and this soon came
to include the drafting of labour for essential wo   about
the same time labour camps were instituted for offenders
sentenced to this form of punishment by the Cheka or by
the ordinary courts, who were to be employed on work at
the direction of Soviet institutions. The severest category
of these camps, known as "concentration camps", was
reserved for those who had engaged in counter-revolutionary
activities in the civil war, and who were to be detailed
for particularly arduous work. But appeals could also be
made to voluntary self-discipline. In May 1919 Lenin called
on the workers for what were named "Communist Saturdays",
when some thousands of workers in Moscow and Petrograd
volunteered to work over-time without pay to speed up the
despatch of troops and supplies to the front; and this precedent
was followed a year later. The institution of *udarniki*, or
shock workers, to carry out specially important work at high
speed dated from this time. Without this combination of harsh
compulsion and spontaneous enthusiasm the civil war could not
have been won.

Early in 1920, with the defeat of Denikin and Kolchak,
the military emergency had been overcome. But it made
way for the equally grave problems of almost total
economic collapse; and it seemed logical that these problems
should be met by the same forms of discipline which had
brought victory in the field. Trotsky as People's Commissar
for War made himself the champion of the conscription
and "militarization" of labour to pave the way for
economic revival. During the period of war communism
the trade unions had been brushed aside. Labour had been
conscripted for work behind the military fronts; and, when
fighting ceased, military units were converted into "labour
battalions" for necessary work of reconstruction. The first
"revolutionary army of labour" was formed in the Urals
in January 1920. Now, however, that the civil war was
over, the mood changed. Those who from the first had looked
askance at measures of compulsion applied to the workers,
those who stood for the independence of the trade unions,
and those who for other reasons resented Trotsky's pre-

eminence in the party, joined in attacking his masterful procedures. He defended his policies in face of mounting opposition
at the party congress in March 1920, and secured Lenin's
support. The outbreak of the Polish war stilled the voices
of dissent. But when the war ended in the autumn of 1920,
and the last embers of the civil war had been stamped
out in the south, fierce opposition arose in the party to
the continued conscription of labour and the virtual by-passing
of the trade unions. Trotsky, impressed by the vast and
urgent problems of economic reconstruction, and irritated by
trade union resistance to his plans, added fuel to the flames
by demanding a "shake-up" of the unions. Lenin parted
company with Trotsky on the issue; and a bitter debate
of unprecedented dimensions raged throughout the winter—
only to be resolved when the policies of war communism
were finally abandoned at the party congress of March 1921.

Party attitudes to war communism were divided and ambivalent. The conglomeration of practical policies collectively
known by that name was approved as necessary and proper
by all but a small minority of dissidents. But interpretations
of its character diverged widely—more widely, perhaps, in
retrospect than at the time. The first eight months of Soviet
rule had broken the power of the landlords and the bourgeoisie,
but had not yet brought into being a socialist economic
order. In May 1918 Lenin still spoke of an "intention . . .
to realise the transition to socialism". The sudden introduction
in the summer, under the name of war communism, of measures
which seemed to many Bolsheviks a foretaste of the future
socialist economy, was treated by more prudent party members
simply as a forced response to an emergency, an abandonment
of the cautious advance hitherto pursued, a plunge—necessary,
no doubt, but rash and full of hazards—into uncharted waters.
This view gained in popularity when the civil war ended,
and the burdens of war communism seemed no longer toler-
able; and it became the accepted line when peasant revolt
finally forced a decision to abandon war communism in favour
of NEP.

Other communists, on the other hand, hailed the achievements of war communism as an economic triumph, an advance
into socialism and communism more rapid than had hitherto
been deemed possible, but none the less impressive on that

account. Industry was comprehensively nationalized; and, if industrial production still declined, Bukharin could write complacently of "the revolutionary disintegration of industry" as "a historically necessary stage". The progressive devaluation of the ruble could be described as a blow struck against bourgeois capitalists, and a prelude to the moneyless communist society of the future, when everything would be shared according to needs. Already, it was claimed, the market had been largely eliminated as the agency of distribution. Grain surpluses were requisitioned from the peasants; and the main foodstuffs were in principle rationed to the urban population. Industry worked chiefly on government orders. Labour was organized and allocated in response, not to the dictates of the market, but to social and military needs. After the civil war the realities of a desperate economic situation clashed too obviously with this Utopian picture to make it seriously tenable. But many party consciences were troubled by its abandonment; and the divergences of opinion about the character of war communism repeated themselves as divergences about the character and permanence of NEP.

# 4 The Breathing-Space of NEP

WAR communism had been made up of two major elements: on the one hand, a concentration of economic authority and power, including centralized control and management, the substitution of large for small units of production and some measure of unified planning; on the other hand, a flight from commercial and monetary forms of distribution, and the introduction of the supply of basic goods and services free or at fixed prices, rationing, payments in kind, and production for direct use rather than for a hypothetical market. Between these two elements, however, a fairly clear distinction could be drawn. The processes of concentration and centralization, though they flourished exceedingly in the forcing-house of war communism, were a continuation of processes already set in motion during the first period of the revolution, and indeed during the European war. Here war communism was building on a foundation of what had gone before, and many of its achievements stood the test; only in their detailed application were its policies afterwards subject to rejection and reversal. The second element of war communism, the substitution of a "natural" for a "market" economy, had no such foundations. Far from developing logically out of the policies of the initial period of the revolution, it was a direct abandonment of those policies—an unprepared plunge into the unknown. These aspects of war communism were decisively rejected by NEP; and it was these aspects which most of all discredited it in the eyes of its critics.

Between the two major elements of war communism there was, moreover, a further distinction. The policies of concentration and centralization were applied almost exclusively in industry; attempts to transfer them to agriculture met with no success. It was here that the revolution had the main social basis of its support, and that the Russian economy showed some of the features of a developed capitalism. The policies of the flight from money and the substitution of a "natural" economy arose, not from any preconceived plan, but from inability to solve the problems of a backward peasant agriculture which occupied more than 80 per cent of the population. They were an expression of the fundamental difficulty of attempting to run in double harness the anti-feudal revolution of a peasantry with petty-bourgeois aspirations and the anti-bourgeois, anti-capitalist revolution of a factory proletariat, and of coping with the conflict between town and country inherent in the attempt. These were the incompatibilities which eventually brought the revolt against war communism and destroyed it.

By the autumn of 1920, when the fighting was over, the whole economy was grinding to a halt. Nothing in the theory or practice of war communism offered any clue how to re-start processes of production and exchange which had come to a standstill. The nodal point, as always in the Russian economy, was grain. The policy of requisitions, which had worked after a fashion during the civil war, was bankrupt. The peasant retreated into a subsistence economy, and had no incentive to produce surpluses which would be seized by the authorities. Widespread peasant disorders occurred in central Russia during the winter of 1920–1921. Gangs of demobilized soldiers roamed the countryside in search of food, and lived by banditry. It was imperative, if the rest of the country was not to starve, to provide the peasant with the incentives which were denied to him under a system of requisition. Nor was all well within the party. A dissentient group calling itself a "Workers' Opposition" was formed under the leadership of Shlyapnikov, a former metal worker who had been People's Commissar for Labour in the first Soviet Government, and Alexandra Kollontai, who enjoyed some prestige in the early days of the revolution. Its programme was directed mainly against the proliferation of economic and political controls and the growing power of the party and state machine; it claimed to uphold the purity of the original ideals of the revolution, and recalled the opposition of 1918 to the surrender of Brest-Litovsk. The leadership of the group was not very impressive. But it enjoyed wide sympathy and support in the party ranks.

A change of front was now urgently necessary. The essence of the new policy worked out during the winter of 1920–1921 was to permit the peasant, after the delivery of a fixed proportion of his output to state organs (a "tax in kind"), to sell the rest on the market. To make this possible, encouragement must be given to industry, especially small artisan industry, to produce the goods which the peasant would want to buy—a reversal of the emphasis under war communism on large-scale heavy industry. Private trade must be allowed to revive; here much reliance was placed on the cooperatives—one of the few pre-revolutionary institutions to retain some degree of vitality and popularity. Finally, all this implied—though the point was not grasped till somewhat later—a halt to the headlong fall of the ruble and the establishment of a stable currency. The package known as the New Economic Policy (NEP), with particular emphasis on concessions to the peasant, was approved by the central committee for presentation by Lenin to the historic tenth party congress in March 1921.

On the eve of the congress its proceedings were overshadowed by a sinister and ominous disaster. The sailors of the Red fleet based on the fortress of Kronstadt rose in revolt, demanding concessions for workers and peasants and the free election of Soviets. The mutiny had no direct association with the Workers' Opposition, but reflected the same deep feelings of discontent with the trend of party policy. Such leadership as there was appears to have been anarchist; the suspicion of the Bolsheviks that it had been planned or inspired by White *émigrés* was unfounded, though they afterwards made much capital out of it. Parleys and calls to surrender were fruitless. On March 17, while the congress was debating Lenin's proposals, units of the Red Army advanced on the fortress across the ice. After a bloody battle, fought on both sides with great tenacity, the rebels were overpowered and the fortress seized. But this massive revolt of men hitherto honoured as heroes of the revolution was a staggering blow to the prestige and confidence of the party. It may well have increased the readiness of the congress to accept the New Economic Policy, as well as proposals to tighten party discipline and provide stronger safeguards against dissent, within and without.

When Lenin submitted the resolution embodying the NEP proposals to the congress, the debate was perfunctory. Disenchantment with war communism was general; and the crisis was too acute to brook delay. Doubters were consoled by Lenin's assurance that "the commanding heights" of industry would remain in the firm hands of the state, and that the monopoly of foreign trade would be maintained intact. The resolution was accepted, if not with enthusiasm, with good grace and formal unanimity. The sharpest difference of opinion at the congress arose out of the heated controversy on the trade union question which had raged throughout the winter. Trotsky, inspired by the experience of the civil war, and supported after some hesitation by Bukharin, once more propounded his plan for transforming the trade unions into "production unions", and making them part of "the apparatus of the workers' state". At the opposite end of the spectrum, the Workers' Opposition wished to place the organization and control of production in the hands of the workers, as represented in the trade unions—a quasi-syndicalist view. Manoeuvring between the two embattled factions, Lenin finally succeeded in rallying the centre of the party round a resolution which, however, skirted the crucial issues without solving them. The taint of "militarization" was avoided. The trade unions were recognized as "mass non-party organizations" which had to be won over. It would be an error to incorporate them in the state machine. Persuasion, not force, was their proper instrument, though "proletarian compulsion" was not ruled out. The trade unions had always professed a concern for production; as early as 1920 the trade union central council established a Central Labour Institute for the study of, and training in, methods and techniques designed to improve the productivity of workers. This aspect of their responsibilities was emphasized in the resolution. It was their function to maintain labour discipline and combat absenteeism; but this should be done through "comradely courts", not by organs of the state. The resolution was carried by a large majority, but not without some minority votes being cast for two dissentient drafts.

The bitterness of the controversy shocked the party, and left its mark on the congress. Lenin spoke of the "fever" which had shaken the party, and of "the luxury of discussions" and "disputes" which the party could ill afford. The congress adopted a special resolution bearing the title "On the Syndicalist and Anarchist Deviation in our Party", which declared dissemination of the programme of the Workers' Opposition to be incompatible with party membership, as well as a general resolution "On the Unity of the Party". This demanded "the complete abolition of all fractionalism"; disputed issues could be discussed by all members of the party, but the formation of groups with "platforms" of their own was banned. Once a decision had been taken, unconditional obedience to it was obligatory. Infringement of this rule could lead to expulsion from the party. A final clause, which was kept secret and published only three years later, laid it down that even members of the party central committee could be expelled on these grounds by a majority of not less than two-thirds of members of the committee. These provisions, designed to ensure loyalty and uniformity of opinion in the party, seemed necessary and reasonable at the time. As Lenin put it, "during a retreat discipline is a hundred times more necessary". But the vesting of what was in effect a monopoly of power in the central organization of the party was to have far-reaching consequences. Lenin at the height of the civil war had acclaimed "the dictatorship of the party", and maintained that "the dictatorship of the working class is carried into effect by the party". The corollary, drawn by the tenth congress, was the concentration of authority in the central organs of the party. The congress conceded to the trade unions a measure of autonomy *vis-à-vis* the organs of the workers' state. But the rôle which they were to play was determined by the monopoly of power vested in the party organization.

The stringent ban on opposition within the party was the product of the crisis which accompanied the introduction of NEP. The same process logically overtook the two Left opposition parties which had survived the revolution: the SRs and the Mensheviks. The dissolution of the Constituent Assembly in January 1918 had proclaimed the determination of the Bolsheviks to exercise supreme power, and laid the foundations of the one-party state. But during the next three years—the period covered by the civil war—mutual relations between the Soviet Government and the two Left parties were ambiguous and fluctuating, and measures taken against them inconclusive. A few weeks after the revolution a group of Left SRs broke away from the main party, and formed a coalition with the Bolsheviks; three Left SRs were appointed People's Commissars. The signature of the Brest-Litovsk treaty in March 1918, which was bitterly denounced both by SRs and by Mensheviks, led to their resignation. The Right SRs now came out openly against the régime, and were held responsible for the disorders in Moscow in the summer of 1918, as well as for the assassination of the German Ambassador and of two leading Bolsheviks in Petrograd, and for the attempt on Lenin's life (see p. 20) above. On June 14, 1918, the Right SRs and the Mensheviks were banned on the ground of their association with "notorious counter-revolutionaries". Their newspapers were suppressed from time to time, but often re-appeared under other names; even a Kadet newspaper was published for some months after the revolution. Intermittent harassment, rather than the enforcement of a total ban, reflected ambivalence and hesitation on the part of the authorities.

The civil war, which made the plight of the régime more desperate, at first somewhat improved the standing of the two parties. The Mensheviks emphatically, the SRs less consistently, denounced the action of the Whites and of the Allied governments which aided and abetted them, and thus implicitly supported the régime, while continuing to attack its internal policies. The ban on the Mensheviks was withdrawn in November 1918, on the SRs in February 1919; and Menshevik and SR delegates spoke at sessions of the All-Russian Congress of Soviets in 1919 and 1920, though apparently without the right to vote. During the civil war many Mensheviks, and some SRs, joined the Bolshevik party; many more entered the service of the régime and worked in Soviet institutions. The mass following of both parties, persistently harassed by the authorities, began to disintegrate. When the civil war ended, there was no further basis for coalition or compromise. Two thousand Mensheviks, including the whole of the party central committee, were said to have been arrested on the eve of the introduction of the NEP, the extinction of the Menshevik opposition coinciding with the suppression of dissent within the ruling Bolshevik party. Many of those arrested were later released, and the leading Mensheviks allowed to go abroad. But a hard core of SR leaders were put on trial in 1922 for counter-revolutionary activities, and sentenced to death (these sentences were not carried out) or long-term imprisonment.

The benefits offered by NEP to the peasant, which in any case came too late to affect the sowings for 1921, were retarded by a natural calamity. Severe drought ruined the harvest over a large area, especially in central Russia and in the Volga basin. The famine was more widespread, and worked greater havoc on a much tried and enfeebled population, than the last great Russian famine of 1891. The horrors of the ensuing winter, when millions starved, were partly mitigated by supplies from foreign relief missions, notably the American Relief Administration. Sowings for 1922 were extended. The harvests for that year and for 1923 were excellent, and appeared to herald a revival of Soviet agriculture: small quantities of grain were actually exported. It was remarked that NEP, by re-introducing market processes to the countryside, had reversed the levelling policies of war communism, and encouraged the re-emergence of the rich peasant, or *kulak*, as the key figure in the rural economy. The poor peasant produced for the subsistence of himself and his family. He consumed what he produced; if he came to the market, it was more often as a buyer than as a seller. The *kulak* produced for the market and became a small capitalist; this was the essence of NEP. The right to lease land and to employ hired labour, theoretically prohibited since the early days of the régime, was conceded with some formal restrictions in the new agricultural code of 1922. But, so long as the peasants had enough to eat, and provided surpluses sufficient to feed the towns, few even of the most devoted party members were in a hurry to challenge the derogations from the principles and ideals of the revolution which had yielded these fortunate results. If NEP had done little or nothing to help industry or the industrial worker, and less than nothing to promote the cause of a planned economy, these problems could safely be left to the future.

It was at this point that the underlying differences in the party about the character of war communism began to be reflected in differences about the practical implications and consequences of NEP. When, in the crisis atmosphere of March 1921, the substitution of NEP for the more extreme policies of war communism was unanimously accepted as a welcome and necessary relief, these divergences were shelved, but not wholly reconciled. In so far as war communism was thought of, not as an advance on the road to socialism, but as an aberration dictated by military necessities, a forced response to the civil war emergency, NEP was a retracing of steps from a regrettable, though no doubt enforced, digression, and a return to the safer and more cautious path which was being followed before June 1918. In so far as war communism was treated as an over-rash, over-enthusiastic dash forward into the higher reaches of socialism, premature no doubt but otherwise correctly conceived, NEP was a temporary withdrawal from positions which it had proved impossible to hold at the moment, but which would have sooner or later to be regained; and it was in this sense that Lenin, whose position was not altogether consistent, called NEP "a defeat" and "a retreat—for a new attack". When Lenin at the tenth congress said that NEP was intended "seriously, and for a long time" (but added, in reply to a question, that an estimate of 25 years was "too pessimistic"), he gave hostages both to the view that it was a desirable and necessary correction of the errors of war communism, and to the view that it would itself have in the future to be corrected and superseded. The unspoken premise of the first view was the practical necessity of taking account of a backward peasant economy and peasant mentality; the unspoken premise of the second was the need to build up industry and not further depress the position of the industrial workers who formed the main bulwark of the revolution. These differences, muted for the moment by thankfulness that the acute party crisis of the winter of 1920–1921 had been successfully surmounted, re-appeared in a further economic and party crisis two years later.

# 5 The New Soviet Order

THE coming of NEP, which had the unpremeditated consequence of strengthening the central authority of the party, also encouraged the centralizing forces already at work in the formation of the Soviet state. The mass enthusiasm of 1917 for the destruction of state power had faded into the world of unrealized dreams. These continued to haunt the memories of many party members. But since Brest-Litovsk, and since the civil war, the need to create a state power strong enough to cope with these emergencies had been perforce accepted; and it was now reinforced by the need to rebuild the devastated and shattered national economy. The NEP period not only shaped what was to become the permanent constitutional structure of the USSR, but determined the lines to be followed for many years in its relations with foreign countries.

It was time to stabilize the fluid constitutional arrangements of the Soviet régime. A constitution of the Russian Socialist Federal Soviet Republic (RSFSR) had been promulgated in July 1918. It opened with the "Declaration of Rights of the Toiling and Exploited People", proclaimed by the All-Russian Congress of Soviets six months earlier (see p. 9 above). It vested supreme authority in an All-Russian Congress of Soviets composed of delegates elected by city and provincial Soviets, representation being heavily weighted in favour of the cities, the home of the workers. The franchise was confined to those who "earn their living by production or socially useful labour", together with soldiers and disabled persons. The congress elected an All-Russian Central Executive Committee (VTsIK) to exercise authority on its behalf in the intervals between sessions; and VTsIK in turn appointed a Council of People's Commissars (Sovnarkom), whose main functions were administrative, but which was also entitled to issue orders and decrees, so that no clear line of demarcation was drawn between the powers of Sovnarkom and VTsIK. The constitution also enunciated such general principles as the separation of church and state; freedom of speech, opinion and assembly for the workers; the obligation for all citizens to work on the principle, "He who does not work, neither shall he eat"; liability to military service for the defence of the republic; and abolition of all discrimination on grounds of race or nationality. The chaos of the civil war precluded any definition of the territory of the republic. The term "federal" in the title of the republic had no exact meaning; it covered both the incorporation in the RSFSR of "autonomous" republics and regions inhabited mainly by non-Russian populations, and the establishment of links between the RSFSR and other Soviet republics which had been, or would be, proclaimed in other parts of the former Russian Empire. These links took at first the form of alliance rather than federation. The RSFSR concluded treaties of alliance with Azerbaijani and Ukrainian Soviet republics in September and December 1920, and with Belorussian, Armenian and Georgian republics in 1921. Resistance to the process of unification was encountered in the Ukraine, where a national anti-Soviet government had been one of several rival authorities during the civil war, and in Georgia, where a Menshevik government had installed itself. Military power was used to expel the dissidents, and set up unimpeachably Bolshevik governments. The use of force could be more easily justified in the Ukraine, which had been deeply involved in the civil war, and where rival armies had reduced much of the country to anarchy, than in Georgia, which long remained a restive and recalcitrant member of the federation of Soviet republics.

As the whole country advanced towards economic recovery, and sought to renew contacts with the outside world, it seemed natural and necessary that it should function for these purposes as a single unit. While the form, and some of the reality, of local autonomy was carefully pursued, the Russian Communist Party, to which regional parties were affiliated, maintained a uniform discipline; and major decisions of economic and foreign policy were taken in Moscow. The first step was to persuade the three Transcaucasian republics—Armenia, Georgia and Azerbaijan—to unite in a Transcaucasian Socialist Federal Republic. Then, in December 1922, congresses of the four republics—the RSFSR and the Ukrainian, Belorussian and Transcaucasian republics—meeting separately, voted to form a union of Soviet socialist republics (USSR). Finally, delegates of the four republics met together, constituted themselves as the first Congress of Soviets of the USSR, and elected a committee with instructions to draft a constitution. The constitution of the USSR was approved by the committee in July 1923, and formally ratified by the second Congress of Soviets of the USSR in January 1924.

The constitution was modelled on the original constitution of the RSFSR. The sovereign Union Congress of Soviets was composed of delegates of the congresses of Soviets of the constituent republics, representation being proportionate to the population of each republic. The congress elected a central executive committee (TsIK), which appointed a Sovnarkom of the USSR. The organization of People's Commissariats was complicated. Foreign affairs, foreign trade, military affairs, and "the conduct of the struggle against counter-revolution" by the Cheka, now renamed OGPU ("Unified State Political Administration"), were reserved exclusively to the Union authorities; each republic had its GPU, which was, however, directly subordinate to the OGPU. Most economic affairs were subject to a system of "unified" commissariats; there were commissariats of the Union and commissariats of the republics, the latter enjoying a certain degree of independence. In other fields of administration, including agriculture, internal affairs, health and education, the republics alone had commissariats without any Union counterpart. In form the USSR was a federation of republics. But the omission of the word "federal" from its title was perhaps significant, since its unifying tendencies were apparent from the outset. The RSFSR accounted for more than 75 per cent of the population of the Union, and 90 per cent of its area. The other republics had some reason to suspect that the USSR was little more than the RSFSR writ large, and represented an extension over them of the central authority of Moscow. Voices of dissent were heard, especially from Ukrainian and Belorussian delegates, in the committee which drafted the new constitution.

An attempt to meet these objections led to one notable innovation, designed to recognize the formal equality of all the republics. The TsIK of the USSR, was divided into two chambers. The first and much larger chamber, the Council of the Union, consisted of delegates elected proportionately to the population of the republics; this recognized the enormous preponderance of the RSFSR. Delegates to the second chamber, the Council of Nationalities, were elected on the basis of equality of national groups, five from each of the four main republics and each of the autonomous republics, one from each autonomous region. But, since both chambers normally met only to listen to, and comment favourably on, statements of official policy (on occasion they met jointly to hear important speeches), and since contentious issues were seldom raised, and never voted on, these complicated arrangements had no practical significance in the process of policy-making. The periodical sessions of the congress and of TsIK, whose membership was enlarged as time went on, took no decisions. But they provided an important means of making contact with representatives of the outlying and often primitive regions of the Union, and of popularizing and making known throughout the Union major policies decided in Moscow; their principal function was not to debate, but to instruct, persuade and exhort. The constitutions of the USSR and of its constituent units served quite different purposes from the constitutions of western countries, to which they had only the most superficial resemblance.

The complex ethnic structure of Central Asia, and its affiliations with the Muslim world, made it a special problem. The Central Asian republics of Bokhara and Khorezm, though they had been brought within the orbit of Moscow by treaties of alliance with the RSFSR, were excluded from these constitutional arrangements on the ground that they were not yet socialist. It was not till 1925 that Central Asia was re-organized on national lines; Uzbek and Turkmen Socialist Soviet Republics, with subordinate autonomous units, were incorporated in the USSR as its fifth and sixth constituent republics.

The structure of the party organization was no less important a factor in the course of events than the structure of the Soviets. Between party congresses the supreme authority was vested in the party central committee. The committee which

took the vital decisions to launch the rising in October 1917,
and later to sign the Brest-Litovsk treaty, consisted of 22
members. In the period of acute crisis which followed, this
body was too unwieldy for rapid action, and decisions on
crucial issues rested in practice with Lenin in consultation
with other top leaders. The eighth party congress in March
1919 elected a central committee of nineteen full members
with eight candidates, who were entitled to attend meetings,
but not to vote. But it appointed a Politburo of five, to
be responsible for political decisions, and an Orgburo to take
control of questions of party organization; and this marked
the atrophy of the central committee as an effective source of
authority. The ninth congress in 1920 reorganized the secretariat,
placing it under the management of three "permanent" secretaries, who were members of the party central committee;
and in the ensuing period the refurbished secretariat underwent
a rapid expansion, acquiring a staff of several hundred officials,
divided into departments charged with different branches of
party activity. The party structure assumed the shape which
it was to retain throughout the nineteen-twenties, though
the processes at work took some years to develop to their
full extent. The creation of a powerful party machine later
provided an instrument for Stalin's dictatorship. Party congresses met annually till 1925, and thereafter at less regular
intervals, alternating with smaller and less formal party conferences; and the party central committee held three or four
sessions a year. These bodies continued to serve as a forum
where important issues were debated, though manipulation
by the secretariat of the election of delegates soon made
the results a foregone conclusion. Only the Politburo, increased
in number to seven, and later to nine, with several candidates,
remained throughout the nineteen-twenties a source of decisions
at the highest level; and, since the authority of the party
in a one-party state was mandatory for all decisions and
activities of the Soviet Government, the party Politburo became
the supreme policy-making organ of the USSR.

The strengthening of party and Soviet organization was
matched by a consolidation of Soviet relations with the outside
world. Even in the days of war communism, when thoughts

of world revolution were uppermost in Moscow, the rare
opportunities of direct contact with the governments of western
countries were not neglected. In January 1920 representatives
of the Russian cooperatives in Paris discussed with representatives of Western governments the resumption of an exchange
of goods with Soviet Russia; and Litvinov in Copenhagen
negotiated an agreement for the mutual repatriation of prisoners. A treaty of peace with Estonia was signed on February
2, 1920; and Lenin commented that "we have opened a
window on Europe, which we shall try to utilise as extensively
as possible". At the party congress in March 1920 Lenin
spoke of the need "to manoeuvre in our international policy".
A few days later Krasin, the one leading Bolshevik who
had foreign industrial and commercial experience, set out
with a large delegation of "trade experts" for Scandinavia,
and in May was politely received in London. These overtures
were cut short by the Polish war, which inspired a recrudes-
cence of revolutionary hopes in Moscow and a fresh outbreak
of apprehension and animosity in the west. But by the autumn
of 1920 peace was restored. A Russian trading company was
registered in London under the name Arcos (All-Russian Cooperative Society); and Krasin spent most of the winter in
London negotiating with the British Government and with
firms interested in orders for Soviet Russia. Finally, just a
week after Lenin had introduced NEP to the party congress
in Moscow, an Anglo-Soviet trade agreement was signed in
London on March 16, 1921.

The trade agreement was rightly hailed as a break-through
and a turning-point in Soviet policy. The parties agreed
to put no obstacles in the way of trade with one another,
and, in default of formal diplomatic recognition, to exchange
official trade representatives. The most important clause from
the British point of view was one in which each party undertook
to "refrain from action or undertakings" and from "official
propaganda, direct or indirect", against the other. "Action
or propaganda to encourage any of the peoples of Asia in
any form of hostile action against British interests or the
British Empire" was specially mentioned. A pledge to refrain
from hostile propaganda had been given in a less elaborate
form in the Brest-Litovsk treaty. But the circumstances were
different. That treaty had been concluded in conditions which

were not expected to last, and did not last. The Anglo-Soviet agreement was designed, like NEP, "seriously and for a long time". It heralded a change of emphasis in Soviet policy. Pronouncements about world revolution continued to be made, but were consciously or unconsciously regarded more and more as a prescribed ritual, which did not affect the normal conduct of affairs. The latent incompatibility between the policies of the People's Commissariat of Foreign Affairs (Narkomindel) and of Comintern began to come to the surface.

The background of the Soviet *rapprochement* with Great Britain was economic: desire to facilitate mutually profitable trade. The background of the *rapprochement* with Germany was primarily political, being rooted in common opposition to the Versailles treaty and common antipathy to the claims of Poland. Radek, who spent most of 1919 in prison or under house-arrest in Berlin, contrived to make contact with Germans from many different *milieux*, to all of whom he preached the virtues of German–Soviet cooperation. Official German–Soviet relations had been severed since the assassination of the German Ambassador in Moscow in 1918. In the summer of 1920 a Soviet representative was once more received in Berlin, and a German representative in Moscow. The Polish war gave a powerful stimulus to friendly relations between Poland's two neighbours. Trotsky was reported to favour an agreement with Germany; and Lenin in a public speech in November 1920 noted that, "though the bourgeois German Government madly hates the Bolsheviks", nevertheless "the interests of the international situation are pushing it towards peace with Soviet Russia against its will". Soviet policy was still ambivalent, being divided between the pursuit of revolution and diplomacy. On March 17, 1921, the German Communist Party began an armed rising against the government, known in party history as the "March action". The enterprise was certainly supported, perhaps prompted, by Zinoviev and Comintern officials; the involvement of the other Soviet leaders, heavily preoccupied at the moment by the Kronstadt revolt and the party congress, is doubtful. But the defeat of the German rising must have further diminished the waning hopes in Moscow of revolutions in the west, and strengthened the hand of those who saw a diplomatic accommodation with the capitalist countries as the immediate goal.

A feature of German–Soviet relations at this time was the quest for military collaboration, arising out of the prohibition under the Versailles treaty on the manufacture of armaments in Germany. In April 1921 Kopp, the Soviet representative in Berlin, after secret discussions with the Reichswehr, brought back to Moscow a scheme for the manufacture in Soviet Russia by German firms of guns and shells, aeroplanes and submarines. The response was favourable, and a German military delegation visited Moscow during the summer. An agreement was clinched at meetings in Berlin in September 1921 at which Krasin and Seeckt, the head of the Reichswehr, were the principal negotiators; it seems to have been at this moment that Seeckt first divulged to the civilian German Government what was on foot. The submarine project was dropped. But German factories in Soviet Russia were soon engaged in the production of guns, shells and aeroplanes. Tanks were added to the programme; and experiments were conducted in gas warfare. The products of these enterprises were supplied both to the Reichswehr and to the Red Army. Later German officers trained Red Army personnel in tank warfare and in military aviation. These arrangements were veiled in the utmost secrecy. No mention was made of them in the Soviet press; and they were for a long time successfully concealed from the German public and German politicians, as well as from the western Allies. It was a far cry from the days when, on the morrow of the revolution, the Bolsheviks had denounced the secret treaties concluded by the Tsarist government with the Allies during the war. Meanwhile, German–Soviet economic relations were cemented by the setting up of "mixed companies" and the granting of "concessions" in Soviet Russia to German firms.

Early in 1922 both the Soviet and the German Governments were invited to attend an international conference, which met at Genoa on April 10. The conference was a bold attempt by Lloyd George, its most active promoter, to re-forge links with Germany and Soviet Russia, hitherto outcasts from the European community. Lenin greeted the invitation with guarded enthusiasm. "We go to it", he explained, "as merchants, because trade with the capitalist countries (so long as they have not altogether collapsed) is unconditionally necessary for us, and we go there to discuss . . . the appropriate political conditions for this trade". Chicherin, Krasin and Litvinov led the Soviet delegation, the first of its kind to attend an international conference on equal terms with the delegations of other major Powers. The conference was a failure, partly owing to unyielding French opposition to Lloyd George's aims, partly owing to the inability of British and Soviet negotiators to reach agreement on the question of Soviet debts and liabilities. The Soviet Government was ready in principle to recognize pre-war debts (though not the war debts) of the former Russian Government, but only provided a substantial foreign loan were granted to facilitate their settlement. The Soviet Government refused to rescind decrees nationalizing foreign enterprises, but was prepared in certain conditions to allow foreign firms to re-occupy their former enterprises in the guise of "concessions". No amount of in-genuity could bridge these gaps.

The deadlock in negotiations paradoxically produced the only concrete result of the conference. For some time, Soviet and German diplomats in Berlin had been discussing the terms of a political treaty. The Soviet delegation at Genoa, having failed to make any impression on the western Allies, now pressed the German delegation, headed by the Foreign Minister, Rathenau, to complete and sign the treaty forthwith; and the German delegation, equally disillusioned by the pro-ceedings of the conference, agreed. The treaty was signed, hastily and secretly, at Rapallo on April 16, 1922. The contents of the Rapallo treaty were not remarkable. The only operative clauses provided for a mutual renunciation of financial claims, and the establishment of diplomatic and consular relations. But, as a demonstration of solidarity against the Western Allies, it shattered the conference, and made a lasting impact on the international scene. Soviet Russia had secured for herself a bargaining position among the European Powers. Manoeuvres originally conceived as expedients to tide over a crisis were becoming accepted procedure.

In Comintern, signs of the change of mood were apparent as early as its third congress in June 1921. The effervescent revolutionary enthusiasm of the second congress a year earlier had evaporated. What the Bolsheviks initially thought of as impossible had happened: the socialist Soviet republic had maintained itself, and showed every sign of continuing to maintain itself, in a capitalist environment. Lenin found himself on the defensive at the congress both in domestic and in international affairs. He took pains to explain the necessity of NEP and of the link with the peasantry to an audience some of whose foreign members were plainly sceptical of this interpretation of proletarian revolution. He admitted that the progress of world revolution had not been "in the straight line which we expected", and recommended "a profound study of its concrete development". Trotsky remarked that, while in 1919 world revolution had seemed "a question of months", it was now "perhaps a question of years". Practical caution had replaced the unrestrained enthusiasm of the previous congress.

Much time was spent analysing the failure of the "March action" in Germany, and the internecine divisions in the Italian Left. The "21 conditions" of admission to Comintern drawn up by the second congress had split some of the principal foreign parties, and led to the exclusion of sympathizers who were not prepared to accept the rigid discipline imposed by them. Once the first revolutionary wave had receded, only a minority of workers in western countries felt any specific allegiance to communism. The danger was seen that communist parties might degenerate into small sects bound by rigid doctrine and isolated from the main body of workers; the British and American parties, in particular, were warned that it was "a matter of life and death not to remain a sect". A new emphasis was placed on the need to woo "the masses". Six months after the congress IKKI issued a pronouncement on "the united workers' front". This was a call to communists to cooperate with other workers and members of Left parties on joint platforms for specific purposes. Since, however, it was an imperative condition that communists should not sacrifice their independence or their right to criticize, the conception of the united front remained ambiguous, and gave rise to much friction and misunderstanding in the years to come.

The new turn in foreign policy which accompanied the introduction of NEP extended to Soviet relations with eastern countries. Treaties with Afghanistan and Persia were signed in February 1921, and a treaty with Turkey on the same day as the Anglo-Soviet agreement, March 16, 1921. The

Persian treaty seemed difficult to reconcile with the support
given at that very moment by Soviet agents to a rebel leader
who was seeking to set up an independent republic in northern
Persia. But during the summer this support was withdrawn,
and the revolt collapsed. The Turkish treaty, which proclaimed
the solidarity of the two countries "in the struggle against
imperialism", caused greater and more lasting embarrassment.
Three months before its signature the leader of the illegal
Turkish Communist Party had been murdered, and other
Turkish communists killed or arrested, by Kemal's agents;
and the suppression of communism was a well-advertised aim
of Kemal's régime. This was glossed over in the common
interest of resistance to British intervention in Turkey. The
obligation undertaken in the Anglo-Soviet treaty to refrain
from propaganda against the British Empire in Asia also
imposed some measure of public restraint. Though Lenin
assured the third congress of Comintern that "the revolutionary
movement among hundreds of millions of oppressed peoples
of the east grows with remarkable vigour", the congress
itself, unlike its predecessor, was silent on eastern affairs.
Lenin, in the peroration of his last speech to a congress of
Comintern in November 1922 (he was now a sick man),
concluded that "the most important task in the period now
beginning is to study in order to achieve organization, structure,
method and content in revolutionary work". It was a low-key
ending.

On the other hand, the Soviet Government appeared more
decisively than hitherto as the defender of traditional Russian
interests. For an almost land-locked country the passage from
the Black Sea through the Straits to the Mediterranean had
always been a sensitive point. The Soviet-Turkish treaty of
March 16, 1921, had guaranteed free passage "for the com-
merce of all nations". But the crux was the passage of warships.
Turkey had protested against the use of the Straits by foreign
warships without Turkish permission as an infringement of
her sovereignty. Soviet Russia, with her depleted naval forces
and fear of foreign incursions in the Black Sea, vigorously
endorsed the protest. A conference was to meet at Lausanne
in the autumn of 1922 to settle terms of peace between
the western Powers and Turkey, at which this issue would
inevitably be raised; and, rather unexpectedly, the Soviet

Government was invited to participate "in the discussion of the question of the Straits". Chicherin led the Soviet delegation, and his confrontation with Curzon, then regarded as the main champion of British imperialism in the east, was widely publicized. The issue was settled by a compromise; and the Soviet Government signed, but never ratified, the resulting convention. What had been achieved was general recognition of Soviet Russia as the heir to the rights and interests of the former Russian Empire.

# 6 The Scissors Crisis

THE "link with the peasant" which NEP was designed to establish remained the watchword of Soviety policy for several years. Few doubted its necessity. "Only an agreement with the peasantry", Lenin had said at the tenth congress, "can save the socialist revolution in Russia until the revolution has occurred in other countries". When, after the terrible famine of 1921–1922, agriculture quickly revived, and recovery began to spread to other sectors of the economy, NEP had been triumphantly vindicated. Yet, once the danger was over, and memories of the privations of war communism receded into the past, the mood of relief and acquiescence slowly faded, and was overtaken by a sense of uneasiness at so radical a departure from the hopes and expectations of an advance into socialism which had inspired the early triumphs of the revolution. In the long run someone carried the cost of concessions made to the peasant; and some consequences of NEP, direct or indirect, were unlooked-for and unwelcome. In little more than two years the country was in the throes of a fresh crisis which, though less dramatic than the crisis preceding the introduction of NEP, deeply affected every sector of a now expanding economy.

The impact of NEP on industry was less direct than on agriculture, and mainly negative. Its first effect was to stimulate the recovery of rural and artisan industries, both because they had suffered less than factory industry in the civil war, and could more easily be brought back into production, and because they were the main suppliers of the simple consumer goods which the peasant wanted to purchase with the proceeds of his sale of agricultural products. The campaign for the nationalization of industry was halted. Large-scale industry

(Lenin's "commanding heights") remained in state hands, but with two important modifications. In the first place, a large measure of devolution was practised. State industry was divided into three categories, "Union", "republican" and "local". "Union" industry was administered by the Vesenkha of the USSR, "republican" industry by the Vesenkhas of the constituent republics; and, within the republics, provinces and regions set up their own Councils of National Economy (Sovnarkhozy) which were responsible for "local" industry. A fluctuating degree of supervision was exercised by the higher over the lower organs. But practical considerations dictated a large measure of autonomy. At lower levels private industry was encouraged. Enterprises employing less than 20 workers were exempt from nationalization. Larger enterprises which had already been taken over might be leased back to individual *entrepreneurs*, often to their original owners. Rural, artisan and cooperative industries operated and expanded with official approval.

Secondly, the direct administration of factory industry by Vesenkha through its *glavki* and centres was abolished. Industries were organized in trusts, which operated a group of enterprises as a single entity; the average number of enterprises in a trust was ten. The largest trusts were in the textile and metallurgical industries; the largest textile trust employed over 50,000 workers. The essential feature of the trusts was that they were no longer financed from the state budget, but were instructed to work on principles of commercial accounting (*khozraschet*), and to earn profits which were paid, subject to some deductions, to the state as the owner of the fixed capital of the enterprises. Some essential industries were still obliged to deliver a proportion of their output to state institutions. Otherwise industry, like the peasant, was free to sell its products on the market at whatever price they would fetch. These arrangements were consonant with the spirit of NEP. But they were criticized in some party circles; a blunt instruction from Vesenkha to the trusts in 1923 to earn "maximum profits" excited unfavourable publicity.

A year after the introduction of NEP the stimulus given by it to the availability and circulation of commodities of all kinds could be regarded with some degree of complacency.

Lenin had been aware of the dangers of "freedom of trade", which, as he said at the tenth congress, "inevitably leads to the victory of capital, to its full restoration". He seems at first to have envisaged the exchange of goods between town and country as a grandiose system of organized barter. But, as he later admitted, "the exchange of goods broke loose", and "turned into buying and selling"; and he shocked some party stalwarts by telling his hearers to "learn to trade". In 1922 a Commercial Bourse was established in Moscow. The intention was doubtless to exercise some form of public control over the processes of trade. The result was to facilitate the operations of a new class of merchants who quickly came to be characterized as "Nepmen". Petty private trade had never been completely extinguished, even under war communism; the famous Sukharevka market in Moscow was a known, and tolerated, abuse. The rising class of Nepmen were no longer petty traders, but large-scale commercial *entrepreneurs* who spread their tentacles into every sector of the economy. The big industrial trusts were still able to control the wholesale market in their products. Retail shops known as GUM (State Universal Store) were opened under Vesenkha auspices in Moscow and some other cities. But they were not at first very successful; and existing consumer cooperatives made little progress. Retail trade everywhere was dominated and fostered by Nepmen. As trade began to flow in increasing abundance, an air of prosperity returned to the well-to-do quarters of the capital. Many once-familiar features, banished by the revolution, now re-appeared in the landscape. Krasin on a visit to the city in September 1922 wrote to his wife that "Moscow looks all right, in some parts as it was before the war". Foreign visitors commented, sourly or triumphantly, according to their bent, on the revival of such "capitalist" phenomena as prostitutes on the streets, and subservient waiters and cabmen soliciting tips. For the beneficiaries of NEP prospects looked rosy. The worst seemed over. The shortages and tensions of war communism had been relaxed. Recovery was on its way.

Before long, however, the deeper implications of NEP revealed themselves in several interconnected crises. The first was a crisis of prices. Now that the controls of war communism had been lifted, prices fluctuated wildly. A prices committee appointed in August 1921, and a commission for internal trade set up in May 1922, proved wholly ineffective. The hunger of the cities for agricultural products outstripped the hunger of the peasant for the products of industry, so that agricultural prices at first soared in relation to industrial prices. Industry, denuded of working capital and deprived of sources of credit, could finance itself only by selling its products on a falling market, thus depressing industrial prices still further. This process, which reached its height in the summer of 1922, resulted in a crisis of labour. Under war communism labour, like every commodity, was scarce, and unemployment unthinkable. Compulsory labour service had the advantage of ensuring food rations for mobilized workers. Now compulsory labour, except in the penal labour camps, was gradually abandoned, and free employment for wages returned; collective contracts began to be negotiated by trade unions on behalf of their members. But the number of jobs was now smaller than the number of workers seeking them. Employers continued for a long time to supply food rations to their workers; but these were now payments in kind calculated at market prices in lieu of wages. The vagaries of the price-index made wage-rates a constant subject of haggling, in which the worker had a poor bargaining position. Wages frequently fell into arrears owing to the inability of enterprises to find the cash to pay them.

The status of the trade unions was governed by the rather hollow compromise reached at the tenth party congress in March 1921, the limitations of which were shown up at the trade union congress two months later. Tomsky, having failed to resist an attempt to re-open the issues decided at the party congress, was severely reprimanded, relieved at the behest of the party authorities of his post as president of the trade union central council, and despatched on a mission to Central Asia. It may have been significant that Tomsky was succeeded as president by Andreev, originally a supporter of Trotsky's trade union platform. But this did not restore peace in the unions. In January 1922 the Politburo once more intervened with a resolution which recognized the existence of "a series of contradictions between different tasks of the trade unions"—notably a contradiction between "the defence of the interests of the toiling masses" and the rôle of the unions as "sharers of state power and builders of the national economy as a whole". This formula seems to have paved the way for a reprieve of Tomsky, who at the next trade union congress in September 1922 was reinstated in his former post as president. The congress once more attempted to define the role of the unions. It was their function "unconditionally to protect the interests of the workers". On the other hand, the obligation rested on them to maintain and improve productivity, seen as the contribution of the workers to the building of a socialist order; and, though strikes were not formally prohibited, the right way to settle disputes was by negotiations between the trade union and the employer or economic administration concerned. It is noticeable that no distinction of substance appears to have been drawn at any time between the rôle of the trade unions in state and in private enterprises. Both contributed to essential production; and it was important that this process should not be disrupted.

Discontent among the workers was fanned by the rising status and influence of the so-called "Red managers". In the civil war, former Tsarist officers had been employed to rebuild and command the Red Army; so also, in order to revive essential industries, former factory managers, and sometimes factory owners, had been pressed into service, in the guise of "specialists", as managers of nationalized enterprises, sometimes under the supervision of party members or workers. The system met the need for managerial skills, and was standardized and extended under NEP, when autonomous trusts and syndicates took the place of the *glavki* and centres of war communism. The group of "Red managers", in spite of their predominantly bourgeois origin and affiliations, acquired a recognized and respected place in the Soviet hierarchy; some of them were admitted to party membership—a reward for distinguished service. They received special rates of remuneration outside the normal wage-scales, and far in excess of them; and they exercised an increasingly powerful voice in industrial administration and industrial policy. Frequent and not unjustified accusations of their brutal and dictatorial attitude to the workers, reminiscent of the methods of the old régime, were symptomatic of the jealousies and resentments provoked by this apparent reversal of everything that the revolution had stood for in the factories.

It was, however, the onset of unemployment which made the worker most conscious of his lowered status in the NEP economy. The continued stagnation of heavy industry, the prices crisis in the consumer industries, the call for rationalization of production, the insistence on *khozraschet* and on earning profits—all these set up strong pressures for the dismissal of redundant workers. Unemployment resumed its normal rôle under a market economy as an instrument of labour discipline and pressure on wages. Statistics were few and unreliable. In 1923 the number of unemployed was said to have reached a million; but official returns related to members of trade unions and those registered at the labour exchanges, who were entitled to exiguous relief payments, and took no account of a mass of unskilled workers, mainly peasants, seeking casual work in the towns, especially in the building industry. If NEP had rescued the peasant from disaster, it had reduced industry and the labour market to conditions bordering on chaos. An underground opposition group in the party, which called itself the "Workers' Group", and declared that the letters NEP stood for "new exploitation of the proletariat", was denounced at the party congress in April. When NEP was freely described as a policy of concessions to the peasant, the question which nobody had asked was at whose expense these concessions were being made. The proletariat, the heroic standard-bearer of the revolution, had suffered dispersal, disintegration and a drastic reduction of numbers under the impact of civil war and industrial chaos. The industrial worker had become the step-child of NEP.

The other crisis, or aspect of the crisis, was financial. The financial consequences of NEP were quite unpremeditated. Once NEP had established the principle of a free market on which goods were bought and sold, these transactions could not be conducted in terms of a constantly declining, and now almost valueless, ruble. The autumn of 1921 saw the introduction of a number of financial reforms. It was decided to draw up the state budget in pre-war rubles, the value of the current ruble being adjusted month by month to this standard. This was in effect a price-index ruble, sometimes referred to as a "goods" or "commodity" ruble, and was used in the calculation of wage-rates. A State Bank was set up to manage the currency, to re-establish credit, and to lay the foundations of a banking system. At the end of 1921 a party conference advocated the establishment of a currency based on gold; and a few months later the fluctuating "commodity ruble" was replaced by a hypothetical "gold ruble" as the standard of value. In the autumn of 1922 the State Bank began to issue notes in a new denomination; the chervonets, equivalent to ten gold rubles. But the issue was at first small. For another year the chervonets served as a unit of account, and payments were made in the old paper rubles at the constantly declining current rate.

A major economic crisis resulting from all these conditions broke in the summer and autumn of 1923. The collapse of industrial prices in the previous year had impelled the leaders of industry to combine in their own defence. The industrial trusts formed selling syndicates to maintain orderly conditions of marketing and hold up prices. These organizations were remarkably successful in achieving their purpose. By September 1922 the relation between industrial and agricultural prices had been restored to its pre-war balance; and from this time industrial prices rose dramatically at the expense of agricultural prices. Trotsky in his report at the twelfth party congress in April 1923 produced a diagram which showed pictorially how the "scissors", representing the blades of agricultural and industrial prices, had opened more and more widely in the past six months. Everyone deplored these violent price fluctuations; but how to prevent them within the framework of NEP was less clear. The party was still deeply committed to the policy of indulgence for the peasant, which was the essence of NEP. Yet the current trend was wholly adverse to the agricultural producer. When in October 1923 the scissors opened to their widest extent, the ratio of industrial prices to agricultural prices was three times as high as in 1913. Meanwhile further monetary problems threatened the economy. To finance the abundant harvest it had been necessary to resume the unlimited printing of ruble notes, thus further depreciating the old paper currency. Attempts were made to substitute the "gold ruble" for the "commodity ruble" in calculating wage payments; and this was said to reduce actual payments by as much as 40 per cent. This and other grievances of the workers produced a wave of unrest and strikes in the autumn of 1923.

The party leaders took alarm at the gathering storm; and the central committee appointed a so-called "scissors committee" of 17 members to report on the crisis, with special reference to prices. Trotsky had hitherto been careful not to dissent openly from his colleagues, and perhaps for that reason refused an invitation to serve on the scissors committee. But, while it was deliberating, he lost patience, and on October 8 addressed to the party central committee a letter denouncing "flagrant radical errors of economic policy"; decisions were being taken without regard to any "economic plan". Trotsky condemned "*attempts to command prices in the style of war communism*". The right approach to the peasant was through the proletariat; the rationalization of state industry was the key to the closing of the scissors. The letter was followed a week later by the issue of a "platform of the 46", signed by 46 party members, some followers of Trotsky, some of other opposition groups. This spoke of a "grave economic crisis", brought on by "the casual, unconsidered and unsystematic character of the decisions of the central committee". Both Trotsky's letter and the "platform" went on from these criticisms of economic mismanagement to attack the oppressive régime which stifled opinions in the party.

The "platform" had demanded a broad party conference to debate these issues. The central committee responded by opening the columns of *Pravda* to a controversial discussion—the last of its kind in Soviet history—which lasted for more than a month without participation by any of the leaders, growing more and more confused and heated as it went on. Meanwhile the scissors committee pursued its difficult task. The experience of the past year had convinced almost everyone that prices could not be left to the free play of the market. The committee readily accepted control of wholesale prices. Retail prices presented more difficulty. But it was pointed out that to control wholesale and not retail prices would merely swell the profits of middlemen, identified with the now increasingly unpopular Nepmen. The committee reconciled itself to selective controls of retail prices. But the complexity of the problem, and the timidity of the committee, were such that it did not report till December.

By this time the economic situation had undergone a favourable change. Industrial prices, having reached their peak in October, fell back sharply. The scissors began to close. The harvest, always a major indicator in the primitive Russian economy, was excellent for the second year in succession. Industry, far from being damaged by lower prices, was able to increase its efficiency and enlarge its market. Idle factories and plant were brought back into production. Even pressure on wages was somewhat relaxed. The economic tension of the past six months was eclipsed by a new political tension; this was the moment when the campaign against Trotsky began in earnest. In these circumstances the Politburo adopted a resolution on the report of the scissors committee which was a skilful compromise. The predominance of peasant agriculture was emphasized; nothing must be said to justify Trotsky's insistence on priority for industry. Industry was exhorted to keep prices down, to rationalize itself, and to increase productivity. Control of wholesale prices of articles of mass consumption was to be extended to retail prices: legal maximum prices were to be fixed at once for salt, paraffin and sugar. Concessions were promised on wages, which were to rise "in proportion to a rise in industry and in the productivity of labour". Finally there were gestures of support for the financing of heavy industry and for the strengthening of Gosplan. The proposals were endorsed by a party conference in January 1924, a few days before Lenin's death.

The resolution on the report of the scissors committee, for all its caution, gave a certain fillip to industry; by 1924 industry had climbed out of the depths of stagnation and depression in which it floundered when NEP was introduced in 1921. But the revival was one-sided. Light consumer industries directly serving the peasant market prospered. But in NEP conditions nothing stimulated the heavy industries concerned with the production of the means of production, and these lagged behind. According to Gosplan figures, industrial production for the year ended October 1, 1924, while two-and-a-half times as great as in 1920, reached only 40 per cent of the pre-war level, and the metal industries reached only 28·7 per cent. This deficiency began to excite anxiety in the party, notably in opposition circles. The scissors resolution of December 1923 expressed the view that the metal industry should "be advanced to the front rank and receive from the state support of all kinds"; and this was endorsed by the party conference in January 1924. But nothing was done to implement the pious aspiration. Dzerzhinsky's appointment in February 1924 as president of Vesenkha drew fresh attention to the problem. Three months later Dzerzhinsky reported to the thirteenth party congress that an investment of from 100 to 200 million gold rubles would be required over the next five years to put heavy industry on its feet; and Zinoviev rhetorically exclaimed that it was now "the turn for metal, the turn for an improvement in the production of means of production, the turn for a revival of heavy industry". These fine words had no immediate counterpart in action, but they marked a change in the climate of opinion which held out promise for the future.

The spring and summer of 1924 were a time of recovery and growing confidence. Agriculture under NEP had emerged from the disasters of the recent past; some indulgence was even shown for the *kulak*. Industry steadily revived, though the advance was uneven. The currency reform was completed in March 1924, when the gold-based chervonets currency was universally adopted, and the old Soviet ruble notes withdrawn. In May a People's Commissariat of Internal Trade, headed by Kamenev, was set up for the main purpose of operating price controls. The ratio of industrial to agricultural prices had now returned approximately to its 1913 level. Control of industrial prices, both wholesale and retail, seems to have been partially effective, but agricultural prices proved recalcitrant. Foreign trade, managed under the monopoly of foreign trade by a separate commissariat under Krasin, reached sizable dimensions for the first time in the year 1923–1924. Of exports 75 per cent were agricultural products, including grain; the other principal items were timber products and oil. Of imports, nearly 75 per cent were taken by industry, in the form of cotton and other raw materials or semi-manufactured products. These impressive results had been achieved under the régime of NEP, and could not have been achieved without it; they were hailed as a triumphant vindication of NEP. Yet the scissors crisis had been overcome only by measures—especially price controls—which contravened the market principles of NEP; these too had been an essential condition of recovery. Nor was everyone in the party happy about the conspicuous rôle of the *kulak* in the villages or of the Nepman in the towns. But the revival in every sector of the economy encouraged the postponement of these baffling problems to a later period. The struggle between the elements of a market economy and of a managed economy went on throughout the nineteen-twenties.

# 7   Lenin's Last Days

THE process of economic recovery inaugurated by NEP was overshadowed in 1922 by the onset of Lenin's prolonged and fatal illness. In May 1922 he had a stroke which incapacitated him for many weeks. He returned to work and delivered several speeches during the autumn. But his physical powers were manifestly under strain. On December 12, on medical advice, he withdrew to his apartment in the Kremlin, and there four days later he had a second and severer stroke which permanently paralysed his right side. For the next three months physical incapacity did not affect his mental faculties; and, though none of the other leaders were apparently allowed to see him, he continued to dictate notes and articles on party affairs. These included the famous "testament" of December 25 with its postscript of January 4, 1923. But on March 9, 1923, a third stroke deprived him of speech; and, though he lived for ten months longer, he never worked again.

After his third stroke hopes of Lenin's eventual recovery gradually faded. The question of the succession loomed ahead, and clouded every other issue. The tightening of party discipline at the tenth party congress in March 1921 had been followed by a party purge, and was further emphasized at the eleventh congress a year later, when 22 dissidents, most of them members of the former Workers' Opposition, were censured, and two of their five leaders expelled from the party; Lenin had asked for the expulsion of all five. This fresh crisis called for a further strengthening of the party machine. The three co-equal secretaries of the party central committee appointed in 1920 (see p. 42 above) had proved ineffective, and were removed from office. On April 4, 1922, a few days after the eleventh congress, it was announced that Stalin had been appointed general secretary, with Molotov and Kuibyshev as secretaries. Nobody found the announcement particularly significant. Stalin was known as a hard-working, efficient and loyal party official.

When Lenin returned to work after his first stroke, he was evidently alarmed by the way in which Stalin had patiently built up both the power and authority of his office, and his own personal standing; he was now for the first time a leading figure in the party. Lenin did not like either of these developments. He was much preoccupied at this time with the growth of bureaucracy in the state and in the party; and he became acutely mistrustful of Stalin's personality. The testament was dictated, a few days after the second stroke which put in doubt his chances of recovery, in a mood of an anxious foreboding. Lenin began with the danger of a split between "the two classes"—the proletariat and the peasantry—on whose alliance the party rested. This he dismissed as remote. The split which he envisaged as a threat for the "near future" was between members of the central committee; and the relation between Stalin and Trotsky was "a big half of the danger of that split". Stalin had "concentrated an enormous power in his hands", and did not "always know how to use that power with sufficient caution". Trotsky, though "the most able man in the present central committee", showed "too far-reaching self-confidence and a disposition to be too much attracted by the purely administrative side of affairs". Other leading members of the committee did not escape criticism. The hesitation of Zinoviev and Kamenev at the critical moment in October 1917 was recalled; this was "not, of course, accidental, but ... ought as little to be used against them personally as the non-Bolshevism of Trotsky". Bukharin, though "the biggest and most valuable theoretician in the party" and "a favourite of the whole party", had never fully understood the dialectic, and his views could "only with the very greatest doubt be regarded as fully Marxist". It was an unexpected verdict on the man whose *ABC of Communism*, written in conjunction with Preobrazhensky, and *Theory of Historical Materialism* were still widely circulated party textbooks. But, however perspicacious Lenin's diagnosis of the shortcomings of his colleagues, the only cure prescribed in the testament was a proposal to increase the membership of the central committee to 50 or 100; and this was unlikely to touch the root of the problem.

Lenin's attention had been drawn in the autumn of 1922 to what was happening in Georgia, where procedures for the incorporation of the Georgian republic into the USSR had encountered stiff resistance from the Georgian party committee. A commission headed by Dzerzhinsky visited Georgia in September, and returned to Moscow with the two dissident leaders. At this point Lenin intervened, overruled Stalin who was in charge of the question, and believed himself to have secured a compromise. But he did not follow up the matter, and relations with the Georgians again became embittered. Ordzhonikidze now visited Tiflis and, after a violent struggle, dismissed the rebel leaders, and forced the committee to accept Stalin's proposals. A few days after dictating the testament, Lenin, under what impulse is not clear, returned to the Georgian question. He dictated a memorandum in which he confessed himself "seriously to blame before the workers of Russia" for having failed to intervene effectively at an earlier stage. He denounced the recent proceedings as an example of "Great-Russian chauvinism", referred to Stalin's "hastiness and administrative impulsiveness", and severely censured him, Dzerzhinsky and Ordzhonikidze by name. Then, on January 4, 1923, Lenin's mistrust of Stalin again burst out, and he added a postscript to the testament. Stalin, he now said, was "too rude", and should be replaced as general secretary by someone "more patient, more loyal, more polite, and more attentive to comrades, less capricious etc."; and as the motive for this recommendation he once more cited the danger of a split, and "the relation between Stalin and Trotsky". Finally, early in March, after an occasion on which Stalin was said to have insulted Krupskaya (who had presumably refused him access to Lenin), Lenin wrote a letter to Stalin breaking off "comradely relations". Three days later came the third stroke which ended Lenin's active life.

The approach of the twelfth party congress, which met on April 17, 1923, was a source of embarrassment. Who was to don the mantle of leadership which Lenin had worn without challenge at previous congresses? Lenin's eventual

recovery was not yet despaired of. But even an interim choice
might pre-judge the future succession. Trotsky, a newcomer
to the party with a record of past dissent, owed his commanding
position since 1917 to Lenin's unfailing support. Deprived
of this, he was an isolated figure, and did not and could
not aspire to lead the party. He was regarded with jealous
dislike by his immediate colleagues, whom he treated with
a certain haughtiness; and his past advocacy of the militarization of labour made him suspect in trade union circles. The
three other most prominent leaders—Zinoviev, Kamenev and
Stalin—drew together in a determination to block any aggran-
dizement of Trotsky's rôle. In this provisional triumvirate
Stalin was the junior partner; and he was keenly conscious
of the need to live down Lenin's personal hostility, which
was probably by this time known to the other leaders, if
not to the rank and file of the party. Kamenev had more
intelligence than force of character. Zinoviev, weak, vain and
ambitious, was only too eager to occupy the empty throne.
He presided and spoke at the congress in terms of fulsome
subservience to the authority of the absent leader, contriving
at the same time to suggest that he was the authorized
exponent of Lenin's wisdom. Stalin, by way of contrast,
assumed a rôle of calculated modesty. Claiming nothing for
himself, he repeatedly referred to Lenin as his "teacher",
whose every word he studied and sought to interpret aright.
Speaking on organization, he repeated Lenin's strictures against
bureaucracy, hypocritically ignoring the fact that these shafts
had been aimed in large part at himself. In his report on
the national question he emphatically endorsed Lenin's attacks
on "Great-Russian chauvinism", and gently exculpated himself
from the charge of "hastiness". Trotsky, clearly anxious to
avoid any direct confrontation, absented himself from the
debate on the national question. His rôle at the congress
was confined to the presentation of a weighty report on
the economic situation, which stated the case for industry
and for the "single economic plan", but did not directly
assail current policies. Latent disagreement with Zinoviev was
carefully concealed.

Throughout the summer of 1923 personal animosities sim-
mered beneath the surface while the economic crisis mounted,
and hopes of Lenin's recovery gradually faded away. Though

Trotsky was not a candidate for the formal rôle of leadership, his powerful personality, his record in the civil war, his cogency in argument, and his brilliant oratorical gifts won him widespread popularity in the rank and file of the party, and made him a formidable adversary in any debate on policy. The triumvirate of Zinoviev, Kamenev and Stalin had successfully conspired at the party congress in April to block his advance. They now decided that the moment had come to crush him. The campaign was launched with the utmost caution—partly because Zinoviev and Stalin already, perhaps, did not fully trust one another.

The provocation came from Trotsky's letter of October 8, 1923 (see p. 57 above), which, after its caustic criticism of current economic policies, launched into an attack on the "incorrect and unhealthy régime in the party". Nomination had replaced election in appointments to key posts in the party organization; and appointments went to those committed to the maintenance of the existing régime. A "secretarial apparatus created from above" had gathered all the threads into its hands, and rendered participation by the rank and file "illusory". The letter concluded by demanding that "secretarial bureaucratism" should be replaced by "party democracy". Coming from a member of the Politburo, it was a formidable indictment, and its cutting edge was pointed unmistakably at Stalin. A few days later the "platform of the 46" deplored the rift between the "secretarial hierarchy" and ordinary members of the party. The "dictatorship within the party" which silenced all criticism was traced back to the emergency decisions of the tenth party congress in March 1921; this régime had "outlived itself". The triumvirate could not ignore this open challenge to its authority.

It was at this moment, by a strange fatality, that Trotsky succumbed to the first attack of an intermittent and undiagnosed fever, which continued to afflict him at intervals during the next two or three years. On October 25 the party central committee, in Trotsky's absence through illness, passed a resolution condemning his letter of October 8 as "a profound political error" which had "served as the signal for a fractional grouping (the platform of the 46)". Throughout November animated discussion of the economic and political issues in the columns of *Pravda* provoked no intervention either by

Trotsky or by the triumvirate. Trotsky's persistent indisposition condemned him to a passive rôle. But early in December he held parleys with the three leaders, which resulted in an agreed resolution of the Politburo of December 5, 1923. The tactics of the triumvirate were to make maximum concessions to Trotsky on points of principle in order to isolate him from the opposition. The resolution spoke of "the unique importance of Gosplan", of the danger of "bureaucratization" and "the degeneration under NEP of a section of party workers", and of the need for more "workers' democracy". The existing preponderance of "non-proletarian" elements in the party was to be remedied by "an influx of new cadres of industrial workers"; this was regarded as a guarantee of "party democracy". But the earlier resolution of October 25, in which the party central committee had condemned both Trotsky's letter of October 8 and the platform of the 46, was specifically re-affirmed, so that Trotsky appeared both to renounce his own previous stand, and to acquiesce in the condemnation of those who had come out in his support. Trotsky none the less regarded it as a victory for his principles.

So artificial a compromise could not last. Three days later Trotsky, still unable to appear in public, expounded his interpretation of the resolution in an open letter which was read at party meetings and published in *Pravda*. He criticized "conservatively minded comrades who are inclined to over-rate the rôle of the machine and under-rate the independence of the party". He cited the German social-democrats before 1914 as an example of an "old guard" which had lapsed into "opportunism", and he appealed to the rising generation, which "reacts most sharply against party bureaucracy". In a postscript he referred "the dangers of NEP", closely connected with "the *protracted* character of the international revolution". The triumvirate still hesitated. At a meeting of the Moscow party organization on December 11, several supporters of Trotsky spoke, including Preobrazhensky and Radek; and Zinoviev and Kamenev, while condemning the opposition, handled Trotsky with cautious politeness.

A few days later all inhibitions were removed, and the triumvirate had decided to treat Trotsky's open letter as a declaration of war. On December 15, Stalin in an article in *Pravda* launched a full-scale attack on the opposition, ending with bitter personal gibes against Trotsky. This was the signal for a campaign of vituperation in a series of speeches and articles by Zinoviev, who seems to have coined the term "Trotskyism", Kamenev, Bukharin and lesser party figures. Articles favourable to the opposition no longer appeared in *Pravda*. Students demonstrated for the opposition; and a purge of the central committee of the Komsomol was conducted in order to bring that organization to heel. But at party meetings in Moscow and Petrograd only a small minority of workers spoke or voted against the official line. Trotsky's earlier advocacy of the militarization of labour made it difficult for him to appear as a champion of the workers' cause. The growing power of the party organization, the lack of any positive or popularly presented alternative programme, fear of victimization in a period of widespread unemployment, the weakness in numbers and in radical traditions of the Russian working class, all contributed to the rout of the opposition. A protest by Trotsky, Radek and Pyatakov against the discriminatory attitude of *Pravda* produced a reply from the party control commission that "the organ of the central committee is obliged to carry out the perfectly definite line of the central committee". The decision was final and absolute. Thereafter *Pravda* spoke exclusively with the official voice of the central organs of the party.

The process of the personal denigration of Trotsky quickly gathered strength. At a session of IKKI early in January 1924 Zinoviev delivered a further uninhibited attack on his character, his party record and his opinions. Trotsky, dogged by illness, gave up the unequal struggle, and departed on medical advice for the Caucasus in the middle of January 1924. A few days later a party conference by an overwhelming majority (the delegates had, no doubt, been carefully sifted) condemned the opposition, and held Trotsky personally responsible for the campaign against the party leaders. These events immediately preceded the death of Lenin, which took place on January 21, 1924.

# 8 The Rise of Stalin

THE death of Lenin brought into the open the issue which had long preoccupied the party leaders. Zinoviev had already assumed without hesitation the provisional mantle of the succession. Stalin had studiously refrained from disclosing his ambitions. At a commemorative session of the Union Congress of Soviets on January 26, 1924, the eve of the funeral, Stalin's tribute was distinguished from those of his colleagues by a fervent strain of worshipful devotion still unfamiliar in the Marxist or Bolshevik vocabulary: "we communists" were humble and loyal disciples, pledged to carry out every injunction of the dead master. Two notable decisions were taken. One was to re-name Petrograd "Leningrad"; Lenin had superseded and eclipsed Peter in moulding the fortunes of the fatherland. The other was to strengthen the party by a mass recruitment of "workers from the bench", which was dubbed "the Lenin enrolment". The demand for a larger representation of workers in the party had figured in Trotsky's letter of October 8 and in the Politburo resolution of December 5, 1923 (see p. 66 above), and could be justified by much that Lenin himself had written. Its execution was now in the hands of Stalin, the general secretary of the party.

The Bolshevik party in 1917 had a membership of not more than 25,000. During the revolution and the civil war its numbers were progressively swelled by mass admissions. Statistics for this early period are unreliable. But early in 1921 it had reached a total of 600,000 or perhaps 700,000. The purge ordered by the tenth party congress in March 1921 was drastic. Some members, recruited in the enthusiasm of the revolution and the civil war, drifted away; others were expelled as unsuitable. By the beginning of 1924, the membership had been reduced to 350,000. The Lenin enrolment, which in two years added 240,000 new members to the party, increasing its numbers by more than two-thirds, was hailed both as a move towards more democracy and as an assertion of the rightful predominance of genuine workers in the party, though its later stages also included a substantial enrolment of peasants. Its historical rôle was quite different. It was the symbol of a gradual change in the character of the party which had deeper causes. Almost unnoticed a new conception emerged which differentiated the party of Stalin from the party of Lenin.

Lenin before the revolution had envisaged the party as a small homogeneous group of devoted revolutionaries pledged to the overthrow of a régime of inequality and oppression. Even after the revolution, he continued to think of the party as an élite group of dedicated workers; and he was more concerned to purge the unfit than to open a wide door to recruitment. The sharp reduction in the number of party members between 1921 and 1924 was certainly due to his insistence. Lenin, though he had moved a long way from the Utopian views expressed in *State and Revolution*, still looked forward, in the words of the party programme of 1919, to "a simplification of the functions of administration, accompanied by a rise in the cultural level of the workers", and seemed unaware, till the very end of his life, of the vast complexities and problems of public administration. By this time the conception of an élite party was an anachronism. In 1920, 53 per cent of party members were said to be working in Soviet institutions of one kind or another, and 27 per cent were in the Red Army. Gradually and insensibly, the party had been transformed into a machine geared to conduct and supervise the affairs of a great state. It was the plain duty of rank-and-file members—and especially of new members who lacked the revolutionary grounding of the pre-1917 generation—to support the leaders loyally in this formidable task; and party membership carried with it certain undeclared privileges which made the performance of this duty worth while. The Lenin enrolment was accompanied by a further purge of undesirable members; and, since both the purge and the enrolment were controlled by the party secretariat, it may be guessed that adherence to

the new party orthodoxy was one of the main criteria applied.
The Lenin enrolment, and the whole process of which it
formed part, enhanced the power of the party machine and
of the general secretary who manipulated it. Molotov spoke
no more than the truth when he observed at the party
congress of 1924 that "the development of the party in the
future will undoubtedly be based on this Lenin enrolment'.

Another and more subtle change followed the replacement
of Lenin's élite party by the mass party of Stalin. The party
statute imposed on members the obligation, once a policy
decision had been taken, to speak in support of it with
a united voice. Loyalty to the party meant acceptance of
its discipline. But it was assumed that the decision would
have been taken by democratic procedures after free discussion
among party members. Nor did anyone suggest that the party
was infallible; Lenin often drew attention to mistakes that
had been made, and admitted errors of his own. When his
fiftieth birthday was celebrated in April 1920, at the moment
of victory in the civil war, he rather strangely spoke, in
his reply to the greeting of his comrades, of the danger
of the party "giving itself airs". The angry controversies
which divided the party on the eve of the introduction of
NEP shocked Lenin and other party leaders into a realization
of the hazards involved in the unfettered toleration of dissent;
and the Kronstadt mutiny increased the sense of alarm. The
disciplinary measures adopted by the tenth congress were an
ominous landmark in party history. But Lenin never made
his peace with the conception of a central party organization
announcing infallible edicts and imposing silence on all dissent
within the party and outside it. When at the last party
congress which he was to attend, in March 1922, he observed
that the party had enough political and enough economic
power, and that "what is lacking is culture", he already
showed a troubled consciousness of the dangers that lay ahead.
In the last tormented months of Lenin's active life he was
preoccupied both by mistrust of Stalin's personality and by
the need to struggle against "bureaucracy" in the party
as well as in the state. Belief in the infallibility of the party,
in the infallibility of Lenin, and eventually in the infallibility
of Stalin himself, was a later development, the seeds of which

were sown in the first weeks after Lenin's death.

While the Lenin enrolment was in progress, Stalin took a further step to distinguish himself as Lenin's most faithful disciple. He delivered at the Sverdlov University six lectures "On the Foundations of Leninism", which were published in *Pravda*. They were clear, schematic and entirely conventional. One sentence only might, in the light of subsequent developments, have attracted attention:

> For the final victory of socialism, for the organization of socialist production, the efforts of one country, particularly of a peasant country like Russia, are insufficient; for that, the efforts of the proletarians of several advanced countries are required.

But this was merely the recital of a familiar item in the party creed. The lectures passed without comment. The other leaders showed no interest in Stalin's incursion into the field of theory where he had hitherto rarely sought to shine. What was significant in Stalin's initiative was the consecration of a specific cult of "Leninism". If the term was current during Lenin's lifetime, it was used, like "Trotskyism" later, as a term of opprobrium by opponents eager to discredit it. Henceforth, on the lips of Stalin and of other party leaders, Leninism was a vaguely defined, but infallible, body of doctrine, which distinguished the official party line from the heresies of its critics.

The embarrassment of Lenin's testament had still to be overcome. Fortunately for Stalin, his embarrassment was shared by the other leaders, none of whom escaped unscathed. At what precise moment they became aware of its contents is not recorded. But on May 22, 1924, on the eve of the thirteenth party congress, a gathering of prominent party members heard it read by Kamenev, who presided. Then Zinoviev spoke, in terms of fulsome devotion to the dead leader, ending with the verdict that "on one point" Lenin's apprehensions had proved unfounded, and that it was not necessary to remove Stalin from his post. Kamenev supported Zinoviev. Nobody expressed any other view. Trotsky, just back from the Caucasus, sat silent through the proceedings.

The only clash arose over Krupskaya's insistent demand that the testament should be read to the congress. The meeting decided, by a majority of 30 to 10, that it would be sufficient to communicate it confidentially to the leading delegates.

The problem of the opposition loomed large at the congress. Zinoviev restrained himself in his main report, ending with a rhetorical appeal to members of the opposition to come to the tribune to confess their error, and admit that the party was right. Many delegates denounced the opposition, and Trotsky by name. Trotsky rose painfully and reluctantly to meet Zinoviev's challenge. "One cannot be right against the party," he now proclaimed. The party could make "particular mistakes"; and he continued to believe that the resolution of the January conference condemning him was "incorrect and unjust". Nevertheless as a loyal party member he was bound to say: "Just or unjust, this is my party, and I bear the consequences of its decision to the end." Whether one regards it as the source of the inhibition which prevented Trotsky from giving battle, or as the rationalization of an inhibition which had deeper psychological roots, this declaration of submission, coupled with a refusal to confess error, was significant for his attitude at this time. It was only two years later—when it was already too late—that he regained his freedom of action, struck boldly at his enemies, and rallied his friends for his defence. The congress heard a plea from Krupskaya for peace between the factions and for "an end to further discussion". This went unheeded. Stalin and Zinoviev wound up the proceedings with speeches full of vituperation of Trotsky. He was, however, re-elected to the party central committee—apparently by a narrow margin. It is said that Zinoviev and Kamenev sought to exclude Trotsky from the Politburo, but that the proposal foundered on the opposition of Stalin, anxious to preserve his reputation as a moderate.

During the rest of the year Trotsky's literary prowess added fuel to the flames. In a commemorative pamphlet *On Lenin* he described his close personal association with Lenin at the time of the revolution in terms which seemed to inflate his own importance, and to relegate other participants to a secondary place. In October 1924, he published a long essay entitled *Lessons of October*, pillorying Kamenev and other "old Bolsheviks" for their resistance to Lenin's April theses on Lenin's return to Petrograd in April 1917, and the opposition of Zinoviev and Kamenev to the seizure of power in October, which had been cited by Lenin in the testament, with the qualification equating it with Trotsky's non-Bolshevik record as things which should not be brought up against them (see p. 62 above). This onslaught provoked a spate of controversial replies, and encouraged the triumvirate and their followers to delve, deeply and spitefully, into Trotsky's own record. Kamenev delivered a lengthy speech, published as a pamphlet under the title *Leninism or Trotskyism?*, in which he accused Trotsky of Menshevism, recounted his many sharp exchanges with Lenin, and added the henceforth familiar charge of "under-estimating the peasantry". Stalin followed, more briefly and incisively, in the same vein. Denunciation of Trotsky became a routine exercise in the press and in party meetings. The most savage blow was the discovery and publication of a forgotten letter written by Trotsky in 1913, full of crude and angry invective against Lenin. No further evidence was required to prove the incompatibility of "Trotskyism" with "Leninism".

Overwhelmed by this flood of invective Trotsky remained silent. He succumbed once more to the mysterious malady which had afflicted him in the previous winter, and doctors advised his removal to a milder climate. He did not attend the session of the party central committee in January 1925. He addressed a letter to it in which he claimed that his silence in face of "many untrue and even monstrous charges" had been "correct from the standpoint of the general interests of the party"; and "in the interest of our cause" he asked to be released from his duties as president of the Military-Revolutionary Council. He left for the Caucasus while the session was in progress. The committee hesitated over what sanctions to apply to him. Extremists, who included Zinoviev and the Leningrad delegation, proposed to expel him from the party, from the party central committee, or at the very least from the Politburo. Moderates, supported by Stalin, were content to relieve him of his military functions. The latter view prevailed; Trotsky was removed from the post of president of the Military-Revolutionary Council and People's Commissar for War. He was succeeded by Frunze, whose appointment was the signal for a powerful campaign to build up the Red Army, neglected since the end of the civil war.

The controversy provoked by *Lessons of October* led, almost casually, to an important innovation in party doctrine. One of the items on which Lenin and Trotsky had once differed, and which was now brought up against Trotsky by his critics, was the so-called theory of "permanent revolution"—a phrase originally used by Marx. Trotsky in 1905 argued that a revolution breaking out in backward Russia, while in its first stage it would remain a bourgeois anti-feudal revolution, would automatically pass over into the stage of a socialist anti-capitalist revolution. Lenin was unwilling to accept the prospect of this transition unless, as both he and Trotsky expected, revolution in Russia kindled the flame of revolution in the advanced countries of the west. The dispute was of little importance, and had been forgotten long before 1917, when Lenin in his April theses appeared to adopt a position nearer to that of Trotsky. But nobody displayed any interest in the issue till Bukharin, in December 1924, made his contribution to the campaign against Trotsky in an article on "The Theory of Permanent Revolution". Bukharin was concerned merely to spotlight Lenin's dissent from Trotsky, and drew no positive conclusion. But when, a few days later, Stalin also published a lengthy essay on the theme, written as an introduction to a collection of his speeches and articles, he used his denunciation of Trotsky's theory as the springboard for a new doctrine of "socialism in one country".

Stalin now abandoned what he later called "the incomplete and therefore incorrect" formula in his lectures of the previous spring, in which he had held that the efforts of one country were "insufficient for the organization of socialism". Having declared that "Trotsky's 'permanent revolution' is the negation of Lenin's theory of proletarian revolution", he proceeded to argue that Lenin had in several passages in his writings contemplated the possibility of a victory of socialism in one country. Stalin admitted that "for a *complete* victory of socialism, for a *complete* guarantee against a restoration of the old order of things, the combined efforts of the proletariat of several countries are indispensable". But did this mean that "revolutionary Russia could not stand up against conservative Europe", and build a socialist régime in the USSR?

Stalin's answer was a resounding negative. The argument was complicated and casuistical, resting extensively on quotations taken out of context. It was also somewhat unreal, since it was conducted in conditions which neither Lenin nor Trotsky had considered possible—the survival of the revolutionary régime in Russia in the absence of revolution in other countries. But psychologically its impact was enormous. It supplied a positive and definable goal. It dispensed with vain expectations of help from abroad. It flattered national pride by presenting the revolution as a specifically Russian achievement, and the building of socialism as a lofty task in the fulfilment of which the Russian proletariat would set an example to the world. Hitherto the dependence of the prospect for socialism in Russia on socialist revolution in other countries had occupied a central place in party doctrine. Now the order of priority was reversed. Stalin boasted that the victory of the revolution in Russia was "the beginning and the premiss of world revolution". Critics of Stalin's doctrine were, implicitly and explicitly, revealed as faint-hearted, timid and mistrustful of the Russian people, sceptical of their capacity and determination. Socialism in one country was a powerful appeal to national patriotism. Indisputably it put Russia first.

Stalin had created a climate of opinion which he was to exploit to the utmost in his struggle against his rivals. But for the moment nobody took his abstruse excursion into theory very seriously. At the session of the party central committee in January 1925, which condemned Trotsky, socialism in one country was not mentioned. Bukharin hesitatingly reverted to it in a speech three months later, without mentioning Stalin, and in terms which suggested that he himself was one of its authors. It appeared, not very prominently, in the main resolution of the party conference in April 1925, which, on the strength of quotations from Lenin, announced that "in general the victory of socialism (*not* in the sense of *final* victory) is unconditionally possible in one country". When the triumvirate broke up some months later, it was alleged that this passage had been the subject of a clash in the Politburo on the eve of the conference. But the evidence suggests that Zinoviev and Kamenev raised no strong objection, and were indifferent rather than hostile. When Stalin celebrated this modest victory in a speech after the conference, he produced yet another quotation from Lenin:

> Only when the country is electrified, only when industry, agriculture and transport have been put on the technical basis of modern large-scale industry, only then shall we be finally victorious.

Hitherto socialism in one country might have been seen as a continuation of NEP, which had also turned its back on the bleak prospect of international revolution, and marked out the road to socialism through an alliance with the Russian peasant. Now Stalin was groping his way to the very different conception of a self-sufficient Russia, transformed and rendered economically independent through a modernized industry and agriculture. Stalin did not press the point, and was perhaps not yet fully conscious of its implications. But it was a dazzling long-term vision; and it fitted in with changes which were beginning to make themselves felt on the economic scene.

The gradual rise of Stalin to a position of authority after the death of Lenin occurred in a period of acute economic controversy and conflict, which was also a period of economic revival. The resolution of the scissors crisis in December 1923 and subsequent party pronouncements heralded a new attention to the restoration of heavy industry. The doctrine of socialism in one country, whatever the intention of its exponents, lent support to the promotion of heavy industry as a condition of self-sufficiency. But it also implied that this could be achieved with the resources of the backward Russian economy. Here lay the crux. The controversy about industrialization, like every other issue in the Soviet economic scene, was bound up with the problems of agriculture, which once more disturbed the current mood of complacency. The grain harvest of 1924, though impaired by a late summer drought, was fair. Nobody seems to have doubted that the peasant, freed from the burdens of the scissors crisis, would deliver to the state collecting organs, at officially fixed prices, the quantities of grain required to feed the cities. Nothing of the kind happened. The grain collections fell disastrously

1) economic = s/c in Dec 1923

short. Private traders appeared for the first time in large numbers on the market, and the fixed prices had to be abandoned. At the turn of the year prices were rising fast. The price of rye doubled between December 1924 and May 1925. With the return of the free market, the scissors had once more opened, this time in favour of the peasant, and the cities were held to ransom. Moreover, the price mechanism operated to increase disparities of wealth in the countryside. It was the rich peasant, the hated *kulak*, who had large surpluses to sell, and could afford to hold them till prices reached their peak. It was reported that many poor peasants, pressed to realize their crop, had sold cheap in the autumn to *kulaks*, who made their profits by selling dear in the spring.

These developments were the starting-point of a keen controversy in the party. The leaders clung to the guiding principle of NEP—conciliation of the peasant; Zinoviev in July 1924 had launched the slogan "Face to the Countryside". A few days later, Preobrazhensky read to the Communist Academy a paper on "The Fundamental Law of Socialist Accumulation", which was widely recognized as a searching challenge to the official line. Marx had shown that the early stages of capitalist accumulation had required "the separation of the producers from the means of production", i.e. the expropriation of the peasantry; so—argued Preobrazhensky—socialist accumulation "cannot do without the exploitation of small-scale production, without the expropriation of part of the surplus product of the countryside and of artisan labor". He rejected as impracticable the principle of "equivalent exchange" between town and country, and advocated "a price policy consciously directed to the exploitation of the private economy in all its forms". Preobrazhensky did not mince his words; and his outspokenness gave a handle to defenders of the party leadership and of the peasantry. Bukharin published an indignant reply, which denounced the article as "the economic foundation of Trotskyism". But Preobrazhensky had confronted the party in the plainest terms with the harsh dilemma of reconciling the process of industrialization with continued indulgence for the peasant.

Throughout 1925, while Stalin manoeuvred cunningly between the other leaders, an open clash between the two policies was avoided. Pressure was strong for further concessions to the peasant, which meant in practice concessions to the well-to-do peasant or *kulak*. A party conference in April 1925 voted three such measures. The agricultural tax, the sole vehicle of direct taxation in the countryside, was to be reduced, and its incidence changed to make it less progressive. The right to employ hired labour, and the right to acquire land by leasing, still partially though ineffectively restricted by the agrarian code, were to be recognized. It was at this moment that Bukharin delivered a speech which was long quoted as the most outspoken exposition of the policy represented in these decisions. He pleaded the cause of "the well-to-do top layer of the peasantry—the *kulak* and in part the middle peasant", who needed incentives to produce. "To the peasants, to all the peasants", he exclaimed, "we must say: *Enrich yourselves*, develop your farms, and do not fear that constraint will be put on you". He denied that this was "a wager on the *kulak*" (a phrase coined fifteen years earlier to describe the Stolypin reform). But he equally rejected "a sharpening of the class war in the countryside". Bukharin, like his adversary Preobrazhensky, compromised his cause by undiplomatic frankness. Stalin seems to have told other party leaders that "Enrich yourselves" was "not our slogan". But it was some months before it was publicly disowned; and the course charted by Bukharin was followed during the rest of the year.

Side by side, however, with policies designed to provide incentives for peasant production, the needs of heavy industry attracted increasing attention. Hitherto the revival of industry had for the most part meant the bringing back into productive use of plant and machinery which had been idle since the civil war; for this no great capital outlays were required. But by the end of 1924 the process had reached its limit. It was estimated that existing factories and plant were being utilized to 85 per cent of capacity. Industry was beginning to approach the levels of production achieved in 1913, and could contemplate an advance beyond them. But to maintain the rate of industrial growth, and especially to revive heavy industry, demanded large-scale capital investment. The party central committee in January 1925 advocated "budget allocations" to industry as well as "an expansion of credit". Obsolescent equipment must be renewed, and new industries created. Thus encouraged, Vesenkha convened "a special conference on the restoration of fixed capital in industry", which remained active for the next 18 months. The party conference of April 1925, which voted concessions to the peasant, also approved a three-year plan for the metal industry, involving a total investment of 350 million rubles.

The year 1925 was still a period of optimism, when it seemed possible to meet all demands of a rising economy. It was not the harvest itself, the best since the revolution, but the sequel of the harvest, which in the last months of the year showed up the dimensions of the problem inherent in relations between industry and agriculture. The state grain-collecting organs abandoned the "fixed" prices of 1924, and were instructed to work on "directive" prices which could be adjusted from time to time. In spite of the experience of the previous harvest, everyone seems to have assumed that the abundance of the crop would keep prices down, that surplus grain would be available for export, and that the proceeds of the harvest would provide funds for the financing of industry. These hopes were disappointed. After the harvest of 1925 the prosperous peasants held large stocks of grain. But they had no incentive to exchange these for money. The reduction of the agricultural tax had relieved the pressure of taxation; the supply of industrial goods was meagre, and offered little that they wished to buy; and, though the currency had nominally been stabilized, a hoard of grain was a more reliable asset than a packet of bank notes. They could afford to wait. Grain came slowly to the market. Under the influences of short supplies, competition with free-market purchasers, and even competition between different state purchasing organs, prices soared. Hopes of grain exports, or of profits from the harvest to finance industry, evaporated. The harvest had been a success for the peasant. The marketing of the harvest was a disaster for the government. The crisis split the party, and gave the signal for a prolonged and bitter struggle between the claims of industrialization and planning on the one hand, and the peasant-oriented market economy promoted by NEP on the other, which was to dominate the ensuing period.

These events were the background of Stalin's ascent to

a position of supreme authority in the party and in the USSR. The year 1925 was decisive. Fear and jealousy of Trotsky was the cement which held the triumvirate together. After his defeat and demotion in January 1925 it began slowly to crumble. Trotsky spent more than three months convalescing in the south. When he returned to Moscow at the end of April 1925 he faced an embarrassing situation. Eastman, a well-known American communist, had spent the winter of 1923–1924 in Moscow, and was a declared supporter of Trotsky. At the beginning of 1925 he published in New York a small book *Since Lenin Died* which gave a detailed and accurate account, from Trotsky's standpoint, of the intrigues conducted by the triumvirate during the last weeks of Lenin's life and after his death, and quoted Lenin's testament—the first reference to that document to appear anywhere in print. The revelations made a sensation. Anxious members of the British Communist Party wrote and telegraphed to Trotsky asking for his comments for publication. The party leaders in Moscow insistently demanded from him a refutation of Eastman's indictment. Trotsky was once more faced with the dilemma of standing his ground, or refusing to fight on what might be called a secondary issue. He still suffered from the deep inhibition which prevented him from coming out publicly in opposition to a majority of his colleagues: "one cannot be right against the party". If it occurred to him that to retreat meant to compromise his cause and disavow his friends, he stifled these doubts in the name of party discipline. On July 1, 1925, he signed a long statement which, as he wrote three years later, "was *forced on me* by a majority of the Politburo". He described the allegation that the party central committee had "'concealed' from the party a number of extremely important documents written by Lenin in the last period of his life", including "the so-called 'testament'", as "a slander". Lenin had left no testament; everything that he had written, notably "one of Vladimir Ilich's letters containing advice of an organizational character", had been communicated to the delegates at the party congress. Stories of a concealed testament were "a malicious invention". Trotsky's statement was published in the British Left-wing *Sunday Worker* on July 19, and in the Russian party journal *Bol'shevik* on September 1, 1925. It was the last triumph of the united triumvirate.

Trotsky on his return to Moscow had been appointed to two or three minor, and largely nominal, posts connected with industry. During the rest of the year he made a few speeches, and wrote a few articles, on industrial development and planning, stressing the need to "catch up with the west", but offering no direct challenge to party policy. His restraint relaxed the last bond that held the triumvirate together. After some preliminary bickering, open dissension broke out over the grain collections crisis. Zinoviev and Kamenev, reversing their earlier position, came out against the peasant orientation, of which Bukharin remained the most articulate champion. In September Zinoviev submitted for publication in *Pravda* an article entitled "The Philosophy of an Epoch". It took the form of an attack on an *émigré* writer, Ustryalov, who had enthusiastically endorsed Bukharin's support of the *kulak*, and joyfully proclaimed that "the peasant is becoming the only real master of the Soviet land". Zinoviev concluded that "NEP, together with the delay in world revolution, is really pregnant, among other dangers, with the danger of degeneration". The party central committee insisted on the removal of phrases that pointed too directly at Bukharin. But the sense of the article, which ran through two issues of *Pravda*, and was published as a pamphlet, could not be mistaken. In the following month Zinoviev published a volume of essays under the title *Leninism*. One of these repeated the attack on Ustryalov, and denounced the slogan "Enrich yourselves", though still without mentioning Bukharin by name. Another quoted Lenin's denunciation of the *kulaks*, and recalled his description of NEP as a "retreat"; this implied that Soviet industry under NEP was a form of "state capitalism"—a conclusion denied by Bukharin. The most decisive chapter of all was a frontal attack on "socialism in one country"; it was impossible to "remain Leninists if we weaken by a single jot the international factor in Leninism". This was a declaration of war, not only against Bukharin, but against Stalin himself.

Zinoviev's abrupt abandonment of the peasant orientation, and espousal of the cause of industry and the proletariat, had a certain logic. A struggle for mastery between Zinoviev and Stalin was a struggle between the Leningrad party organization controlled by the former and the central party organization in Moscow dominated by the latter. Kamenev was head of the local Moscow organization. But this was overshadowed by the central organization in the same city; Kamenev lacked the authority to assert its independence, and was soon ousted. Leningrad was still the most heavily industrialized city in the USSR. It was the home of the proletariat which had been the vanguard of the revolution, and maintained its proletarian tradition. In Moscow the new proletariat had retained far closer ties with the countryside. Zinoviev could mobilize and lead the Leningrad workers against Moscow only from a platform which upheld the pre-eminent claims of the workers, and rejected with contumely the attempt to exalt the rôle of the peasant. Rivalry between the two capitals, and between the two party organizations, between *Pravda*, which was the organ of the party central committee in Moscow, and *Leningradskaya Pravda*, the newspaper of the Leningrad party organization, played a significant part in the struggle for power between Stalin and Zinoviev.

The battle-ground was the fourteenth party congress which sat during the last fortnight of 1925. Stalin and Zinoviev were the main speakers; Bukharin answered Zinoviev, and was answered by Kamenev. While Zinoviev and Kamenev fiercely denounced the *kulak*, Bukharin stood his ground; and Stalin, whose concern was to defeat his two principal rivals, half-heartedly supported Bukharin. The congress took no significant decision on agricultural policy. But it registered a growing impatience with the favours enjoyed by the *kulak*, and it harped once more on the urgency of industrialization. When the dust of party conflict had settled, it was clear that a major decision lay ahead. Bukharin at the congress, in a phrase which was long remembered, made a desperate attempt to prove that conciliation of the peasant was not incompatible with policies of industrialization: "We shall move forward at a snail's pace, but all the same we shall be building socialism, and we shall build it". But snail's pace industrialization no longer satisfied the growing body of opinion which wanted to transform the USSR into a great industrial country, independent of the west. Paradoxically the victory of Bukharin and the defeat of Zinoviev at the congress did not lead to the victory and defeat of the policies for which they respectively stood. It was not altogether misleading when the congress was later dubbed "the congress of industrialization".

Economic problems did not, however, dominate the debate, which opened in a fairly low key, but became more acrimonious when sensitive political and personal issues were broached. Kamenev criticized "the theory of a 'leader'", and launched a personal attack on Stalin. Krupskaya spoke for the opposition, and made a sensation by challenging the doctrine that "the majority is always right". Molotov and Mikoyan were among those who supported the official line, and Voroshilov eulogized Stalin. The delegates on both sides, nominally elected by their party constituencies, had been hand-picked by the party organizations, and a solid phalanx of Leningraders was isolated in a hostile audience. The resolution endorsing the official line was voted by a majority of 559 to 65. *Leningradskaya Pravda*, hitherto the mouthpiece of the opposition, was taken over, a new editor being appointed from Moscow. After the congress a powerful delegation, which included Molotov, Voroshilov, Kalinin, Rykov, Tomsky, Kirov, and later Bukharin, proceeded to Leningrad, and addressed a series of mass meetings of party members. The means of pressure which had silenced and intimidated the followers of Trotsky were now brought to bear on the supporters of Zinoviev. Mass meetings of workers were induced, by large majorities, to condemn their old leaders and vote approval of the congress decisions. The ground was thus prepared for a Leningrad provincial party conference, at which Bukharin was the principal speaker. The same verdict was repeated, and loyal supporters of the party central committee were elected to the Leningrad party organs; Kirov, a young and popular recruit to the party leadership, became secretary of the Leningrad provincial party committee, the *de facto* head of the Leningrad organization. It was a complete take-over. Zinoviev remained a member of the Politburo and president of Comintern. But, expelled from his base in Leningrad, he lost all effective power. Stalin was the victor. But what his victory portended, either economically or politically, was still unclear.

# 9    The USSR and the West (1923-1927)

THE progress towards the establishment of normal relations with the western Powers, which had followed the introduction of NEP, suffered a setback during the turbulent year 1923. The year opened with the French occupation of the Ruhr in reprisal for a German default on reparations. In Great Britain, the fall of Lloyd George left Curzon in undivided control of foreign policy. In France, the no less inflexible Poincaré was at the height of his power. In May 1923 a number of British protests against Soviet misdemeanours culminated in what came to be known as the "Curzon ultimatum". This rehearsed at length the activities of Soviet agents in Persia, Afghanistan and India in violation of the undertaking given in the Anglo-Soviet trade agreement of March 1921. Failing the abandonment of these activities, and the settlement of a number of minor outstanding claims within ten days, the British Government threatened to annul the trade agreement and withdraw its representative in Moscow. The Soviet Government, frightened by this violent onslaught, agreed to comply with most of the demands, and entered into a mild and inconclusive argument on the propaganda question; and for the time being the storm blew over.

In Germany, the one major country which had so far accorded *de jure* recognition to the Soviet Government, the year was also marked by disquieting events. The German economy and the German currency collapsed under the pressure of the Ruhr occupation; and a series of political crises encouraged optimistic observers in Moscow to scent an opportunity to retrieve the failure of March 1921 (see pp. 19, 44 above). In August Brandler and other leaders of the KPD were summoned to Moscow, and plans were laid for a *coup* to seize power in the autumn. But confidence was sapped by differences about tactics. The whole scheme was bungled in a way which led afterwards to endless recriminations. An isolated communist rising in Hamburg on October 23 was easily crushed. By this time Stresemann was installed as the head of a government pledged to restore the shattered economy; and Seeckt, the head of the Reichswehr, showed every confidence in his ability to maintain order. The paradoxical feature of this episode was that it did not disturb German–Soviet relations. The moral was clear. Seeckt, assured of freedom to deal with German communists, had every incentive to continue and develop military collaboration with Moscow, and Stresemann willingly fell in with this policy. The Soviet Government, in Germany as in Turkey, could not afford to support native communists at the expense of its need for allies and partners in the game of international diplomacy. The same lesson could be drawn from its readiness to cultivate friendly relations with Mussolini's Fascist régime in Italy.

The year 1924 opened under more promising auspices. The advent to power of the first British Labour government brought *de jure* recognition of the Soviet Government on February 1; and Italian recognition followed a few days later. In May elections in France resulted in the formation of a Left coalition under Herriot. But, owing to the powerful opposition of French holders of pre-revolutionary Russian bonds, recognition of the Soviet Government was delayed till October. During the summer negotiations went on in London for an Anglo-Soviet treaty to replace the trade agreement of 1921. A treaty, accompanied by the promise of a loan, was signed in August in the face of stiff opposition from British financial and commercial interests, and from the Conservative Party. At this point the Liberals withdrew their support from the Labour government, which was defeated in the House of Commons. The treaty was not ratified, and in the ensuing elections the Conservatives won a sweeping victory. Their success was aided by the publication, just before the election, of the "Zinoviev letter"—a letter of instruction from Comintern to the CPGB to conduct propaganda in the armed forces and elsewhere. The letter was almost certainly a forgery. But its contents seemed plausible; and it was sufficient to inflame public opinion still further against the USSR and its British friends. The new Conservative government, with Austen Chamberlain as its Foreign Secretary, did not formally break off relations, but virtually suspended all dealings with the Soviet Government throughout 1925. Franco-Soviet negotiations for the settlement of debts and claims reached a similar deadlock.

Meanwhile the balance of forces in Europe was changed by the acceptance in August 1924 of the "Dawes plan", diplomatically and financially supported from the United States, for an agreed settlement of German reparations obligations with the aid of a massive international loan. This was the starting-point of a process of reconciliation between the victors and vanquished of 1918, which culminated in the famous Locarno treaty, initialled at Locarno in October 1925, and signed with much ceremony in London on December 1. The essence of the treaty was a mutual guarantee of Germany's existing western frontiers—a voluntary acceptance by Germany of this part of the Versailles peace treaty, which did not, however, extend to acceptance of Germany's eastern frontiers. It was ill-received in Moscow, where it was seen as proof of a new westward orientation in German foreign policy and a reversal of Rapallo. It was moreover understood that Germany had been promised admission to the League of Nations with a seat on the League Council; and the Soviet Government expressed particular apprehension that Germany, as a member of the League of Nations, might be obliged to participate in sanctions decreed by the League against the USSR. An attempt was made to meet these fears by a declaration, signed by all the parties to the Locarno treaty, that a member of the League could be required to participate in sanctions only "to an extent which is compatible with its military situation, and takes its geographical position into account". On these terms Germany finally entered the League in September 1926.

Assurances to the contrary notwithstanding, the Locarno treaty was rightly assessed in Moscow as an attempt to re-integrate Germany into the western world, to wean her from the Soviet entanglement, and to isolate the USSR as an alien element in the society of nations. The attempt was not wholly successful. Germany, still smarting under the humiliation of 1918, was conscious of an inferior status among the western Powers, and did not wish to become exclusively dependent on them. Association with the USSR was no longer as intimate as in the days when the Rapallo treaty brought the two outcasts together. But it remained for Germany a bargaining counter in relations with the west, and an important factor in the European balance of power. Common mistrust of Poland remained a firm link between the two countries. The secret German–Soviet military arrangements were working well; and the Reichswehr would have strongly resisted anything that tended to disrupt them. Economic relations were profitable to both countries. At the very moment when Stresemann was negotiating with Chamberlain and Briand at Locarno, a German–Soviet trade agreement, carrying with it a substantial credit from a group of German banks, was signed in Moscow. For the USSR Germany was its largest and most reliable trading partner.

This was not, however, the only demonstration of German concern to maintain a foothold in eastern Europe. The Soviet Government, not content with denouncing British efforts to build up an anti-Soviet coalition of states, sought at this time to establish special relations with other states which might be interested to resist this design. But, since it was unwilling to undertake any military commitment, and was concerned primarily to forestall combined action against the USSR, the formula proposed was a mutual undertaking by each party not to participate in hostile action, military or economic, against the other, and to remain neutral in the event of a war arising from aggression against the other. A treaty with Turkey on this basis was signed in December 1925. The same formula, with verbal variants, was embodied in a German–Soviet treaty of April 24, 1926. Some Germans invoked the precedent of Bismarck's "reinsurance treaty" with Russia in 1887; and the treaty caused considerable annoyance in the west. Angry interludes from time to time disturbed normal intercourse between Moscow and Berlin. The most serious of these incidents occurred in December 1926, when Soviet shipments of war material to Germany under the secret military agreements came to the knowledge of the German social-democrats, who made a public protest in the Reichstag, to the grave embarrassment both of the German and Soviet Governments, and especially of the German communists and

Right-wing nationalists. But fears of Allied reprisals did not materialize; the western Powers were too much involved in maintaining the good relations with Germany established by the Locarno treaty to raise this awkward question. The storm subsided; and during the next few years, while Soviet relations with western Europe were almost a blank, relations with Germany, political, military, economic and cultural, remained far closer and more fruitful than with any other country.

The revolutionary element in policy and outlook in the relations of the USSR with the outside world, embodied institutionally in Comintern, still sometimes appeared to conflict with the diplomatic activities conducted by Narkomindel in a way which created momentary embarrassment. But the illusory character of the supposed clash between the claims of revolution and diplomacy, encouraged by the pretence that the Soviet Government had no responsibility for the proceedings of Comintern, was revealed in the argument, constantly repeated, that the USSR was the one solid bulwark of world revolution, whose prospects depended on its strength and security. The interests of international revolution and the national interests of the USSR were on this hypothesis inseparable. A corollary of this view was the dependence of all other communist parties, often referred to as "sections" of Comintern, on the Russian party. Any clash between Comintern and the Russian party was unthinkable. When in the spring of 1922 twenty-two members of the Workers' Opposition appealed to Comintern against their treatment by the Russian party, as the statutes entitled them to do, the appeal was rejected out of hand by a commission which included the Bulgarian, Kolarov, and the German, Klara Zetkin. The Russian party alone had led a victorious revolution. It had acquired the right and duty to lead and instruct other parties on the road to revolution. The historical fact that Comintern had developed as an institution built on a Russian model, and centred round the Russian party, lent support to this argument.

The relation of communist parties to the central organs of Comintern was the key-note of its fifth congress which met in June 1924. The KPD leaders who had bungled the

October rising in Germany were condemned as Rightists, and replaced by new leaders from the Left, Ruth Fischer and Maslow. A similar shift occurred in the French and Polish parties, whose leaders, now branded as Rightists, had declared in favour of Trotsky. But, amid much rhetoric at the congress about the virtues of the Left, it was apparent that the main quality demanded of the new Left leaders was disciplined obedience to decisions taken in Moscow. Zinoviev launched the slogan of the "Bolshevization" of the parties, defined in a resolution of the congress as "the transmission to our sections of everything that was and is international, and of general significance, in Russian Bolshevism". Its adoption seemed a matter of course. It was the automatic product of the delay of revolution in other countries; and it drew fresh reinforcement from the doctrine of socialism in one country, which registered the role of the USSR as the unique exemplar of a successful socialist revolution. Stalin, who had hitherto taken no part in the work of Comintern, modestly attended the fifth congress, but left the limelight to Zinoviev, spoke in some of the commissions, though not in the plenary sessions, and made himself known to foreign delegates. Trotsky, who was present, and drafted a manifesto of the congress on the approaching tenth anniversary of the war of 1914, did not speak.

For the next three years the isolation of the USSR in a capitalist world was a source of growing anxiety in Moscow. The capitalist economies of Europe, severely shaken by the war of 1914–1918, had by the middle nineteen-twenties regained their equilibrium, and were enjoying a wave of prosperity, stimulated by American investment. Recognition by Comintern that the western countries had achieved a state of "capitalist stabilization" was qualified by attaching to it the epithets "relative" and "temporary", and was matched by insistence on "Soviet stabilization". But these considerations inspired a mood of caution. Left leaders of foreign parties who had enjoyed favour at the fifth congress were removed within the next two years, and succeeded by moderates. Annual congresses of Comintern were abandoned, being replaced by "enlarged" sessions of IKKI; the sixth congress was not convened till 1928. Visions of the coming revolution were still evoked, but with diminishing conviction. Revolutionary propaganda was conducted, but mainly as a defensive weapon against governments whose hostility was known and feared. The rise of Stalin was greeted with some satisfaction in the west, since it represented the eclipse of revolutionary firebrands like Trotsky and Zinoviev by a moderate and cautious leader, primarily devoted to restoring the fortunes of his own country.

This period was the heyday of the united front, when cooperation of communists with other Left-wing parties and groups was assiduously preached, and of the organization of international "fronts", not ostensibly communist, though encouraged and partially financed from Moscow, which recruited Left sympathizers of heterogenous groups or parties to support causes favoured by Comintern. The most famous and successful of these was the League against Imperialism, whose founding congress in Brussels in February 1927 brought together for the first time delegates from China, India and Indonesia, from the Middle East, from many parts of Africa, from Latin America, and from the Negroes in the United States, on a platform of protest against the tyrannical rule of the imperialist Powers over subject peoples. The Moscow celebrations of the tenth anniversary of the revolution in November 1927, attended by a galaxy of distinguished foreign guests, were the occasion for the foundation of an international society of Friends of the Soviet Union. Organizations like the International Workers' Aid and the International Class War Prisoners' Aid, centred in Moscow but with branches in the other principal countries, served the same purpose of maintaining contacts with the non-communist Left and of wooing sympathy for the USSR.

Relations with the British labour movement were from the first anomalous. The CPGB had been formed in 1920 by the amalgamation of several splinter groups of the extreme Left; its total membership in the middle nineteen-twenties was about 5000. Its weakness was offset by the unique strength of the British trade unions, which formed the hard core of the workers' movement, and had a dominant influence in the Labour Party. Moreover, the unions had shown on more than one occasion warm and effective sympathy for the Russian revolution and the Soviet régime. To win over the trade unions in capitalist countries was the task of the

Red International of Labour Unions (Profintern or RILU) set up in Moscow in 1921. In France and in Czechoslovakia, its efforts were successful in splitting the movement more or less equally between trade unions affiliated to the existing International Federation of Trade Unions (IFTU), commonly called the Amsterdam International, and unions affiliated to Profintern. In Germany no split occurred, and members of the KPD exercised considerable influence in the unions affiliated to Amsterdam. In Great Britain the trade unions, with very few exceptions, remained loyal to Amsterdam. But a majority of British trade unions continued for many years to deplore the split in the international movement, and to call for a reconciliation between the two rival federations. Acute jealousies, as well as deep ideological differences, between Amsterdam and Moscow made this a hopeless ambition.

Profintern was founded at the very moment when Comintern was turning to united front policies. When Lenin at the second congress in 1920 first adumbrated the ideas which took shape a year later under the catchword of the "united front" (see p. 16 above), his remarks were directed primarily to British affairs, and to the need for British communists to support the "MacDonalds and Hendersons" of the Labour Party, whose peculiar constitution made it possible and normal for members of the CPGB to remain at the same time members of the Labour Party. But in Britain the trade unions provided the most natural ground on which the appeal to sympathizing non-communist workers could be made. The typical British communist was said to carry three membership cards in his pocket: of the CPGB, of his trade union and of the Labour Party. Profintern set up a bureau in London; and, responding to this stimulus, the CPGB promoted two united front organizations—the National Minority Movement (NMM) to act as a ginger group within the trade unions, and the National Unemployed Workers Movement (NUWM) to conduct propaganda and agitation, under communist leadership but with broad workers' participation, on one of the major ills of the period. Though the Labour Party rejected repeated requests from the CPGB for affiliation, its rank-and-file members were not initially inhospitable to individual communists. In the 1922 elections two communists were elected to parliament, one as the official Labour Party candidate, the other with tacit Labour support.

Reaction came more swiftly in the Labour Party than in the trade unions. In 1924 the Labour Party prohibited the selection of communists as official Labour candidates. A decision to ban members of the CPGB from Labour Party congresses was taken, but could not be enforced so long as trade unions included them in their delegations. Sympathy for the USSR in the unions was a hardier growth. Tomsky, the Soviet trade union leader, spoke amid scenes of enthusiasm at the British trade union congresses of 1924 and 1925, and a British delegation attended the Soviet trade union congress in December 1924—just after the Zinoviev letter and the defeat of the Labour government. Early in 1925 a joint Anglo-Russian trade union committee was formed with the aim of fostering cooperation between the unions of the two countries. But the project under-estimated the discrepancies and differences of outlook between Soviet and British trade union leaders, and the unwillingness of the latter to place themselves in opposition to the Amsterdam International. The meetings of the committee were the occasion of increasingly sharp recriminations between Soviet and British delegates. The activities of Profintern, and many tough Soviet criticisms of the British leaders, were resented; and the aggressive tactics of the NMM and the NUWM caused continual irritation. In the General Council of the TUC an anti-Soviet majority confronted a dwindling pro-Soviet minority.

The dividing line was the British general strike of May 1926. In Soviet eyes, a general strike was a political act, a bid for power, an act of class warfare and the beginning of a proletarian revolution. On the British side, it remained, as it had begun, a dispute about wages. The trade union leaders, and a vast majority of the workers, were seeking to extract a fairer share of benefits from the existing system, not to overthrow it. The exhortations to revolution radiated from Moscow alarmed and alienated them; and they refused the financial aid offered by the Soviet unions on the plea that it would prejudice their cause—an insult for which the British leaders were never forgiven by their Soviet counterparts. When after ten days they acknowledged defeat and called off the general strike, leaving the miners, whose wrongs had been its original cause and inspiration, to struggle on helplessly alone, this seemed in Soviet eyes conclusive proof that the British trade union leaders had sold out to the bourgeoisie, and that the only hope lay in raising the rank and file of the workers in revolt against a treacherous trade union bureaucracy. Henceforth Soviet animosity against the British leaders was implacable; and failure to shake the loyalty of the majority of British trade unionists to their leaders embittered and frustrated Soviet relations with the movement for many years.

The general strike, and the financial aid to the strikers proffered from Moscow, added fuel to the anti-Soviet campaign conducted by prominent Conservative politicians with increasing vehemence ever since the autumn of 1924. During the winter of 1926–1927 the demand in Conservative circles to break off relations with the USSR became irresistible. In May 1927 the premises of Arcos, which contained some offices of the Soviet trade delegation in London, were raided by the police. The seized documents produced no sensational revelations. The purpose of the exercise was, however, clear and was not to be frustrated. On May 24 Baldwin announced the severance of diplomatic relations with the USSR and the annulment of the trade agreement. No other government followed the British example. But the British presence still dominated the European diplomatic scene. The gesture was sufficient to create widespread anxiety. Fears of war, or at the least of an economic and financial blockade, were rife in Moscow. Pilsudski had seized power in Poland in the previous year; and apprehension was felt that Britain might instigate, or support, military action by him against the USSR. The British TUC added to the discomfiture of the Soviet leaders by voting, at its annual congress in September 1927, to dissolve the Anglo-Russian trade union committee, which had long been a target of attack by Trotsky and the opposition in Moscow. No ray of light appeared on the horizon. A grain collections crisis of formidable dimensions followed the harvest. The battle with the opposition in the party reached its peak of bitterness. Even in Asia Soviet fortunes were at their lowest ebb.

Throughout this period the United States Government inflexibly refused to recognize the Soviet Government or to have any relations with it. This attitude was reiterated by successive

Presidents and Secretaries of State, and was challenged only
by a handful of radical intellectuals and by a few bankers
and businessmen interested in a revival of trade with the
USSR. After an official embargo on trade had been removed,
a ban on loans to the USSR, a veto on the acceptance
of Soviet gold on the alleged ground of contested ownership,
and a refusal by the banks to grant credit, constituted an
effective prohibition on any large transaction. But a trickle
of trade began to flow. In 1924 the Soviet authorities set
up a trading corporation in New York under the name Amtorg,
the counterpart of Arcos in London. An unofficial Soviet
emissary resided in Washington, and occasionally visited the
State Department in a private capacity. In 1925 the American
financier Harriman secured a concession to work the manganese
mines in the Caucasus. Though the project was not a success,
and the concession was later cancelled, it was a breaking
of the ice. But it was not till after 1927, when industrialization
was on the way in the USSR, that American industrialists
became seriously interested in the Soviet market.

# 10  The USSR and the East (1923-1927)

THE non-European countries occupied only a peripheral place in Marx's thought, and were neglected by the First and Second Internationals. When Lenin, in his famous work published in 1916, diagnosed "imperialism" as the highest, and last, phase of capitalism, he was more concerned with its implications for the imperialist countries than for their colonial subjects. The proclamations to the peoples of Asia during the first year of the revolution were for the most part incitements to revolt against foreign, and in particular British, rule; and the founding congress of Comintern in March 1919 included in its manifesto an appeal to the "colonial slaves of Asia and Africa". It was the second congress in June 1920 which first sought to lay down a policy for what were called "the colonial and semi-colonial countries". Theses drafted by Lenin called for "a close alliance of all national and colonial liberation movements with Soviet Russia". Whether the national movements with which this alliance would be struck would be bourgeois-democratic or proletarian-communist depended on the stage of development of the country concerned. In backward countries communists must be prepared to support every "national-revolutionary" movement of liberation, even of a bourgeois-democratic character. It was a commonsense solution, which continued to present many practical problems.

After the congress, Comintern took its first major initiative in eastern affairs by convening a "congress of peoples of the east" at Baku, which mustered nearly 2000 delegates, most of them from Central Asia, and predominantly Muslim. Throughout this area it was not difficult to depict British imperialism as the major enemy; and this was the main theme of orators at the congress. But embarrassments arose both from the religious susceptibilities of many Muslim delegates, and from the presence of Enver, a leader of the Young Turk nationalist revolution of 1908, who was widely held responsible for the massacres of Armenians, and whose socialist or democratic credentials were conspicuously defective. The congress had no sequel, and yielded no lasting results. A year later a similar congress of Far Eastern peoples was projected at Irkutsk. The plan fell through, and the congress was eventually held in Moscow in January 1922. But by this time enthusiasm had waned, and it proved less impressive than its predecessor at Baku. In the Far East Japan was the country where industrialization had progressed far on a western model, which possessed a numerous proletariat, and therefore seemed to offer the most promising prospect of revolution. But no Japanese delegates appeared at the founding congress of Comintern; and capitalist Japan was even more impenetrable to the impact of communism than the capitalist countries of the west. It was China, where a growing national movement for liberation from imperialist domination was directed against the "unequal treaties" and foreign settlements in the "treaty ports", which proved the most fruitful field for communist propaganda and Soviet diplomacy.

Lenin, in an article of 1912 inspired by the Chinese revolution of that year, had declared that "the hundreds of millions of toilers in Asia have a reliable ally in the proletariat of all civilized countries", and predicted that the victory of the proletariat "will free the peoples of Europe and the peoples of Asia"; and he described Sun Yat-sen, the Chinese nationalist leader, as a *narodnik* with a "revolutionary-democratic core" in his programme. When in 1918 Sun Yat-sen set up a dissident nationalist government in Canton, which made him the recognized head of the national movement, mutual sympathy between the two revolutionary centres was demonstrated in an exchange of letters and telegrams between Sun and Chicherin. Early in the nineteen-twenties Soviet diplomacy first became active in China. Japanese troops had lingered in Siberia long after the other Powers active in the civil war withdrew their units. But by 1921, under American pressure, they were on the way out. Soviet forces moved gradually eastwards, expelled a White Russian army which had occupied Outer Mongolia, and in November 1921 proclaimed a Mongolian People's Republic under Soviet patronage and control. In the summer of 1922 Joffe was despatched from Moscow in an attempt to clear up relations with the shadowy and largely impotent Chinese Government in Peking. The attempt failed. But in January 1923 Joffe had a meeting in Shanghai with Sun Yat-sen, who had been recently driven out of Canton. It was a moment when the principles of the united front and of cooperation with national movements to resist imperialism were firmly implanted in Soviet policy. A joint declaration signed at the end of the meeting recorded Joffe's acceptance of Sun Yat-sen's view that "neither the communist order nor the Soviet system can actually be introduced into China, because there do not exist there the conditions necessary for the successful establishment of either communism or Sovietism". But it was agreed that "China's paramount and most pressing problem is to achieve national unification and attain full national independence"; and Joffe gave an assurance that China could count on the warmest sympathy and support from Russia in this task.

Two months later Sun Yat-sen regained power in Canton; and the agreement with Joffe was the starting-point of a long and fruitful period of Soviet cooperation with Sun and his party, the Kuomintang. In the autumn of 1923 Chiang Kai-shek, one of Sun's lieutenants, was sent to Moscow to negotiate for the supply of arms and equipment; and Borodin, a Russian, American-born, English-speaking communist, arrived in Canton to act as adviser to Sun. During the next year Borodin succeeded in cementing a close alliance between himself and Sun, and between the Soviet Government and Kuomintang, the common aim being to liberate China from the domination of the imperialist Powers—Britain, Japan and the United States. Sun, since his return to Canton, had established there a nationalist government, which planned one day to launch a military "northern expedition" to reunite China and drive out the privileged foreign intruders. Military supplies reached Canton in modest but increasing volume from the USSR; Soviet military advisers helped to build up the Canton army, and to equip and staff a new Military Academy. Sun, with guidance from Borodin, tightened up the loose organization of Kuomintang. The Chinese Communist Party (CCP), founded in 1921, had at this time scarcely more than a thousand members, mainly Marxist intellectuals. Before Borodin's arrival, and apparently at the instigation of Comintern, an agreement had been reached under which members of the CCP were also to become members of Kuomintang. The model was apparently the dual status of many members of the CPGB as members of the Labour Party; and the intention was that this disciplined and devoted group should add a stiffening to the larger and looser organization. All these arrangements masked the discrepancies between Marxist doctrine and the "three principles" of Sun Yat-sen— "nationality", "democracy" and "people's livelihood". This was easy so long as everything else was subordinated to the national revolution against imperialism. It was only when Borodin pressed for the inclusion of the expropriation of landlords in the Kuomintang programme that Sun stubbornly resisted, and Borodin had to give way.

At the end of 1924 Sun Yat-sen embarked on a journey to Japan and northern China to take stock of the situation. He fell ill on the way, and died in Peking on March 12, 1925. The succession seemed most likely to fall on Wang Ching-wei, a clever but weak man, who belonged to the Left wing of Kuomintang. Chiang Kai-shek's military capacities, and the prestige which he had acquired by his visit to Moscow, gave him a commanding position. But for the moment he revealed no political ambitions, and leaned heavily on Soviet support in building up the national army. The most sensational event of 1925 occurred on May 30 in Shanghai, when municipal police under British command fired on a demonstration of striking workers and students, killing several of them. This act provoked a general strike and mass labour disorders which lasted for two months, and spread to Canton. For the first time an effective trade union organization was formed in Shanghai under CCP leadership; and membership of the CCP leapt up in a few weeks to 10,000. One result of these first symptoms of workers' revolt in China was to sharpen mutual animosity between Britain and the USSR. Another was to encourage the growth in Kuomintang of a Right wing committed to the cause of national liberation, but hostile to social revolution. Chiang Kai-shek watched events, and manoeuvred quietly between Left and Right.

Concern for the national-revolutionary movement centred on Canton did not exhaust Soviet interest in China. It was northern China which abutted directly on Soviet territory. In August 1923 Karakhan had arrived in Peking as diplomatic representative to the Chinese Government, and concluded in May 1924 a treaty for the regularization of Sino-Soviet relations. The Soviet Government had already renounced the extra-territorial rights and concessions which Russia, in common with the other major Powers, had formerly enjoyed in China. The remaining bones of contention were Outer Mongolia, over which the the Chinese Government still claimed sovereignty, and the Russian-built Chinese Eastern Railway (CER), which traversed the length of Manchuria on its way to Vladivostok. Outer Mongolia was recognized by the treaty as "an integral part" of China; but no date was fixed for the withdrawal of Soviet troops or administrators, and the USSR was determined to keep a firm hand over the Mongolian People's Republic. The CER was placed under the control of a board consisting of five Chinese and five Russian members; but the general manager of the line was appointed by the Soviet Government—an arrangement which caused much friction in the years to come. The Soviet Government was conscious of no incompatibility between the defence of its interests in north China and the promotion of the revolutionary cause in the south. But some circles in Kuomintang keenly resented the conclusion of these agreements by the USSR with sworn enemies of the nationalist movement.

The Chinese Government in Peking which had negotiated the Sino-Soviet treaty was under the loose control of Wu Pei-fu, the warlord who had for some time dominated central China, and enjoyed British support. In the autumn of 1924 hostilities broke out between Wu and Chang Tso-lin, the warlord of Manchuria and a protégé of Japan. Wu's defeat was hastened by the desertion of Feng Yü-hsiang, who held a large area in north-western China. Hitherto a subordinate of Wu, Feng now announced his sympathy with Kuomintang and the nationalist government in Canton—a change of front which may have been encouraged by subsidies and offers of support from Moscow. After the decline of Wu's authority Feng sought to assert his own control over Peking and the adjacent provinces. But this ambition was thwarted by Chang Tso-lin, who drove him out at the end of 1925. Thereafter, the hapless Peking government became the puppet of Chang.

There were now only two major military forces in China—those of Chang Tso-lin in the north, and the rapidly expanding nationalist forces commanded by Chiang Kai-shek in the south. Much of central China was a prey to the disintegrating armies which had once owed allegiance to Wu Pei-fu. It was in these conditions that Chiang took, at the beginning of 1926, the momentous decision to start the long-projected "northern expedition" in the summer. It was not welcomed by Borodin or by the Soviet advisers. The northern expedition had been talked of continually as the ultimate objective of the military preparations, and applauded in principle. But, presented as a concrete plan for the immediate future, it inspired apprehension. Its success was uncertain, and it seemed likely to provoke intervention by the imperialist Powers. The Soviet Government was much alarmed at this time by a dispute with Chang Tso-lin over the CER, wanted no trouble elsewhere, and paid no great attention to events in Canton. Borodin left Canton in January 1926 for a visit to Peking and to Feng's headquarters; and, while he was away, a quarrel broke out between Chiang and the senior Soviet military advisers, who were tactlessly sceptical of the projected enterprise. On March 20, 1926, a trumped-up incident, arising out of the movements of a Chinese gun-boat whose commander was a communist, gave Chiang an excuse for confining several Soviet advisers to their quarters and arresting Chinese communists attached to the armed forces. The advisers were quickly released; but Chiang peremptorily demanded the departure of those who had disputed his authority. When Borodin returned to Canton at the end of April, peace had been restored and honour saved all round. The offending advisers were withdrawn. Blyukher (*alias* Galin), a Red Army officer who had previously served in China and was *persona grata* to Chiang, arrived to take charge of an enlarged team of Soviet military advisers. Everyone now accepted the imminence of the northern expedition, and Blyukher and his staff worked actively to plan and organize it. But the balance of forces had changed. Chiang was firmly in command.

Early in July 1926 the nationalist army 70,000 strong,

with a full complement of Soviet advisers, marched northwards from Canton. The campaign was a brilliant success. Not only was no resistance encountered, but large reinforcements— units from Wu Pei-fu's disbanded armies, and groups of armed peasants living on the plunder of landlords' estates—joined the march. When Chiang at the beginning of September entered Hankow, the great industrial city of central China and the former capital of Wu's dominions, his force numbered some 250,000. A few weeks later he moved eastward to set up his head-quarters at Nanchang—a first step on the road to Shanghai. In November the Kuomintang authorities left behind in Canton, together with Borodin and his staff, journeyed to Hankow, where a national-revolutionary government was proclaimed amid scenes of enthusiasm. The city was enlarged by the accretion of two adjacent industrial centres and renamed Wuhan. It was a moment of triumph, in Wuhan and in Moscow.

Victory concealed, however, the seeds of calamity. So long as the revolutionary movement remained within its nationalist framework, and preached liberation from foreign imperialism, unity prevailed. But, when some of its sponsors began to speak of the liberation of peasants or workers from feudal or capitalist oppression, jarring notes recurred. Kuomintang was predominantly petty bourgeois. It had more small land-owners than landless peasants among its members; most officers in the nationalist forces were said to own land. Nor had it any specific links with the workers, or with the trade union movement in Shanghai initiated by the events of May 30, 1925. The session of IKKI in Moscow in November 1926, which hailed the victory of the Chinese revolution, gave an uncertain lead. It looked forward to the next stage of the revolution, in which the proletariat would take the lead; and it proclaimed the importance of agrarian revolution in China. It instructed Chinese communists to remain in Kuomintang and support the national movement. The CCP was divided and hesitant. But Borodin interpreted the views of Moscow correctly when he insisted on its loyal support for Kuomintang, even if this involved postponement of the demands of workers and peasants to a more convenient season.

The crisis came through a split in Kuomintang itself. The Wuhan government, representing the Left wing of Kuomintang and strongly influenced by Borodin, combined support of the national revolution with much lip-service to the aims of social revolution. Peasant revolts were rife in Hunan, the province to the south of Wuhan; and this was the moment when Mao Tse-tung first became prominent as the champion of the peasants. In Nanchang, Chiang Kai-shek and his generals moved sharply to the Right, expressing open hostility to the communists and to the demands of unruly peasants and workers, which interfered with his nationalist ambitions. These developments were assisted by the changed attitude of the British Government, which, impressed by the sweeping success of the nationalist forces, concluded that it might be wiser to come to terms with them than to fight them. It paved the way to an agreement by returning to Chinese control the British concessions in Hankow and Kiukiang, and proposing to relax or abolish other servitudes imposed on China by the unequal treaties of the past. Chiang, who had long been impatient of Soviet tutelage, and was now strong enough to dispense with it, perceived a dazzling opportunity of realizing his ambitions with the blessing of the imperialists, whose antipathy to the communists and to their programme of social revolution ran parallel with his own.

The full implications of the change were not at once realized. Shanghai was controlled at this time by a minor warlord, Sun Ch'uan-fang, who was clearly in a vulnerable position. In February 1927 the trade unions in Shanghai organized a workers' rising, counting on aid from Chiang Kai-shek, whom they still looked on as a liberator. Chiang made no move; and Sun easily suppressed the rising. A few weeks later Sun's forces were defeated by those of Chiang in a pitched battle outside Shanghai. Once more the workers in Shanghai rose, set up organs of local self-government, and prepared to welcome the entry of nationalist forces into the city. When Chiang eventually arrived, his disapproval of these proceedings was made manifest. Order was enforced by the troops, and organs of government disbanded. Then, on April 12, when everything was ready, Chiang let loose a large-scale organized massacre of communists and militant workers throughout the city. The CCP and the trade unions were wiped out. This time the message was unmistakable. Chiang was fiercely denounced in Wuhan and in Moscow. But these protests did not alter the fact that Chiang commanded the one effective army in central and southern China, and had won the sympathy and toleration of the foreign Powers.

A few days earlier another disaster had overtaken Soviet policy and Soviet prestige in China. On the orders of Chang Tso-lin, and with the complicity of the diplomatic corps, the Peking government conducted a raid on the Soviet Embassy. The Ambassador's residence was spared, but the outlying buildings were ransacked, employees arrested, and a mass of papers seized. The Chinese employees were summarily executed, the Soviet employees held in prison for many months awaiting trial. Large numbers of documents, some genuine, some suitably doctored, were published in various languages by way of demonstrating the communist conspiracy against the established order. Soviet protests fell on deaf ears, and diplomatic relations were broken off. These events preceded by a month the Arcos raid in London and the rupture of Anglo-Soviet relations.

In the summer of 1927 Soviet fortunes in China reached their nadir. In Wuhan, the local warlord declared his independence of Chiang. But he had no more sympathy than Chiang for social revolution, and carried out a massacre of peasants in Changsha, the capital of Hunan. Borodin and the Wuhan government counted on the loyalty of Feng Yü-hsiang, who had just returned from a long and apparently enthusiastic visit to Moscow. But Feng preferred to do a deal with Chiang, as a result of which he dismissed his Soviet advisers, and debarred communists from working in his army. The CCP held a congress at Wuhan in April–May 1927, at which it claimed a membership of 55,000. But its impotence was apparent. The Wuhan government slowly disintegrated. One of its last acts was to demand the recall of Borodin. He left China at the end of July; and the last Soviet military advisers and members of other Soviet missions also took their departure. Of four years of feverish effort directed from Moscow nothing seemed to survive. Blows had been struck from which even the most optimistic observers could see small hope of recovery. During these years a vast revolutionary ferment had indeed been generated all over China. But it remained, for a long time to come, effectively crushed under the iron heel of Chiang Kai-shek.

Ambitious schemes were mooted from time to time to extend communist propaganda and influence over the Pacific area, seamen being regarded as the most promising agents for such work. A conference of Pacific transport workers (mainly seamen, though some railway workers were also represented) met in Canton in the summer of 1924, apparently under mixed communist and Kuomintang auspices. More than twenty delegates were present from north and south China, from Indonesia and from the Philippines; Japanese delegates were prevented from making the journey. The conference sent greetings to Comintern and Profintern. But its platform seems to have been anti-imperialist rather than specifically communist. Nothing further happened till the summer of 1927, when another Pacific conference was held in Wuhan. This time Lozovsky, the president of Profintern, had come from Moscow, and the conference proceeded under his masterful direction. Delegates attended from the USSR and China, from Japan, Indonesia and Korea, and from Britain, France and the United States; delegates from Australia and India failed to arrive owing to the veto of their respective governments. The conference proclaimed its support of the Chinese revolution, demanded independence for Korea, Formosa, Indonesia and the Philippines, and set up a permanent Pan-Pacific Secretariat which led a rather shadowy existence for some years in different centres, and published a periodical called the *Pacific Worker*.

Other parts of the eastern world were less open in this period to the activity either of the Soviet Government or of Comintern. Soviet relations with Japan were not unlike those with other capitalist countries. Once Japanese troops had been withdrawn from the mainland of Siberia, the most important Soviet demands were for the evacuation of northern Sakhalin and for diplomatic recognition. Both these were belatedly achieved in a treaty of January 1925. But the questions of fishery rights and of competition between the CER, which fed Vladivostok, and the Japanese South Manchurian Railway, which fed the Japanese-controlled port of Dairen, were constant causes of friction; and mutual suspicion continued to cloud relations. Initial faith in the revolutionary potential of the Japanese proletariat was not fulfilled. The Japanese police was ruthless and efficient; and the first Japanese

Communist Party dissolved itself early in 1924. It was reconstituted as an illegal organization in December 1926. Some trade unions joined a dissident federation with Left or communist affiliations. But these efforts achieved little except, from time to time, to exacerbate Soviet–Japanese relations; and the party was once more virtually stamped out by wholesale arrests in 1929.

Elsewhere there was little to record. The cause of Indian communism enjoyed little success, except among Indians living in Europe. A small communist party led a precarious existence, constantly harassed by the British authorities. Provincial workers' and peasants' parties promoted by communists showed more promise. The demands of the Indian National Congress for independence or autonomy were widely supported; and protests against the dilatory and half-hearted concessions offered by the British Government were frequent. Some strikes were said to have been fomented by communist propaganda. But the government had the situation well in hand. In Indonesia, a small communist party was reinforced by a popular Muslim nationalist organization and by an incipient trade union movement. In November 1926, apparently without prompting or support from Comintern, it staged a mass rising, which was crushed within a few days. Executions and mass deportations followed, and put an effective end to the Indonesian party for many years. The Middle East offered still fewer opportunities for Soviet diplomacy or for communist infiltration. Relations with Turkey and Persia were designed to counteract the influence of the western Powers, and particularly of Britain, in these countries, and to develop trade between them and the USSR. Occasional embarrassments in dealing with régimes fiercely repressive of all movements of the Left did not disturb the course of Soviet policy. In Egypt the national movement of revolt against British domination grew slowly, and had no affiliations with the USSR. The Arab countries, as well as Palestine, were still too firmly under western control to permit of any significant Soviet or communist activity.

# 11 The Beginnings of Planning

THE conception of a socialist planned economy to replace the market economy of capitalism was deeply embedded in Marxist thought, though little had been done by Marx or by his successors to develop it in detail. But the concept of planning was not specifically socialist; it was inherent in any reaction from the laissez-faire economy of the nineteenth century. The underlying theme of Witte's famous memorandum to the Tsar of 1899 was the need to plan the development of the Russian economy, though nothing was worked out precisely. The Bolsheviks in the crisis of the revolution and the civil war had no time for the theory of planning. But Lenin among others had been impressed by the degree to which the German war economy conformed to a pattern of centralized control and planning. Nor was this accidental. The final stage towards which capitalism was moving before the war by its own inner development was monopoly capitalism. By what Lenin called "the dialectic of history", war was hastening the transformation of monopoly capitalism into "state monopoly capitalism", which constituted "the fullest *material* preparation for socialism". "*Without the big banks*", wrote Lenin with emphasis in September 1917, "*socialism would be unrealizable*". The application of the German model to Russia presented all the difficulties inherent in the building of socialism in a backward economy. Though the recent growth of industry in Russia had been highly concentrated, and dependent directly or indirectly on the state, it was still in a primitive stage of organization, and had little theoretical or practical assistance or guidance to offer to socialist planners. But the principle of planning met with no resistance. The party programme of 1919 demanded "one general state plan" for the economy; and from this time party and Soviet resolutions on economic affairs regularly included the call for "a single economic plan".

For the present, however, plans for particular industries were a more promising approach. The most famous of these was the work of a commission for the electrification of Russia (Goelro) set up in February 1920. This plan had a special fascination for Lenin, who coined the aphorism: "Communism is Soviet power, plus electrification of the whole country". It was just a year later, on the eve of the introduction of NEP, that the decision was taken to establish a "State General Planning Commission (Gosplan)". But Lenin showed little enthusiasm at this time for current discussions of a general plan, which he dismissed as "idle talk and pedantry". While Goelro at once embarked on the practical task of planning and constructing a network of power stations, which later made an important contribution to the process of industrialization, Gosplan was confined for some years to academic exercises in comprehensive planning. Pronouncements were constantly made on the need for a single economic plan. But the party leaders, wedded to NEP and to priority for agriculture, remained lukewarm. From 1920 onwards the most active champions of planning were Trotsky and other critics of the official line. Planning was primarily a policy for industry, with remote and uncertain implications for agriculture; and its practical application meant more and more sweeping inroads into the market economy of NEP. In these conditions progress was slow. Plans for particular branches of production, including agriculture, were drawn up by the departments concerned. But these, unlike the Goelro plan, had no authority; nor was any attempt made to coordinate them. The president of Gosplan complained in the summer of 1924 that, three years after its foundation, there was still no "single economic plan".

The case for comprehensive planning did not go unchallenged. Planning had been much discussed in general terms, but its practical implications had not been explored. A planned economy was a new and untried concept, which defied in hitherto unrecognized ways the traditional rules of a market economy. The aims of the planners were countered by formidable arguments drawn from the armoury of classical economics.

Industry, and especially heavy industry, in the USSR was an inefficient high-cost producer; agriculture with its unlimited supply of peasant labour was a relatively low-cost producer. The maximum return on capital would be obtained by investing it in agriculture, by developing agricultural surpluses for export, and thus financing the import of industrial goods, including capital goods for the eventual development of industry. Even in the field of industrial production, in a country like the USSR where capital was scarce and unskilled labour superabundant, the rational course was to give priority to industries producing simple consumer goods which were labour-intensive, and not to industries producing capital goods which were capital-intensive. But a policy of priority for agriculture and for light consumer industry, however consonant with traditional economic analysis and with the principles of NEP, was the very antithesis of the ambition of the planners to speed the transformation of the USSR into a modern industrial country matching the industrial countries of the west. The arguments of the planners were political rather than economic, or perhaps belonged to a novel and unfamiliar kind of "development economics". The resistance to them, conscious and unconscious, of a large body of economists trained in the old school was strong and persistent.

It was the scissors crisis of the autumn of 1923 which, by revealing the inadequacies of NEP, brought about measures of state intervention in the economy which were the first steps on the road to comprehensive planning. Wildly fluctuating prices disrupted orderly relations between country and town; heavy industry stagnated; figures of unemployment persistently rose. Price controls were introduced at the end of 1923. In January 1924 the party conference which called for a revival of the metal industry also, pursuing a perhaps unconscious train of thought, instructed Gosplan to "establish a general perspective plan of the economic activity of the USSR for a number of years (five or ten)". But the planners, though supported by Vesenkha as the champion of industry, still encountered the powerful opposition of Narkomzem and Narkomfin, the custodians of the market economy and of financial orthodoxy; and it was not till the following year that some advance was made. In August 1925 Gosplan issued its "Control Figures of the National Economy" (in essence, preliminary estimates) for the year beginning October 1, 1925. The figures were a mere outline, occupying with explanations and commentary less than a hundred pages; and they were marked by the resolute optimism which continued to inspire the efforts of Soviet planners. They were not mandatory; the economic departments were merely invited to take account of them in framing plans and programmes. The sceptics derided the figures as pure speculation. Sokolnikov, the People's Commissar for Finance, called the proposals for an increased emission of currency to finance the plan "a formula of inflation"; and the excessive attention given to industry was attacked by Narkomzem. Of the party leaders, only Trotsky greeted the "dry columns of figures" with enthusiasm as "the glorious music of the rise of socialism". The other leaders received them with, at best, polite indifference. The difficulties of the grain collections after the 1925 harvest (see p. 79 above) thwarted the optimistic estimates of the planners and discredited their work.

In these circumstances it was not surprising that the important fourteenth party congress in December 1925, which ended in the defeat of Zinoviev and Kamenev, ignored the control figures, and had little to say about planning. Nevertheless, it was a turning-point. It was significant that Stalin should have attacked Sokolnikov as the principal advocate of keeping the USSR an agrarian country dependent on imports of industrial goods from abroad. The congress heralded the gradual abandonment by Stalin, once Zinoviev and Kamenev had been eliminated, of the peasant orientation inherent in NEP, and his conversion to far-reaching projects of industrialization. The congress resolution expressed determination to "ensure the economic independence of the country, the development of the production of means of production, and the formation of reserves for economic manoeuvre". All this, though its advocates may not have realized it, was a commitment to planning, and gave a strong stimulus to Gosplan and to the regional planning commissions which had been set up in many parts of the country. Hitherto the plans for particular industries and for agriculture had been drawn up by the departments concerned without any attempt at coordination. Now planning was to become comprehensive, for the economy as a whole. A new period had opened.

The question was no longer whether to industrialize, but how to industrialize. Before 1925 industrial production had been climbing slowly out of the trough of the revolution and the civil war to reach its former levels. Hitherto the goal had been to restore what had been lost or destroyed. Progress in industrial technology in the capitalist countries since 1914 had actually enlarged the gap between the USSR and the industrialized countries of the west. New construction and new technological equipment were a crying need. Now that the way was clear for a fresh advance, major decisions of policy were required, which would have to be based on a broad plan for the whole economy.

During the next two years the authority and prestige of Gosplan steadily increased. In March 1926, at a first Union planning congress, the task of Gosplan was divided into three branches—a "general" long-term plan, a "perspective" five-year plan, and annual operational plans; and a month later the party central committee, in a resolution on industrialization, demanded "the reinforcement of the planning principle and the introduction of planning discipline". The "general plan" proved to be an abortive enterprise. It was never completed, though it continued for some time to encourage visions of a long-term transformation of the economy. But the idea of planning for a five-year period caught the imagination, and stimulated the ambitions, of the planners. It compelled them to confine vague and remote prospects within the term of a fixed period; on the other hand, it was easier to produce optimistic estimates which were to be realized five years ahead than to limit oneself to the prospects of a single year. Alternative plans drafted by Gosplan and Vesenkha rivalled one another in their predictions of industrial development, and continued to excite controversy. The control figures of 1926 and 1927 were both fuller and more cautious than those of 1925. But interest in Gosplan shifted to the more ambitious projects of the five-year plan; and it came to be understood that the control figures were to be geared to this still hypothetical plan. The order was given to base the operational plans (called "production and finance plans") of particular industries on the estimates in the control figures. The structure of planning gradually took shape.

At this point a sharp division of opinion manifested itself

in Gosplan between what were called the "genetic" and the "teleological" schools. It was significant that the former consisted mainly of non-party economists, most of them former Mensheviks, employed in Gosplan, and the latter of party members or of economists sensitive to the official party line. The "geneticists" argued that planning estimates must be based on the "objective tendencies" inherent in the economic situation, and were limited by those tendencies. The advocates of "teleology" maintained that the decisive factor in planning was the goal in view, and that one of its aims was to transform the economic situation and the tendencies inherent in it. Directives, not prediction, were the basis of the plan. This made planning a political, and not purely an economic, activity. Evidently both elements were present in all planning, and decisions rested on some balance or compromise between them. In practice the "teleologists" tended to reject the rules of a market economy, and claimed to override them by positive action; and this meant that they paid less attention to the conciliation of the peasant. These attitudes constituted, though this was rarely admitted, a direct challenge to NEP. In the later stages the effect of the "teleological" approach was to encourage the belief that, given sufficient determination and enthusiasm, no planning target was too high to attain. This mood came to dominate the preparation of the final version of the first five-year plan.

The identification of planning with industrialization was manifest from the outset. The underlying motive and driving-force was to develop Soviet industry, to catch up with the west, to make the USSR self-sufficient and capable of confronting the capitalist world on equal terms. An industry comparable to the industry of the western world had still to be created. The party congress in December 1925 accepted without question the principle of priority for the production of "means of production" over the production of consumer goods. This meant large investment in heavy industry which brought no immediate benefit to the consumer. To create reserves for investment from within industry itself, the costs of production were subjected to a "régime of economy", and brought within the scope of planning. Since, however, other opportunities of reducing costs were limited, the régime of economy bore most heavily on the workers; productivity must go up, or wages must come down. At the same time persistent attempts were made to force down retail prices by decree. But this resulted in increasing shortages of goods at the official prices, and left the consumer, especially in rural areas, at the mercy of the private trader, who still flourished under NEP conditions. The burden and discomforts of planning for industry began to come to the surface.

At first nobody tried to press these issues too hard. The costs of industrialization had not yet been fully counted. When Dzerzhinsky, the president of Vesenkha, died in July 1926, in the midst of a sharp controversy about the rate of investment in industry, his successor, Kuibyshev, revealed himself as a fervent advocate of what came to be known as "forced industrialization". Restraint was still imposed by the fact that the united opposition, Trotsky and Zinoviev, consistently pressed for more industrialization, and were at this time denounced by Stalin and Bukharin as "super-industrializers". What divided the two camps in the latter part of 1926 was not so much a difference about the desirability or the pace of industrialization, but the optimistic assumption of the majority, not shared by the opposition, that these policies could be pursued without severe strain on the economy, and in particular on its peasant sector. Opposition criticism was however silenced by the charge of lack of faith in the Soviet régime or in the working class. It was at this time that two major construction projects were approved—Dneprostroi, the great dam on the Dnieper river, and the Turksib railway connecting Central Asia with Siberia (see pp. 145–147 below).

The optimism of the last months of 1926 was succeeded by the anxieties of the following spring and summer, when the hostility of the west seemed to threaten the USSR with blockade or war. But this reversal of mood, far from calling a halt to the haste for industrialization, strengthened the determination to make the USSR self-sufficient, and to enable it to face a hostile capitalist world. Successive draft plans were prepared and circulated; and those who protested that the targets set were unrealistically high were soon outnumbered by those who called for more rapid and intensive progress. The "régime of economy" was followed by a campaign for the "rationalization of production"—a term which covered a variety of pressures on workers and managers to increase efficiency and lower costs. "Rationalization" in several different forms could raise the productivity of labour, i.e. the output per worker employed. It could do so by tightening up organization, in management or on the shop-floor, by concentrating production in the most efficient units, by standardizing production and reducing the number of models produced. It could do so by arranging for the more efficient and economical utilization of existing plant and machinery. It could do so, above all, by modernizing and mechanizing the processes of production, in which the USSR lagged very far behind the major industrial countries. All these methods of rationalization were extensively tried from 1926 onwards, and achieved some success in reducing costs. But in a country like the USSR with scarce capital resources their scope was limited. In particular, the mechanization of industry, the largest source of rationalization, depended in this period mainly on the importation of machines from abroad, and very often on the employment of foreign personnel to give instruction in manning them. These conditions meant that the productivity of labour depended to a greater extent in the USSR than in the west on the physical energy of the workers. Productivity had to be raised primarily by harder, more efficient, better disciplined physical work; and every form of persuasion and pressure was directed to ensure this result.

The implications of planning for other sectors of the economy were also disquieting, and were faced with reluctance. The cult of the peasant, wholeheartedly upheld by Bukharin, was still powerful throughout 1927; and the influence of Narkomzem, though now on the wane, still put a brake on the aspirations of the planners. Narkomfin continued to resist the assumption that unlimited credits could be made available for industrial expansion, and waged a stubborn struggle for what was dubbed "the dictatorship of finance" against "the dictatorship of industry". This raised the issue of "financial" controls, through manipulation of the supply of credit and the monetary system, as against "physical" controls through state decrees, which were exemplified in the heavy industries working directly on state orders, and in the monopoly of foreign trade. It was only gradually, even in the minds of the planners, that the financial instruments were recognized as inadequate, and replaced by direct "physical" controls. These controversies turned ultimately on the attitude to be adopted to the market economy which was the foundation of NEP. It was at first assumed that the planners would work within the market economy. Slowly and painfully, the incompatibilities between planning and industrialization, on the one hand, and NEP and the market economy on the other, came to light.

# 12 The Defeat of the Opposition

THE period between the fourteenth party congress in December 1925 and the fifteenth in December 1927, which was marked by the beginnings of effective planning, the first steps in a programme of intensive industrialization, and the ripening of the agricultural crisis, also saw the culmination of an embittered party conflict, in which Trotsky fiercely and unsuccessfully challenged Stalin's growing monopoly of power. When the triumvirate broke up, and Stalin defeated his rivals at the fourteenth congress, Trotsky remained haughtily silent; Zinoviev and Kamenev had in the past equalled, and sometimes outdone, Stalin in the vehemence of their attacks on him. But, when Zinoviev and Kamenev took up the cause of industrialization against the peasant orientation of Stalin and Bukharin, and when Stalin's personal ambitions became more open and more menacing, neutrality was no longer possible. In the summer of 1926, Trotsky, Zinoviev and Kamenev with their followers constituted themselves as a "united opposition", and appeared as such at the July session of the party central committee. The sequel showed the strength of Stalin's control of the party machine. Trotsky was at first cautiously handled. But Zinoviev lost his seat in the Politburo, and Kamenev his government offices. The united opposition enjoyed much sympathy in the party ranks. But its active supporters were not more than a few thousand; and these on various pretexts were constantly harassed by the authorities.

Lack of internal cohesion and of mutual confidence added to the handicaps of the opposition, which took the field without any clear-cut line other than denunciation of the party leaders. The public withdrawal of the mutual accusations which Trotsky, Zinoviev and Kamenev had levelled at one another in the past three years invited ridicule. Zinoviev's vacillating temperament and proneness to compromise made him uncongenial to Trotsky, who, having cast off earlier inhibitions, called for an unflinching offensive against Stalin. Scarcely had the united opposition been formed when, by an unfortunate coincidence, the *New York Times* published for the first time the text of Lenin's testament. Though Trotsky was certainly not privy to the publication, the supposition that knowledge of the document had come originally from him, or from sources close to him, was not unfounded. Bitterness between the two protagonists in the struggle reached its peak. At a heated session of the Politburo Trotsky branded Stalin as "the grave-digger of the revolution"; and the party central committee, reacting to the growing tension, dismissed Trotsky from his membership of the Politburo. At a party conference in October 1926 and a session of IKKI a month later, Stalin attacked Trotsky in language of increasing virulence, vindictively exhuming his pre-1914 record of flirtation with Menshevism and acrimonious exchanges with Lenin. The opposition was indicted not only for "fractionalism"—a sin condemned by the party congress of 1921—but for a "social-democratic deviation". Stalin was, however, still content to bide his time, and did not bring the issue to breaking-point.

In the spring of 1927 the turn of events in China spurred Trotsky to fresh protests; and in May the opposition issued a document, drafted mainly by Trotsky, and known from the number of its original signatories as "the declaration of the 83", which offered the fullest *exposé* hitherto available of its views. Apart from its excursion into foreign affairs, the declaration denounced current agricultural policy for ignoring the process of "differentiation" among the peasantry, and for neglecting the poor peasant in order to bolster up the *kulak*. In general terms, it accused the party leaders of substituting "the petty-bourgeois theory of socialism in one country" for "Marxist analysis of the real situation of the proletarian dictatorship in the USSR", and of favouring "Rightist, non-proletarian and anti-proletarian elements" inside and outside the party. It also demanded full publicity for the views of the opposition. Coming at a moment when the leaders had been severely shaken by Chiang Kai-shek's *volte-face* in China and by the rupture of relations with Britain, this was a telling blow. A month later, on flimsy pretexts, Trotsky and Zinoviev were summoned before the party control commission, the organ entrusted with the maintenance of party discipline, and threatened with expulsion from the party. After angry exchanges, the question was referred to the party central committee where the battle continued, both Trotsky and Stalin speaking more than once. The only novel feature of the debate was the charge against Trotsky of disloyalty to the Soviet state in face of its enemies. He was now branded not merely as a heretic, but as a traitor ("the united front from Chamberlain to Trotsky"). Finally the opposition was induced to sign a declaration re-affirming its unconditional loyalty to the national defence of the USSR, and disclaiming any desire to split the party or found a new party. On these terms the proposal to expel Trotsky and Zinoviev was shelved.

This respite did not, however, mean any remission in the hounding of the opposition. The struggle against Trotsky was the occasion for the introduction or perfection of many of the instruments of control characteristic of Stalin's dictatorship. Since the first attacks on Trotsky at the end of 1924, the access of the opposition to the press had been severely restricted. Zinoviev had been muzzled when his *Leningradskaya Pravda* was taken over in January 1926. Now the ban became absolute. Articles on the Chinese crisis submitted by Trotsky in April 1927 to *Pravda* and *Bol'shevik* were rejected. Throughout the summer attacks of increasing violence on him and his supporters were published in the press without any right of reply. Opposition meetings were interrupted and broken up by hooligans. The opposition submitted to the party central committee an extensive "platform" of its views, once more drafted mainly by Trotsky, and demanded that it should be printed and circulated in preparation for the party congress, now fixed for December 1927; this was refused. Attempts were made to print it illegally. On September 12 the OGPU discovered the illicit press, and arrested those engaged in the work. Fourteen members of the party were expelled; and Preobrazhensky, who admitted complicity, was added to the number. The occasion was significantly remembered as the first time when the police power of the OGPU had been invoked to quell dissent in the party.

From this point events moved steadily to their predestined conclusion. Mass meetings were organized to denounce the opposition and demand the expulsion of its leaders. Well-known supporters of the opposition were removed from the scene of action by appointments to posts in distant parts of the USSR or to diplomatic posts abroad. At a session of the presidium of IKKI on September 29, Trotsky delivered a two-hour indictment of Stalin's policies. He was then voted out of IKKI with only two dissentients. The same experience was repeated a month later, amid scenes of violence, at the party central committee. Stalin himself proposed the removal of Trotsky and Zinoviev from the committee; this was carried, apparently without a vote. The Moscow police were active at the tenth anniversary celebrations of the revolution on November 7, harassing Trotsky and other opposition leaders as they drove round the city, and seizing banners with opposition slogans. Zinoviev met similar treatment in Leningrad. These public appearances of the opposition leaders were denounced as hostile demonstrations. A week later Trotsky and Zinoviev were expelled from the party by vote of the party central committee; and Kamenev and several others were dropped from the committee.

When therefore the party congress assembled in December 1927, Trotsky and Zinoviev were absent, and the occasion was something of an anti-climax. Twelve opposition members were removed from the party central committee. Kamenev and Rakovsky, who made the principal speeches for the opposition, were frequently interrupted; and their case was weakened by would-be conciliatory approaches behind the scenes to the party leaders, which were contemptuously repulsed. The congress expelled from the party 75 "active workers of the Trotskyite opposition" and 15 other dissidents. Trotsky and Zinoviev were replaced in the Politburo by Kuibyshev and Rudzutak, both stalwarts of the official line. But Trotsky, though expelled, had not been silenced and was still dangerous. The Politburo decided to remove him and about 30 of his chief supporters from Moscow. Most of these were assigned to minor official posts in Siberia or Central Asia. Trotsky refused such an assignment, and was forcibly deported under an article of the criminal code relating to counter-revolutionary

activities. Exceptionally—for they were recognized as presenting no danger—Zinoviev and Kamenev were banished to
Kaluga, only a few hundred miles from Moscow; and even
this sentence was not rigidly enforced. Trotsky's place of
exile was Alma-Ata, a town on the furthest confines of Soviet
Central Asia, remote even from the railway. Here he remained
till his deportation from the USSR a year later, conducting
a slow, but voluminous, correspondence with members of
the opposition scattered all over Siberia, receiving from time
to time secret reports from supporters still at large in Moscow,
and addressing a flow of protests, personal and political,
to the authorities.

The defeat of the united opposition, and the expulsion
of the only figure in the party whose stature made him
a match for Stalin, was a historical landmark. When the
party congress of 1921 banned "fractionalism" and the propa-
gation of dissentient opinion, the aim was to maintain the
unity of the party and the loyalty of its members. Dissent
in the party carried party sanctions, but was not yet disloyalty
to the state. Party representatives of state institutions were
obliged to follow the party line and to speak with a single
voice. But this obligation did not extend to non-party representatives. By 1927 the distinction between party and state had
been gradually eroded. Economic as well as political emergencies strengthened the need for a firm undivided authority.
"The supreme historical task of building a socialist society",
declared a resolution of the party conference in October
1926, "imperatively demands a concentration of the forces
of party, state and working class on questions of economic
policy". Decrees were now sometimes issued in the joint
name of the party central committee and the central executive
committee of the Congress of Soviets. The power of the
state was available both to enforce party edicts and to enforce
party discipline on party members. Supreme authority in
party and state was concentrated in one institution—the
Politburo of the party; and that authority was absolute. It
was significant that the opposition headed by Trotsky was
the last to be officially designated by that name; the word,
familiar in the practice of western democracy, implied opposition to the ruling party which was not incompatible with
loyalty to the state. In the next stage, dissent was described

as "deviation"—the language not of political differences, but of doctrinal heresy. Finally, dissident groups were simply branded as "anti-party", hostility to the party being unconditionally identified with hostility to the state.

The elimination of legal opposition was part of a process which concentrated and centralized the combined authority of party and state, and made it absolute. The results were often unpremeditated, but were none the less irresistible. The same forces were at work in many fields. The limited licence hitherto accorded in the press and in journals to expressions of independent opinion on peripheral issues (sometimes accompanied by an editorial reservation) now almost entirely disappeared, control being silently achieved not by direct censorship, but by changes in editors and editorial boards. A proliferation of different literary schools—some *avant-garde*, some formalist, some professedly proletarian—had been characteristic of the years after the revolution. A pronouncement of the party central committee in 1925, apparently drafted or inspired by Bukharin, showed a willingness to tolerate these multifarious approaches to literature, none of them directed against the régime, and a reluctance to choose between them. Among these literary organizations was one calling itself the All-Russian Association of Proletarian Writers (VAPP), dominated by an ambitious literary politician named Averbakh, who had good party connexions, and from 1926 onwards conducted a campaign, in the name of a "cultural revolution", to place VAPP in control of all literary productions, and to suppress the publications of other schools. It was not till December 1928, after prolonged resistance, that the party central committee issued a decree placing all publishing under party and state control, which was in practice exercised through VAPP. It seems clear that this consummation had not been planned, or even perhaps desired, by the central committee, and least of all by Stalin. But corruption spread from the top. Petty dictators at lower levels eliminated their rivals by cajoling and flattering the superior authority, and by imitating its methods.

The drive to strengthen and centralize authority was especially conspicuous in the domain of law. The administration of law had originally been reserved to the constituent republics of the USSR, each of which had its own courts and its own People's Commissariat of Justice. But the constitution of the USSR of 1923 provided for a Supreme Court of the USSR with powers to rule on questions of law submitted to it by the Supreme Courts of the republics; and the Praesidium of the TsIK appointed a Procurator whose function it was to supervise the administration of law throughout the USSR. The constitution also established a Unified State Political Administration (OGPU)—the heir of the original Cheka, whose name it often continued to bear in popular speech—to control the GPUs of the republics, which now became local agencies of a powerful central organ. While each republic had its own criminal code (the code of the RSFSR serving in practice as a model for the rest), the USSR issued in 1924 a set of "Foundations of Criminal Legislation", which sought to reserve for the exclusive competence of the USSR "state crimes", alternatively described as "counter-revolutionary crimes", and crimes threatening "the administrative order". The republics were instructed to bring their criminal codes into line with the "foundations". The task was evidently approached with reluctance. It was not completed for the RSFSR till the middle of 1927, and somewhat later for the other republics.

Centralization of authority was accompanied by a gradual modification of current attitudes to law. The Marxist conception of law as an instrument of class rule, destined eventually to wither away with the state, and in the meanwhile to be administered with special indulgence for workers and peasants, was silently abandoned. The market practices of NEP demanded the development and strict enforcement of civil law. The maintenance of law and order under the label of "revolutionary legality" became a major objective. Initial emphasis on the reformatory rather than the punitive aspects of penal policy faded away. These changes reflected the growing economic and political tension. Such episodes as the assassination of the Soviet representative in Warsaw in June 1927, and the explosion of a bomb in Leningrad a few days later, led to a loud outcry against monarchists, *provocateurs* and agents of foreign governments; and the demand for what were officially called "measures of social defence" automatically increased the powers and prestige of the OGPU. The tenth anniversary of the creation of the Cheka was enthusiastically celebrated in December 1927, a few weeks after the tenth anniversary of the revolution. In March 1928 an instruction "On Penal Policy and the Régime of Places of Confinement" paved the way for an extension of the hitherto limited network of "concentration camps" for political offenders under the management of the OGPU, and prescribed the severest measures of repression for "dissidents and professional criminals and recidivists". The year 1928, which followed the defeat of the opposition, and was marked by the growing pressures of industrialization, witnessed throughout Soviet society the imposition from above of a powerful and despotic authority, of a rigid orthodoxy of opinion, and of the harshest penalties on those who offended against it.

# 13 The Dilemma of Agriculture

THE experience of the 1925 harvest (see p. 79 above) showed that the problem facing the planners of agricultural policy was not only to increase production, but to bring the product to the market; and it pointed ominously to the power of the well-to-do peasant and the *kulak*. The marketing crisis had, however, been surmounted, and optimism prevailed. The mood of hoping for the best was encouraged by the record harvest of 1926. When it had been gathered, many peasants had ample resources, and were sellers of grain. The market stringency of the previous year was not repeated, and prices were moderate. A feature of the grain collections was the increased participation of the agricultural trading cooperatives, which, though financed and controlled by the state, proved more popular and more efficient than the state purchasing agencies. The successful outcome of these operations helped to bring about the discomfiture of the opposition at the party conference in October 1926; the crisis predicted by the opposition had not occurred. It also encouraged the party leaders to step up programmes of industrialization, and to neglect the future consequences of this pressure for the peasant market.

In the external crises which overtook the USSR in 1927, and in the first flush of enthusiasm for planning, not much attention was paid to agriculture. The harvest, though lower than that of 1926, was satisfactory, and it was assumed that the grain collections would again proceed smoothly. This confidence was misplaced. The mood had changed since the previous year. The anxieties of the international situation, and talk of war and invasion, had spread to the countryside. After two good harvests the peasant was better off than

at any time since the revolution. The well-to-do peasant
had reserves both of grain and of money. The supply of
industrial goods which he might want to buy was still meagre.
The currency was once more being eroded by inflation; in
a state of uncertainty and alarm, grain was the safest store
of value. For those peasants who held stocks no incentive
remained to put them on the market. The grain collections
in the autumn of 1927, which should have been the best
months, yielded less than half the quantities of 1926. But,
if the well-to-do peasant had turned sour, provocation also
came from the other side. The united opposition ever since
its formation in the summer of 1926 had continued to denounce
the policy of toleration for the *kulak*; and in October 1927
the party central committee, not to be outdone, called for
"a reinforced offensive against the *kulak*". What happened
in the autumn of 1927, though neither side perhaps at first
realized its full import, was a declaration of war between
the authorities and the well-to-do peasant who held the large
available stocks of grain in the countryside.

An atmosphere of false security prevailed at the party congress in December 1927. At the climax of the battle with
the opposition, it would have been inopportune to admit
that the country was in the throes of a grave crisis. Molotov
observed regretfully that "the advantage of the larger scale
of production lies in practice on the side of the well-to-do
peasant and the *kulak*". But Stalin remarked mildly that
"the way out is to unite small and minute peasant holdings,
gradually but surely, not by pressure, but by example and
persuasion, into large holdings based on common, cooperative,
collective cultivation of the land"; and the resolution of the
congress, though it declared it to be "the fundamental task
of the party in the countryside" to bring about "the unification
and conversion of independent peasant holdings into large
collectives", added that this could be done only with the
consent of the "labouring peasants". Hard things were said
at the congress about the *kulaks*. But the resolution went
no further than to recommend higher and more progressive
taxation of well-to-do peasants. No immediate emergency
seemed to be pending. But no sooner was the congress over
than the deadly nature of the threat to the food supplies
of cities and factories was proclaimed in a series of decrees

and emergency measures. Steps were taken—too late—to speed up the supply of textiles to country markets. Leading party members were despatched on tours of the principal grain-producing regions to supervise and enforce the collection of grain. Stalin made a three-weeks' tour of the main centres in western Siberia, where large stocks were believed to exist.

What were called "extraordinary measures" were widely applied. An article of the criminal code was invoked which imposed the penalty of confiscation for concealment of grain. Propaganda and persuasion alternated with direct coercion. The situation was desperate. By hook or by crook, the holders of grain were induced to deliver it to the collecting organs; it was admitted that the recalcitrant holders of grain were not all *kulaks*, and that many so-called "middle peasants" were also compelled to disgorge their reserves. Not much distinguished these procedures from the wholesale requisitions of the days of war communism. Between January and March 1928 very large quantities of grain were obtained, and in March Rykov announced that the grain crisis had been "taken off the agenda". The first battle of the grain had been won by the government, but in conditions which promised that the war would continue, and would be fought out with extreme bitterness. On one side, well-to-do peasants had been harshly, often brutally, treated. On the other, bread queues appeared in the cities; and scarce foreign currency, sorely needed to finance industrialization, had to be spent on imports of grain to make up the deficiency. No easy or acceptable answer could be found to the question who should suffer from the grain shortage.

The harshness of the "extraordinary measures" shook and divided the party. Many workers still had close ties with the countryside, and were well aware of what had been done. Disaffection was said to have spread to the ranks of the Red Army, composed predominantly of peasants. Rykov was apparently the first of the party leaders to express disquiet, and was soon joined by Bukharin, throughout the NEP period the leading advocate of the conciliation of the peasant, and Tomsky, who was now seriously disturbed by the pressures imposed by industrialization on the workers and on the trade unions. At a crucial session of the party central committee in July 1928 the line was drawn between those who wished to relax the pressure on the peasant, even at the cost·of slowing down the pace of industrialization, and those who gave unconditional priority to industrialization, however severe the measures of coercion inflicted on the peasant. Bukharin spoke of "a wave of dissatisfaction" and "outbreaks" in the countryside, and of "a return to war communism". Stalin professed to temporize, admitted that excesses had occurred, and expressed the belief that these would be avoided in the forthcoming grain collections. Some increase in agricultural prices was conceded. The resolution condemned "violations of revolutionary legality" and "the frequent application of methods of requisition". It was a hollow compromise. No doubt remained that the party machine, with Stalin, Molotov and Kuibyshev in command, was now firmly geared to all-out industrialization, and that whatever measures were required to secure supplies of food for the cities and the workers would be taken.

The experience of the grain collections in the autumn of 1928 repeated that of the previous year on a larger scale. The total figure for the harvest had been maintained. But the essential crops for human consumption, wheat and rye, had fallen off. The authorities were more aware than before of the critical situation, and were more determined and ruthless. Organization had improved; a new central organ, Soyuzkhleb, was set up to control the collections. The reserve stocks in the hands of the peasants had been depleted by the raids of the spring of 1928. The peasants were better prepared for a fresh onslaught, and more adept at concealing what they held. More important still, stringency in the cities revived and expanded the black market. Private traders travelled far and wide in rural areas, offering prices for grain much in excess of the modestly increased official prices. The battle on both sides was fiercely engaged. Legal pretexts were once more invoked to justify confiscation. Reprisals were frequent for real or imaginary offences. In the Urals and in Siberia a system was devised by which the village Soviet or the village assembly was induced to agree on a quota for the village, which was then imposed on the well-to-do peasant under threat of severe penalties. This system, nicknamed the "Ural-Siberian method" of grain collection, was subsequently extended to other regions, and was a powerful instrument of victimization. Disorders and mass demonstrations against the grain collections were reported. Greater latitude was apparently allowed to the local authorities to make "decentralized" collections of grain for delivery to towns within the region, so that comparison with the previous year's figures may be misleading. But only 8·3 million tons of grain were collected by the central collecting organs in 1928–1929 against 10·3 millions in 1927–1928; and this included only 5·3 million tons of wheat and rye against 8·2 millions in 1927–1928. What was certain was that nobody delivered grain to the official agencies except under some degree of coercion or fear.

The situation quickly became desperate. Bread was the staple diet of peasant and industrial worker alike; Moscow, with a population less than two-fifths that of Berlin, consumed more bread. With the progress of industrialization the urban population was rapidly increasing. In the winter of 1927–1928 bread queues were familiar in the cities; and butter, cheese and milk were rarely to be had. State stocks of grain were exhausted. The deficiency was made good by importing grain, by mixing barley and maize with wheat and rye in bread-making, by coarse grinding, by bread rationing in the large cities, and by recourse to the black market. The restraints imposed on the private trader in the towns were inoperative in the countryside. Even attempts to discriminate against him in the provision of such facilities as storage and transport proved largely ineffective. Of the marketed grain from the 1928 harvest 23 per cent was taken by private traders. In July 1928 the party central committee, faced with this competition and with the demands of the new "Right" opposition in the party, had decided to concede an increase in the official prices for grain. The prices paid for grain by the official collecting agencies in 1928–1929 were about 20 per cent higher than in the previous year. But prices on the black market soared faster. It was calculated that the prices of agricultural products in private trade, which in 1927–1928 exceeded the official prices by about 40 per cent, were almost double the official prices in the following year. This may well have been an under-estimate. The scarcity was now chronic. Bread cards were introduced in Leningrad in November 1928 and in Moscow in March 1929; these were honoured up to the extent of available supplies. No cards were issued to non-workers, who were left to the mercy of the private market. Belts had to be tightened all round. Nor was there any security for the future. The belief, on which NEP was founded, that the cities could be fed through a combined system of voluntary deliveries to the state and free sales on the market had broken down.

The dilemma brought into the open a fundamental issue hitherto hidden beneath the surface of day-to-day politics. The maintenance of small individual peasant holdings, often divided into widely separated strips, and practising the ancient three-field rotation, was plainly incompatible with an efficient agriculture. Even in a primitive peasant economy some measure of cooperation between cultivators of the soil was demanded by common sense as well as by socialist doctrine. In pre-revolutionary Russia, this was provided over the greater part of the country at two levels. The smallest unit of production was not the individual, but the household or *dvor*. This varied in size, having in the past often been an "extended" family comprising more than one generation, sometimes supplemented by adoption. In most parts of Russia a group of *dvors* formed a land-holding community (*mir* or *obshchina*) which regulated matters of common concern such as pasture, rotation of crops, ditching, fencing and road-building, and in most cases periodically redistributed the land to take account of the changing composition of the *dvors*.

After the revolution the *dvors* increased in number, but declined in importance, owing to the frequent splitting of family units. This was said to be due to the greater insistence on independence by the younger generation, and especially by the women, who on marriage demanded the establishment of a separate household. But the traditional authority of the *mir*, strengthened by the disappearance of the landlord and the weakening of the *dvor*, increased; it was often a successful rival of the newly established village Soviet. The official attitude to the *mir* was ambivalent and inconsistent. On the one hand, the *mir* generally resisted attempts to change such ancient agricultural practices as the three-field rotation or the strip system of land-holding. Sometimes the enterprising peasant, or the *kulak*, was said to dominate the other peasants in the *mir* for his own advantage. Sometimes he left the *mir*, taking his share of land with him, and set up an independent unit of cultivation. In all these ways, the *mir* perpetuated traditions of the past which the revolution aimed to eradicate. On the other hand, the *mir* was by far the most effective existing agency of collective action in a peasant community. *Narodniks* like Herzen regarded the *mir* as a stepping-stone to socialism; and Marx could be quoted (though his very tentative comment related to a now remote period) as contemplating the possibility that, in the event of "a workers' revolution in the west", the Russian *mir* might serve as "a starting-point for communist development". During the nineteen-twenties, the status of the *mir* was much debated in Moscow. But no attempt was made to interfere with it on the spot; and it survived more or less untouched till the moment of collectivization. The power of party and government in the countryside was still extremely weak.

Forms of organization designed to promote collective cultivation were mainly the creation of the Soviet period. Agricultural cooperatives had flourished before the revolution, and continued to exist, but were concerned with collective marketing, and the provision of credit and the purchase of machines, rather than with collective production. Collective farms (Kolkhozy) and Soviet farms (Sovkhozy), which dated from the days of war communism (see pp. 22–23 above), wilted under NEP. They were said to occupy less than 2 per cent of all land in the USSR, and for some years received little support from the authorities. Many Kolkhozy survived as loose cooperatives, with the collective principle enjoying a much diminished respect. Many Sovkhozy became a by-word for inefficiency. The grain crises of the middle nineteen-twenties led to a renewal of interest in both institutions. The large collective unit was more likely to provide surpluses for the market than the individual peasant working primarily for the needs of himself and his family, and was more amenable to the inducements and pressures of the grain collections. The multiplication of small peasant holdings after the revolution had aggravated the stringency. While Bukharin and his disciples still pinned their faith on the agricultural marketing cooperatives, and hoped that these would lead gradually to an extension of collective cultivation, official policy began to swing towards a revival of the Kolkhozy. A central organiza-

tion, Kolkhoztsentr, was set up in 1926. A movement began
to form new Kolkhozy, which multiplied rapidly after the
middle of 1927. These were smaller than the original Kolkhozy
of the period of war communism; and the practice of collective
working among their members did not extend very far. But
they were a significant attempt to overcome the traditional
conservatism of the mass of peasants, as well as the interested
opposition of the prosperous *kulak*.

The Sovkhozy lagged behind the Kolkhozy; their revival
did not begin before 1927, and was connected with the process
sometimes designated by the catchword "the industrialization
of agriculture". The substitution of even the simplest machines
and implements for the primitive tools of the traditional Russian peasant (typified by the wooden plough, which he could
make for himself) had long been recognized as a crying
need, and attempts had been made to meet it through agricultural credit cooperatives and a state-financed agricultural bank.
More ambitiously, Lenin had proclaimed that "100,000
first-class tractors" were required to convert the peasant to
communism. In the early nineteen-twenties the Putilov works
in Leningrad built a few tractors on an American model;
and from 1923 onwards some hundreds of tractors were imported from the United States. In 1925 a plan was first
mooted to build a large tractor factory at Stalingrad; it
was three years before it was finally approved, and a start
made on the work. Official propaganda underlined the intended rôle of the Sovkhozy as model farms, not only setting
the example of modern methods of cultivation for the surround-
ing peasant holdings, but providing them with tractors and
other agricultural machines. These ideals were far from being
fulfilled. Yet it was becoming clear that, if agriculture was
to be made more efficient through the use of tractors and
complex machines, the work must be conducted in larger
units than the individual peasant holding. In spite of party
exhortations, little progress had yet been made either with
mechanization or with collectivization. This was to be the
task of the next period.

# 14 Growing Pains of Industrialization

THROUGHOUT 1927 opinion in the party moved steadily in favour of rapid industrialization and the five-year plan, though hostile or sceptical reactions still made themselves heard, and the full consequences of these ambitious designs were not faced or understood. The expulsion of the opposition at the party congress of December 1927 cleared the ground by making it possible to silence criticism, and to adopt without undue embarrassment policies which the opposition had championed in the past. The grain collections crisis which followed the congress speeded the process. The first condition of industrialization was that the peasant should supply the necessary food for towns and factories at prices which did not put an intolerable strain on wage levels, and without the diversion of more than a minimum of the resources of industry to the manufacture of consumer goods for the peasant market. These problems had bedevilled the grain collections after the harvest of 1927, and seemed at first insoluble. The successful operation of the first months of 1928 was interpreted as showing that, with a sufficient application of force, the coercion of the peasant was practicable as well as indispensable. The peasant, the recalcitrant factor in a planned socialist economy, had been tamed. During 1928 inhibitions were gradually overcome, and industrialization driven forward relentlessly. The way was open. To force the pace required only an iron will to surmount obstacles, if necessary, by the same methods of coercion. Heroic determination and callous brutality were both manifested in the process.

The tensions set up by forced industrialization extended far beyond the world of the peasant. The revolution had installed new men in the seats of power. But it had not had time to rear and train a new generation of officials, experts, scientists, industrial managers, engineers and technicians of all kinds, whose services were indispensable to any régime; and these services were still performed mainly by the same men who had performed them for the last Tsar and for the Provisional Government. The group of officials and experts who manned the People's Commissariats and other Soviet institutions also included a considerable number of ex-Mensheviks and ex-SRs; the former predominated in Gosplan and Narkomfin, the latter in Narkomzem. Most of these non-party servants of the régime, who had reconciled themselves to the principles of NEP, profoundly disliked and mistrusted the new policies, advised against them, and showed no alacrity—sometimes, perhaps, passive resistance—in carrying them out. From this it was a short step to suspicions, widely entertained in party circles, of an active conspiracy to sabotage them. The wholesale dismissal of non-party officials and experts from positions of influence in Narkomfin and Narkomzem, the two commissariats which put up the most stubborn resistance to forced industrialization, began in the spring of 1928. The most sensational episode occurred in March, when 55 engineers and administrators employed in the coal-mines of the Don basin were arrested on a charge of sabotage, allegedly organized from abroad. After a mass public trial, in which many of the defendants made confessions, eleven death sentences were pronounced, and five were carried out. Others received long prison sentences. Three German engineers originally charged with complicity were acquitted. The trial set a pattern for future demonstrative denunciations and show trials. But for the moment the authorities recoiled somewhat from the suspicion and hostility generated against "specialists" of bourgeois background who were essential to the maintenance and expansion of industry, and issued several reassuring pronouncements. The training of workers as qualified engineers proceeded slowly; and the employment of foreign engineers, at first mainly German, later American, on major construction works was a feature of the period.

It was not only the management side of industry which was subjected to the growing pressure. If the first, though still unstated, condition of industrialization was that the peasant should deliver his grain to the towns for a modest return, the second, and openly avowed, condition was that the productivity of the worker should increase faster than his wages, so that industrial expansion could be in part financed out of the profits of industry itself—an alternative to the unbridled exploitation of the peasant. This had been the chief aim of the campaigns of 1926 and 1927 for the "régime of economy" and "the rationalization of production"; and this, in conditions where other forms of rationalization were limited by scarcity of capital and technical resources, meant above all to raise productivity through a greater physical intensity of labour (see pp. 112–113 above). The campaign to increase the efficiency of the worker was waged on all fronts. Drunkenness, absenteeism and malingering were said to be characteristic of peasants drafted into industry from the countryside rather than of true proletarians; but they seem to have been too prevalent to be curbed by threats of instant dismissal. Side by side with the factory schools which combined vocational training with party indoctrination, the Central Institute of Labour established schools in which young workers received intensive instruction in modern factory techniques. Critics condemned these, as Lenin had once criticized "Taylorism" (see p. 25 above), for treating the worker as "an adjunct of the machine, not a creator of production". Other forms of incentive were not neglected. What was called "socialist emulation" between factories or groups of workers was encouraged by propaganda and by the offer of prizes. The title "Hero of Labour", carrying with it certain privileges, was conferred on specially meritorious workers, and the Order of the Red Banner of Labour was created for award to factories, industrial enterprises or workers' collectives. To celebrate the tenth anniversary of the revolution, "Communist Saturdays" in imitation of the Communist Saturdays instituted by Lenin in 1919—over-time without pay—were worked in factories and mines in several parts of the USSR.

A device tried at this time was symptomatic of the intense pressure now applied to the workers. On the eve of the tenth anniversary of the revolution in November 1927 the authorities announced a planned transition to a seven-hour working day. This project, hailed as a great achievement of the revolution, was denounced by the opposition as a demagogic attempt to lull the workers into quiescence with

the unsubstantial vision of a remote future. But it soon trans-
pired that another end was in view. In order to secure
maximum utilization of plant and machinery some factories
already worked two shifts in 24 hours. It was now proposed
that three continuous shifts of seven hours each should be
worked, leaving only a minimum of three hours for cleaning
and maintenance. The three-shift system was disliked both
by managers and workers, and was at first introduced only
in textile factories, which employed almost exclusively women,
the lowest-paid category. Incidentally, this involved a total
abandonment of the prohibition enacted in the first idealistic
days of the revolution, but long honoured in the breach
rather than in the observance, on night work for women.
During the next two years pronouncements were made from
time to time in favour of the extension of the three-shift
system throughout industry. But resistance to the tensions
and pressures involved was strong. It was noted that, where
the system had been introduced, the productivity of the labour
employed progressively declined through the working period;
and it never appears to have been widely adopted outside
the textile industry.

Wages, however, remained the focus of the relation of
the industrial worker to the employer and to the state. Wages
under NEP were in principle fixed by agreement between
worker and employer—normally by a collective contract
between the trade union and the enterprise or institution
concerned. The principle was not affected by the recognition
on both sides of a link between productivity and earnings,
which was written into the contracts. What radically changed
the situation from 1926 onwards was acceptance of the over-riding importance of planning. The wages bill was too vital
an element in the economy to be excluded from the calculations
of the planners, or to be subject to fluctuations determined
by extraneous causes. After much controversy between the
trade unions and Vesenkha in which both sides purported
to recognize the compatibility of planning with collective
contracts, wage-fixing became subject in practice to two distinct
processes. First of all, the highest authority—generally the
Politburo itself—fixed the total wages fund for the coming
year (in an inflationary period some increase in monetary
terms was inevitable), and determined what increases should

be conceded to which industries. It thus not only fixed the limit of wage payments for which provision had to be made in the plan, but decided which industries were to be encouraged to expand. The second stage was the conclusion of collective contracts, which might be between the trade union central committee and an industry as a whole, or between local trade union committees and individual enterprises. But, since wages had to be kept within limits already laid down, little freedom of negotiation remained; and the discussions of collective contracts were more likely to turn on the conditions of labour or on the "norms" of production.

The original limitation on piece-rates had long ago disappeared; and, where piece-rates were inapplicable, bonuses geared to productivity were a regular part of wage payments. These procedures, which were an essential part of the campaign to gear wages to productivity, required the constant fixing of "norms", or the rate for the job. When a general wages increase was granted in the autumn of 1926, Vesenkha began an agitation for a revision of norms. This could be justified in part by measures of rationalization and mechanization, which increased productivity without imposing additional strain on the worker. But to increase norms was more often simply a way to reduce wages. Controversy between Vesenkha and the trade unions raged through 1927, but ended in recognition of the need for a general re-examination of norms. Wage statistics for the period are dispersed, complex and sometimes misleading. In inflationary conditions, unchanged or even increased monetary payments disguised a decline in real wages. It is certain that, whereas the real wages of the worker rose slowly, but steadily, between 1923 and 1927, for several years after 1928 real wages fell, and the worker, no less than other sectors of society, was subjected to the harsh pressures of industrialization, and constricted by the iron hand of the planned economy.

The rôle of the trade unions had been a matter of controversy in the early years of the régime. The compromise of NEP had rejected "the militarization of labour", and kept the unions formally independent of the state. This independence proved, however, illusory. Under NEP the "commanding heights" of industry were firmly held by the state; and it was unthinkable that the trade unions, still ostensibly non-

party, but now entirely controlled by the Bolsheviks, should
place themselves in opposition to the interests and policies
of the workers' state. The first erosion of the independence
of the unions came from their commitment to increased productivity. This obliged them to accept responsibility for maintaining labour discipline, and for preventing such "anarchistic
methods" as strikes and walk-outs. A strike was treated as
proof of the failure of the unions to exercise due vigilance
and to attend to the needs of the workers. But they could
no longer come out unconditionally as supporters of the short-
term demands of the workers; their rôle was rather to serve
as mediators, in high-level debates within the party, between
these demands and the long-term needs of state industry.
At factory level control was in the hands of a "triangle"
consisting of representatives of the unions, of the management
and of the party. But, where the two last were in agreement,
the union representative was in a weak position; and the
unions were sometimes accused of succumbing to a "managerial
deviation".

Moreover, with the rapid expansion of the labour force
and of trade union membership, the character itself of the
unions underwent a subtle change. The assumption that most
factory workers were class-conscious proletarians, with a fair
sprinkling of active party workers, was rapidly ceasing to
be true. Many of the politically active workers had been
promoted to managerial or official positions. Many of the
new recruits to industry were peasants fresh from the countryside, who had everything to learn in the way of party doctrine
and trade union practices. Much emphasis was laid at this
time on the educational rôle of the unions. But another
consequence was a rapid increase in the authority of the
leaders, represented by the trade union central council, over
the rank-and-file members.

The NEP compromise was maintained with growing
difficulty from 1922 to 1928—the period of Tomsky's uncontested leadership of the trade unions. The period was one
of economic recovery, some of the benefits of which, with
the help of the unions, accrued to the workers. It was the
advent of planning which inexorably brought about the full
integration of the unions into the state machine. The organization and remuneration of labour were an important element

in any economic plan. Narkomtrud had by this time become an auxiliary of the trade unions. It was the trade union central council, rather than Narkomtrud, which took its place in major discussions of policy side by side with the economic organs responsible for other elements of the plan. But all alike were subject to the supreme authority of the Politburo, and executed its decisions; by the middle nineteen-twenties high trade union officials were almost invariably party members directly subject to party discipline. As time went on, however, Tomsky and many of his colleagues became increasingly restive under pressures imposed on industrial workers by the plan, and the neglect of time-honoured trade union traditions. It was not altogether paradoxical that the trade unions should have come out in opposition to current policies of industrial expansion. When the party central committee met in July 1928, Tomsky joined Bukharin and Rykov to make up the minority of three in the Politburo who sought to slacken the pace of industrialization.

Rapidly increasing investment in industry, and primarily in heavy industry, inflated the demand for both agricultural and industrial products in short supply. The scissors crisis of 1923 had demonstrated the impracticability of leaving the conditions of exchange to be regulated by the free play of the market. That lesson was learned, and control of prices became a permanent item of policy. Control of agricultural prices was in theory exercised through the official collections of agricultural products at fixed prices. But from the winter of 1927–1928 inadequate supplies of grain at official prices were obtained from the producers, largely by methods of compulsion, and were supplemented by purchases at higher prices on the private market. Control of industrial prices was more effective, but presented problems of great complexity. From 1926 onwards, amid the growing pressures of industrialization, price policy was a matter of constant controversy. All major industry now being in state hands, the control of the wholesale prices of industrial products was straightforward enough. Ever since the scissors crisis the policy of holding down industrial prices in order to maintain the link with the peasantry had been firmly embedded in party doctrine. Pleas to raise wholesale prices and thus increase the profitability of state industry came from the opposition in 1926 and 1927,

and were indignantly rejected as evidence of the opposition's
neglect of the peasant. Successive variants of the five-year
plan were based on estimates of reduced prices for industrial
goods.

Control of wholesale prices was, however, not matched
by an equally effective control of retail prices; and it was
frequently pointed out that a régime of strictly controlled
wholesale prices combined with floating retail prices merely
widened what came to be called "the wholesale–retail price
scissors", and swelled the undesirable profits of middlemen.
Retail prices had been fixed since 1924 for an increasing
number of standard commodities (see p. 58 above). These
prices, rather unwillingly accepted by state and cooperative
shops and selling organizations, were supposed to be obligatory
for private traders. Enforcement was difficult and uneven.
But police measures, and vigorous propaganda against the
unpopular Nepmen, were more successful in the cities than
in the countryside in restricting private trade. Prices were
fixed without regard to the availability or scarcity of supplies.
A decree of July 1926 called for "a reduction of retail prices
of products of state industry in short supply". During 1927
a series of orders and decrees were issued prescribing a reduction of 10 per cent in the retail prices of standard commodities
prevailing on January 1; and, though this ambitious aim
was not achieved, some prices were brought down, and many
Nepmen driven out of business, in the course of the year.

The results of these reductions proved in practice almost
wholly illusory. They did not improve the real ability of
the peasant or the industrial worker to purchase industrial
goods, since they were accompanied by a now chronic shortage
of supplies both in town and in country. Price levels were
no longer a significant indicator of the economic situation.
The year 1927 saw the beginning of a prolonged and progressive decline in standards of living, due to the pressures of
industrialization and the absorption of available resources for
the planned development of heavy industry. Though the dispar-
ity between official prices and black market prices was less
extreme for industrial than for agricultural products, this
brought little advantage to the consumer, since the shortage
of consumer goods was quite as severe as the shortage of
foodstuffs. The consumer of whatever category was called

on to bear a heavy share of the burden of industrialization. The headlong advance of industry, concentrated primarily on the production, not of consumer goods, but of means of production, imposed ever-increasing strains on the peasant, on the worker, on every aspect of the economy. Apathy and resignation rather than active resistance seems to have been the mood of those who carried the heaviest burdens. But the industrializers continued passionately to believe that the achievement was worth the cost, and that the cost would be willingly borne, or could be enforced on the unwilling.

During 1928 doubts began to penetrate the Politburo itself. The clash of opinions which occurred at the session of the party central committee in July 1928 (see pp. 125–126 above) turned ostensibly on agricultural policy and the pressure on the peasant. But the underlying issue was the pace of industrialization, by which this policy was dictated. What was significant was the open split which now declared itself in the committee between a majority in the Politburo committed to forced industrialization and a dissentient minority consisting of Rykov, Bukharin and Tomsky, who sought to relax pressures all round by slowing down the pace. At the end of September Bukharin expounded his views in a major article in *Pravda* entitled "Notes of an Economist". Starting from the grain crisis, he launched a full-scale attack on current plans of industrialization, which destroyed the equilibrium between agriculture and industry, and the link with the peasantry established by NEP. Investment in industry was being absurdly and incongruously accelerated in face of material shortages not only of grain, but of industrial products of every kind. Agriculture must be allowed to catch up, and industry developed "on a basis provided by a rapidly growing agriculture". Bukharin purported to accept the extent of industrialization already achieved. But the strains were now intolerable, and the pace must not be further increased. He ended by criticizing the "mad pressure" contemplated in current drafts of the five-year plan.

"Notes of an Economist", the last public pronouncement of opposition to the headlong course of industrialization, and the last rearguard action in defence of NEP, was fiercely attacked both by official economists and by Trotsky and his supporters. Priority for agriculture was no longer an acceptable theme. Bukharin, who at this point departed on holiday for the Caucasus, returned in time for a crucial session of the party central committee in November. Vesenkha under the direction of Kuibyshev continued to demand ever-increasing capital investment in industry. The call "to catch up with and surpass" the west had already been made by the industrializers. Stalin took up the theme in a major speech to the committee. Technology, he argued, was "simply rushing ahead" in the advanced capitalist countries: "either we achieve this, or they will destroy us". He cited Peter the Great, whose feverish construction of factories to meet the needs of defence had been "an attempt to leap out of the framework of backwardness". It was the backwardness of the Soviet economy, especially of its agricultural sector, and the isolation of the USSR, which made this "a matter of life and death for our development". The committee approved a figure of 1650 million rubles for investment in industry during the year. Bukharin resisted weakly, tendered and then withdrew his resignation, did not challenge a vote, and finally participated in the drafting of the resolution. His defeat was masked by a show of agreement and reconciliation, but was none the less unmistakable. The victory of industrialization was sealed by the completion of the first five-year plan and its submission to the Union Congress of Soviets in May 1929.

# 15 The First Five-Year Plan

THE period from the publication of the first control figures of Gosplan in August 1925 to the approval of the first five-year plan in May 1929 was one of unbroken advance in the principles and practice of planning. About the middle of the period the centre of interest shifted from the annual control figures to the five-year plan, which entailed a purposeful review of Soviet economic policy and of the long-term prospects of economic development. Party pronouncements from time to time expounded the aims of the plan. The fourteenth congress in December 1925 proclaimed the goal of "economic self-sufficiency", which meant converting the USSR "from a country that imports machines and equipment into a country that produces machines and equipment". The party conference in the following autumn called for "reconstruction of the economy on the basis of new and more advanced technology". The principle of priority for the production of means of production rather than of consumer goods was challenged from time to time by those who sought to slow down the pace of industrialization; and in 1927–1928 the production of consumer goods was expanded to meet the needs of the peasant market. But this was a temporary response to an emergency. The party conference of April 1929, which finally approved the plan, put first on the list of its aims "the maximum development of the production of the means of production as the foundation of the industrialization of the country".

The first tentative Gosplan draft of a five-year plan in March 1926 was concerned primarily with state industry—the only sector of the economy as yet within the control of the planners. Here it budgeted for annual increases in industrial production at rates ranging from 40 per cent in the first year, when unused capacity was still available for exploitation, to 15 per cent in the fifth year—a so-called "attenuating curve" of growth. Investment in industry was to rise from 750 million rubles in the first year to 1200 millions in the fifth. The draft attracted little attention at higher levels, being still regarded as a theoretical exercise rather than a set of practical proposals. The second Gosplan draft a year later was a far more detailed and sophisticated document, devoting separate chapters to different sectors of the economy. Its estimates of industrial growth were considerably more modest than those of its predecessor; and the forecast that the industrial labour force would rise by a million workers during the currency of the plan was scaled down by more than a half. On the other hand, its demands for increasing investment in industry were pitched somewhat higher. Additional funds for the expansion of industry were to be provided by reducing the costs of production through an increase in the productivity of labour; and much was expected from the campaign waged by the authorities to force down prices. Planning had now become a crucial issue, and the draft of March 1927 excited bitter controversy. In Gosplan, the Bolshevik economist Strumilin, the main architect of the draft, was confronted by the cautious ex-Menshevik, Groman. It was attacked by economists in Narkomzem and Narkomfin as a dangerous fantasy, and by Kuibyshev in Vesenkha as unduly timid. The opposition, taken unawares by the sharp turn in the official line towards rapid industrialization, confined itself to the charge that the conversion to planning had come too late to be effective.

From this point pressure to raise planning targets was continuous. The opposition in its platform of September 1927 (see p. 117 above) now condemned existing Gosplan proposals as niggardly and inadequate; already a year earlier, at a discussion of the control figures in the Communist Academy, spokesmen of the opposition outbid those of Gosplan and Vesenkha in the demand for a higher rate of industrialization. In October 1927 Gosplan produced a third draft plan which, by way of conciliating both the doubters and the optimists, offered "basic" and "maximum" figures; the latter represented a substantial advance, both in industrial production and in investment, over the estimates in the second draft. Vesenkha now took up the running, and produced estimates well in excess of those of Gosplan; and this led Gosplan once more to revise its estimates upwards. For the time being progress was halted by the hesitations of the party leaders. At the moment of crisis in the struggle against Trotsky and the opposition it would have been embarrassing openly to concede their demand for more rapid industrialization; and it was inexpedient to press too hard issues on which unavowed differences of opinion existed between the leaders. When the party central committee met at the end of October to approve "Directives for the Drafting of the Five-Year Plan" for submission to the forthcoming party congress, the text, while full of unqualified enthusiasm for the plan, betrayed a notable reluctance to take a stand on any of the contentious problems involved. A balance must be struck between "the interests of accumulation" and "the peasant economy", between heavy and light industry; a "*maximum* transfer of resources" from the latter to the former was ruled out as "a violation of the equilibrium of the whole economic system". A "maximum rate of accumulation" in the current year was not necessarily a guarantee of the most rapid development in the long term. No attempt was made to pronounce a verdict on either of the Gosplan variants or on that of Vesenkha. This was the session which expelled Trotsky and Zinoviev from the committee (see p. 118 above). The few remaining spokesmen of the opposition attacked these vague "directives" which did not contain a single figure. But they were interrupted and shouted down by the majority.

The party congress in December 1927 marked the importance of the five-year plan by devoting seven sittings to the debate on it. Bukharin, whose commendation of "snail's pace industrialization" at the previous congress two years earlier was unkindly recalled by one delegate, did not speak. A few sceptical voices were raised, but these were drowned in the general enthusiasm for the principle of the plan. Some ardent supporters of industrialization criticized the timidity of Gosplan, and praised Vesenkha as the front runner in the race. The party leaders were, however, restrained, notably in their references to agriculture (see p. 124 above). The congress was content to accept the cautious "directives" drafted by the party central committee a few weeks earlier, and made no attempt to translate the enthusiasm for the plan into statistical terms. The main business of the congress was to defeat and expel the opposition. No controversial issue must be allowed to mar the unanimity of the party majority in carrying out this task. The only positive decision taken was to prepare the plan in time for its submission to the next Union Congress of Soviets in the spring of 1929.

Once the opposition had been crushed, and its leaders driven from Moscow and dispersed, the inhibitions which had restrained the top party leaders disappeared. The changed mood was reflected in the harshness of the "extraordinary measures" applied in the grain collections of the first months of 1928. Hitherto the main driving force behind the five-year plan had appeared to come from secondary party figures ensconced in Gosplan and Vesenkha, who sought to convince the leaders of the feasibility of their ambitious projects; Stalin in particular had maintained his favourite rôle of moderator between two extremes. Henceforth it was clear that the weight of the party was behind every upward revision of the estimates; the driving force now came from the Politburo and from Stalin himself. Throughout 1928, with this new impetus and at higher levels, the same pattern as before was followed of rivalry between Gosplan and Vesenkha in pursuit of constantly rising targets. At the same time plans became more specific, purporting to cover every sector of the economy, every industry and every region. Calculations were further and further removed from any "genetic" base, and became to an ever-increasing extent an expression of the will and determination to achieve. Politics were intertwined with economics in the debate, and the final decisions were not so much economic as political. The defeat of Bukharin and the condemnation of his "Notes of an Economist" in the autumn of 1929 made it clear that caution would henceforth be treated as the symptom of a Right deviation. After prolonged discussion between Gosplan and Vesenkha the draft of the plan was completed in March 1929. It offered "basic" and "optimum" estimates both of industrial production over the five years of the plan (1928–1929 to 1932–1933) and of the rate of investment in industry. In the optimum variant, the "attenuating curve" in the rate of increase in production had disappeared; the annual rate of increase was to rise progressively from 21·4 per cent in the first year to 23·8 in the fifth. Investment in industry, planned at 1650 million rubles for the first year, was to be almost doubled by the fifth year (basic variant) or more than doubled (optimum variant). While the economists who drafted the plan seem to have thought of the basic variant as the limit of reasonable expectation, and the optimum as a remote potential, the Politburo boldly adopted a resolution endorsing the plan "in its optimum variant" as "fully corresponding to the directives of the fifteenth party congress".

The plan was finally approved by a large party conference at the end of April 1929. Rykov, though now associated with the Right deviators, was one of three *rapporteurs* who commended it to the conference. But his cautious appraisal was compared unfavourably with the eloquent enthusiasm of Krzhizhanovsky, the president of Gosplan, and the cool, matter-of-fact determination of Kuibyshev, the president of Vesenkha. The plan was published in three large volumes a few days after the conference; owing, no doubt, to lack of time for correction, it still contained the two variants adopted by Gosplan in March, though the basic variant was now obsolete. It was an impressive and comprehensive review of the whole economy. Some of its estimates proved crudely over-optimistic, especially when a year later the targets were raised further, and the decision taken to complete the five-year plan in four years. But it gave a powerful impetus to ambitious projects for the development of heavy industry; and it can be argued that, without the great wave of optimism which it generated, these results could not have been achieved. The five-year plan became the pivot round which the whole economy revolved.

Gosplan was the heir of Goelro, the organ set up to carry Lenin's plan of electrification; *energetika* (energy) continued to be one of its key-words. It was appropriate, and something more than a coincidence, that the most famous project promoted by Gosplan, and executed as a vital part of the first five-year plan, should have been the construction of a great dam and hydro-electric station on the Dnieper river, known as Dneprostroi. In the summer of 1926 Cooper, the American engineer who had built the Tennessee Valley dam, accepted an invitation to visit the site, expressed enthusiasm for its potentialities, and eventually agreed to supervise the construction. The project was to be financed from the Soviet budget; Cooper was employed as a consultant and adviser, not as a contractor. But it required the unstinting use of American technology and equipment and the recruitment of a small army of American engineers. It also involved the erection of new industries and factories to use electrical power generated by the scheme. Power was to be supplied to the Donbass mines, and to large new iron and steel works, as well as to works producing aluminium, high-grade steel and ferro-alloys, forming a vast new industrial complex producing means of production. Two new towns were built—Zaporozhie and Dnepropetrovsk. It was not till about 1934 that the dam itself and the factories planned to consume its output were in full operation.

Dneprostroi set a pattern for many of the ambitious projects initiated under the first five-year plan. One-seventh of all industrial investment under the plan went into the production of iron and steel, though some of this was used to modernize existing factories and plants. The development of the automobile industry attracted much publicity. Before the revolution no motor-cars were manufactured in Russia; the first beginnings were made in two or three engineering works which turned out a handful of cars in the middle nineteen-twenties. In 1927, under the enthusiasm generated by the plan, the first Soviet automobile factory was authorized, a small concern near Moscow with a projected output of 10,000 cars a year. It was not till 1929 that an agreement was signed with Ford of Detroit for the construction of an automobile factory at Nizhny-Novgorod with a planned annual output, to be achieved within ten years, of 200,000 vehicles. At first the emphasis was on cars for personal use. Later priority was given to the production of lorries for industrial use. A road-building programme was a corollary of the growth of the automobile industry. A parallel, but separate, development was the production of tractors. The planned output of the tractor factory at Stalingrad (see p. 130 above), several times increased while the work was in progress, was fixed in the final draft of the five-year-plan at 50,000 tractors a year. By the time it went into production in 1930, two further factories had been authorized. From 1928 onwards the tractor played a leading rôle in programmes for the modernization and collectivization of the peasant economy. It was the major contribution of the first five-year plan to the promotion of agricultural production.

The armaments industry was rarely mentioned in public discussions of the five-year plan. After the civil war, the Red Army had been allowed to run down for some years. But in 1926 steps were taken to strengthen and re-equip it; and, after the war scare of the spring of 1927, recognition of the industrial basis of military power made the five-year plan, with its emphasis on heavy industry, a matter of military concern. Stimulus must have been derived from the secret military arrangements with Germany; and a secret and separate five-year plan was said to exist for the war industries. The aircraft industry led the way, and was followed by the production of tanks. Much importance was attached to the development of a modern chemical industry, which served both military and agricultural needs, and was said by its protagonists to play a rôle comparable to that of electricity in the modernization of the economy.

An enterprise which was actually under way before the beginning of the plan, and which, unlike other major projects, did not depend on imported materials and equipment or on foreign technical advisers, was the construction of the Turksib railway linking Central Asia and Kazakhstan with western Siberia. Central Asia was a rich cotton-growing area. But its communications were poor; and the opening of a fresh outlet for its raw cotton was designed to make the textile industry of the USSR independent of imports from abroad. On the other hand, Central Asia produced inadequate food crops and no timber; the new railway would make possible the supply of grain and timber direct from producing areas in Siberia and relieve the pressure on supplies from European Russia. Russian engineers had ample experience in railway building. Allocations from the budget were readily available; and the construction of 1500 kilometres of track in difficult country proceeded with few hitches. The line was opened for regular traffic on January 1, 1931.

An important planning problem, which was constantly debated and sometimes delayed vital decisions, was the location of the new industries. The issue turned to some extent on the relative practical advantages of different sites. But the main trouble came from local rivalries. It was especially conspicuous in the iron and steel industry, partly because this absorbed so large a share of investment under the plan, partly because the Ukrainians fought hard to retain the pre-dominant place in iron and steel production which they had acquired since the eighteen-nineties, mainly owing to the proximity of large deposits of coal. Their claim was contested by a large school of "easterners", who sought to revive the once-flourishing iron and steel industry of the Urals, and to establish new centres of production in Siberia. In 1927 a number of rival projects were being canvassed and investigated. The first, the planning of which was most advanced, was a large new iron and steel complex at Krivoi Rog in the Ukraine. The second was a project of comparable dimensions at Magnitogorsk in the Urals. This would have to draw its supplies of coking coal by rail from the Kuznetsk basin, 2000 kilometres further east, where a third extensive iron and steel works was proposed. Besides these, a large engineering factory was planned at Sverdlovsk in the Urals, and yet another iron and steel complex at Zaporozhie in the neighbourhood of the Dnieper dam. But the Krivoi Rog project was postponed till the end of the first five-year plan; and the progressive increases in planned investment during 1928 represented in the main a victory for the ambition of the "easterners" to extend Soviet power and activity into the empty spaces of Siberia, and to develop and populate these under-utilized regions. The war scare of 1927 had power-fully intensified the anxiety of the planners to locate the future centres of vital Soviet industry in less vulnerable areas than the Ukraine.

Though the drive for industrialization was the focus of the plan, it was a plan for the whole economy, and could not be anything less. The main and well-recognized stumbling-block in the way of the planners was agriculture. As Rykov once observed, the plan was "at the mercy of a shower of rain"; and the choice of the five-year period in planning was justified by the argument that within this period good and bad harvests would balance one another, and that calculations based on an average would therefore be valid. But an even greater obstacle was the unpredictability of peasant behaviour. The peasant family on its small holding, largely self-sufficient at a traditionally low subsistence level, could isolate itself from the national economy, and frustrate the calculations of the planners. It was the problem of collecting the grain and bringing it to the towns and factories, as much as the problem of producing it, which preoccupied the authorities in the middle nineteen-twenties. The impact of the plan on the peasant was therefore two-fold. It sought to bring the production of peasant agriculture within the scope of its prognostications and directives. But it also aimed at replacing the primitive methods of cultivation hitherto in use by the provision of up-to-date machines and implements. Tractors were merely the most advanced and most ambitious of the tools which industry could supply in order to promote more efficient cultivation of the soil. The production of means of production for agriculture might seem an insignificant part of the programme of industrialization. But the output of agriculture was the basis of the whole plan. A leading official at the party congress in December 1927 called for an increase in grain production of from 30 to 40 per cent in the next five years and of 100 per cent in ten years; the figure of 35 per cent eventually appeared in the five-year plan.

The claims of industrialization rendered obsolete the conception of state finance as the criterion of the feasibility of economic policy. Since the stabilization of the new currency in 1924 Narkomfin had been responsible for preparing, not only the annual budget which controlled state expenditure, but also the quarterly credit plan which regulated the supply of credit through the banks and the rate of emission of currency. Once planned industrialization became the permanent aim, these vital elements in the economy could not elude the attention of the planners. It became clear that the restriction of credit which would have been necessary in order to maintain a stable international currency based on gold was incompatible with the expansion of industry. The choice was not in doubt. As early as 1925, while the budget was strictly balanced, expansion of credit for industry and the consequent increase in the currency issue weakened confidence in the chervonets, the gold parity of which could no longer be maintained in international markets. In the

summer of 1926 export of the chervonets and dealings in
it abroad were prohibited; and the currency became henceforth
a purely internal medium of exchange, subject to manipulation
as the interests of the economy required. This abandonment
of the gold standard after less than two years was a blow
to Soviet prestige, and the growing symptoms of inflation
caused alarm. For a year longer Narkomfin succeeded in
keeping some control over credit. But pressure to step up
the pace of industrialization mounted continuously; and to
confine it within a credit strait-jacket imposed by Narkomfin
was wholly unacceptable.

Before the end of 1927 the battle had been won by the
planners, and the traditional policies of financial control were
obsolete. It was laid down that the state budget would be
geared to the control figures of Gosplan; and the budget,
together with the levels of credit and currency emission, became
effectively a part of the five-year plan. Financial operations
were subjected to the discipline of the plan; and credit was
provided for industrial projects approved by Vesenkha and
Gosplan in the face of predictions in Narkomfin of its inflationary consequences. The mood was one of unbounded confidence.
The boldest expectations seemed to have been surpassed. Investment in large-scale industry under the control of Vesenkha
for 1927–1928 amounted to 1300 million rubles—an increase of
more than 20 per cent on the previous year; and industrial
production planned by Vesenkha was said to have risen by
more than 25 per cent. When the contours of the first five-year
plan began to take final shape in the autumn of 1928, an
investment of 1650 million rubles was projected for 1928–1929.
In October 1928 Pyatakov, known as a "super-industrializer",
a former member of the opposition who had since recanted,
was appointed vice-president of the State Bank; and he became
its president early in 1929. The appointment was significant
of a determination to expand credit to whatever limits might
be necessary to finance industrial production. The total of
capital investment in industry was fixed by a process of
argument between Gosplan, Vesenkha and the higher party
authorities. The provision of funds to meet this demand was
an administrative question. While the plan was couched in
terms of state finance, Narkomfin in effect became a revenue-
raising department which no longer controlled expenditure.

Orthodox sources of finance for industrial development were eagerly explored. Direct taxation—the industrial tax on the private sector, the agricultural tax and income tax—almost doubled in monetary terms between 1926 and 1929. But indirect taxation was more important. Excise, which more than doubled in this period, accounted for one-third of all tax revenue. Excise on articles of common consumption was a tax on the poorest; and the large receipts from the vodka monopoly troubled some party consciences. But alternative sources of revenue were hard to find. From 1927 onwards a series of state loans were floated, subscription to which, in spite of official protestations to the contrary, soon acquired a quasi-compulsory character. By these means Narkomfin was enabled each year to present a balanced budget. Deficit financing would have been regarded as inadmissible. But behind this conventional façade finance had been dethroned from its regulatory rôle, and additional credits were pumped into the economy by the State Bank. Money gradually became simply a medium of exchange and an accountancy unit—a foretaste of the time when it would disappear altogether from the future communist society. But, apart from budget allocations and credits from the State Bank, it was assumed that funds for investment in industry would be made available from the profits of industry itself. In view of the over-riding demand to keep down prices, the only way to achieve this was by reducing costs of production. This had been the consistent aim of campaigns for the "régime of economy", for rationalization and for increased productivity of labour (see pp. 111–113 above). Estimates of productivity had been stepped up in each successive version of the five-year plan; and the planned increase was greater in the capital goods sector than in industry as a whole. The plan as eventually adopted in its optimum variant provided for an increase in productivity during the period of the plan of 110 per cent and for a reduction in costs by 35 per cent. It offered to the worker the prospect of an increase in real wages of 47 per cent and a reduction in retail prices of 23 per cent. But these estimates seem to have been based, not on any realistic assessment of the problem, but on the desire to make the plan statistically coherent, and were indicative rather of the immense pressure imposed by the plan on the industrial worker than of any prospect of their fulfilment.

The adoption of the first five-year plan was a landmark in Soviet history. The essence of NEP had been to concede a measure of freedom to the peasant economy. It would have been impolitic to announce its demise. Stalin argued that NEP, while providing "a *certain* freedom for private trade", had also assured "the controlling rôle of the state over the market". The purpose of NEP was to "secure the victory of socialism". It was officially denied that NEP had been abrogated. A free market in the products of small-scale private industry, and above all of agriculture, still remained. But the subordination of every major economic activity to the dictates of the plan, and the increasingly harsh pressures brought to bear on the peasant, made these survivals of NEP both anomalous and precarious. They were tolerated so long as it was convenient to tolerate them, but seemed of little account. The share of the private sector in the national income, which had exceeded 50 per cent in 1926–1927, fell to insignificant dimensions by the end of the five-year plan. The prestige of the plan, and of the USSR as the protagonist of planning, was enhanced by the economic crisis which broke on the capitalist world in the autumn of 1929. It was widely felt, and not only in the USSR, that the Marxist prediction of the collapse of the capitalist order under the weight of its inherent contradictions had been vindicated. The immunity of the USSR from some of the worst symptoms of the crisis—notably from mass unemployment—encouraged a growing belief that no national economy could any longer be left at the mercy of the iron laws of the market. The Soviet five-year plan, though the conditions of its adoption and operation were not much studied or understood, seemed to provide a pioneering model. The demand for an element of planning in the economies of the capitalist countries grew everywhere, and substantially influenced western attitudes to the USSR.

# 16   The Collectivization of the Peasant

ACUTE anxieties over the grain crisis in the spring of 1929 were veiled in complacent professions of faith in the future. On the basis of the spring sowings a good harvest was predicted. A larger yield was promised from Kolkhozy and Sovkhozy; and a higher proportion of the crop would be marketed. A new procedure was introduced for the grain collections. High quotas were fixed in advance for deliveries from different regions to the collecting agencies. Quotas were assigned to districts and to villages; and within the village pressure was placed on the *kulak* to bear the main burden of the quota. When the harvest of 1929 was in progress, brigades of party officials, party members, workers and trade unionists were despatched from Moscow, Leningrad and provincial centres to supervise and stimulate the collections. The number of persons engaged in these operations can only be guessed. But the territory was vast, and estimates ranging from 100,000 to 200,000 are not implausible. The peasants—not merely *kulaks*, but any peasant who had grain that might be thought of as surplus to his own needs—reacted to the campaign by elaborate measures of concealment and by frantic efforts to sell on the free market. Concealment was a criminal offence, and the line between "trade", which was legal, and "speculation", which was not, was blurred. Reprisals were widely and arbitrarily applied. Failure to fill the quotas was in itself a punishable offence. *Kulaks*, and alleged *kulaks*, were fined, sentenced to imprisonment, or simply evicted from the villages. Scenes of violence and brutality occurred. By these means the quotas were filled, and sometimes over-filled. But these results were achieved in conditions of open hostility between the authorities and the peasants, between town and country. Poor peasants were sometimes said to have applauded measures taken against the *kulaks*. But for the most part solidarity among the peasants prevailed, and *kulaks* and poor peasants were in collusion to thwart the collections. Party expectations of fanning class war in the countryside were disappointed.

It was in these unpropitious conditions that the demand for the collective organization of agriculture was insistently pressed, no longer as a distant prospect, but as a solution of current difficulties. The tractor had long been seen as the key to collectivization. In the autumn of 1927 the large Shevchenko Sovkhoz in the Ukraine managed to acquire 60 or 70 tractors, which were organized in "tractor columns" to work its own fields and those of neighbouring Kolkhozy or peasant holdings. The example was imitated elsewhere; and in 1928 Shevchenko established the first Machine Tractor Station (MTS) with a park of tractors to be leased out to Kolkhozy and Sovkhozy in the region. In June 1929 a central office, Traktortsentr, was set up in Moscow to organize and control a network of state MTSs. Peasant prejudices against the innovation, and perhaps against the degree of state intervention involved in it, were hard to overcome. Tractors were sometimes denounced as the work of Anti-Christ. The success of the experiment seemed, however, to have been limited mainly by the supply of tractors; in the autumn of 1929 only 35,000, most of them of American manufacture, were available for the whole of the USSR. Everywhere it came, the tractor was a powerful agent of collectivization.

The revival of the Kolkhozy which started in 1927 had at first led to a proliferation of small and loosely organized Kolkhozy, whose performance was unsatisfactory. In the middle of 1928 a drive began for "large" Kolkhozy, defined as Kolkhozy with a sown area of 2000 hectares, sufficiently large to be worked by tractors. But at this moment the Kolkhozy were outstripped by the Sovkhozy. At the party central committee in July 1928, Stalin called for the creation of large-scale grain-growing Sovkhozy, which were thought of as "grain factories" working on industrial lines. The prototype of the new Sovkhozy was one appropriately named Gigant, which covered 41,000 hectares of hitherto largely uncultivated land in the North Caucasian region; and this was followed by similar enterprises in the Volga, Ural and Siberian regions. The tractor and the MTS were indispensable pre-requisites of this operation, which was later sometimes criticized as "gigantomania". When collectivization began in earnest, enthusiasm for the Sovkhozy waned, and they were once more eclipsed by the Kolkhozy.

One problem keenly debated in party circles was the question what to do with the *kulak*, or the peasant labelled as such by the authorities, the peasant who commonly farmed the largest and best plots of land in the village, was best equipped with animals and machines, produced and held the largest surpluses of grain, and offered the strongest opposition to Soviet policies, including the policy of collectivization. Opinions were sharply divided. If the *kulak*, together with his land and inventory, were incorporated in the Kolkhoz, he would—so some party members argued—make an important contribution to its production and efficiency. But he would also—as others reasonably predicted—exercise a dominating influence over it, and guide it in directions hostile to the purposes of the party and the state. If, however, he were excluded from the Kolkhoz, what was to become of him? He could not be allowed to retain his land and possessions, and constitute an independent unit of production side by side with the Kolkhoz. He would have to be evicted and expelled from the region; and this was a harsh measure which few at first were ready to contemplate. No acceptable solution could be found.

Throughout the summer and autumn of 1929 the drive at the centre for more and more collectivization increased in intensity. But two assumptions continued to be made even by its most enthusiastic promoters. The first, whatever pressure might be put on the peasant by local authorities, was that collectivization would be voluntary; the second, whatever emphasis might be placed on the urgency of the operation, was that it would take, at any rate, some years to complete. By the end of the year, the leaders had talked themselves out of both these assumptions, and were suddenly prepared to take the plunge into forced and immediate collectivization of Soviet agriculture as a whole. The decisive change seems to have been brought about by two pre-disposing factors. The first was a mood of desperation bred by the annual nightmare of the grain collections; apart from the prospect of increased production, Kolkhozy could be compelled, more easily than the individual peasant, to deliver their grain to the official agencies. The second was a mood of elation inspired by the successes of industrialization and by the prospects of the five-year plan. Agriculture was after all a form of industry. If the forcing of the rate of industrialization had fulfilled the hopes even of the most optimistic, it would show a lack of faith to reject the promise of a forced rate of collectivization. Unflinching resolution was the quality required to carry the position by assault.

Stalin, as was usual with him, refused to enter the arena till the issue was clarified by debate, and the moment was ripe for decision. From April to November 1929 he remained silent. Then he published in *Pravda* the customary article on the anniversary of the revolution under the heading "The Year of the Great Break-Through". Having hymned the triumphs of industrialization and the development of heavy industry, Stalin turned to agriculture, which had achieved "a fundamental break-through from small backward *individual* economy to large-scale progressive *collective* agriculture". The middle peasant, he claimed, "*has entered the Kolkhozy*". The *kulak* was barely mentioned. As regards the future:

> If the development of Kolkhozy and Sovkhozy proceeds at an accelerated pace, there are no grounds for doubting that in three years or so our country will become a great grain country, if not the greatest in the world.

The article contained a vision of the future and an analysis of the present, but no call for immediate action. Considering its character as a celebratory pronouncement, it was restrained and cautious. The party still hovered on the brink of a decision which it hesitated to take.

At the session of the party central committee a few days later the tone was already sharper. Stalin repaired the omission in his article by referring to a "mass offensive of poor and middle peasants against the *kulak*". Molotov was the most uncompromising of several speakers who sought to force the pace of collectivization. He rejected the estimate of the five-year plan (which had modestly foreseen the collectivization of 20 per cent of the sown area in the five-year period) as too extended a projection; most regions would be totally collectivized by 1931, some by the autumn of 1930. The *kulak* was denounced as an "undefeated enemy", who should not be allowed to penetrate the Kolkhozy. But none of the speeches were published till collectivization was already under way, so that their increasingly urgent tone was not known to the party or to the public. The resolutions adopted at the end of the session were less precise than Molotov's pronouncement about dates, perhaps reflecting scepticism among some members of the committee, but called for "a decisive offensive against the *kulak*, containing and cutting off attempts of *kulaks* to penetrate the Kolkhozy". The question what to do with the *kulak* was still not faced. During the next few weeks enthusiastic reports poured in from party organs in the principal grain-growing regions on the progress of collectivization; and on December 5, 1929, the Politburo appointed a commission with instructions to submit, within two weeks, a draft decree on the rate of collectivization in various regions. The commission included representatives of the regions, but no member of the Politburo, and was evidently thought of as a technical, not a policy-making, body.

The fragmentary records of the commission published many years later may reflect the confusion of the proceedings. The commission broke up into sub-commissions which canvassed many bold proposals; one of them seems to have coined the phrase "the liquidation of the *kulaks* as a class". The draft submitted to the Politburo by the commission on December 22 was, however, still relatively cautious. It proposed the collectivization of the principal grain-growing regions in from two to three years (stipulating that in some districts and regions progress might be more rapid), and of other regions in from three to four years; a warning was added against "an ecstasy of dictation". It was assumed that *kulaks* could not be admitted to the Kolkhozy; their means of production, i.e. their machines and their animals, were to be transferred to the Kolkhozy, and distant and inferior land was to be allocated to them. Recalcitrant *kulaks* were to be expelled from the region; those who submitted might be allowed to work in some undefined capacity in the Kolkhozy.

Before the Politburo could consider the commission's report, a conference of Agrarian Marxists assembled in Moscow; Stalin seized the occasion to deliver to it his first public speech for many months. It was the most violent attack yet made on the *kulak*. "Dekulakization" or "the liquidation of the *kulaks* as a class" was described as "one of the most decisive turns in our whole policy". About the same time, an active party worker of Kalmyk origin named Ryskulov, who had been a member of the Politburo commission, criticized its report in a note addressed to the Politburo. It was an odd gesture, which could hardly have been risked without higher approval. Ryskulov called for an increase in the pace of collectivization, and its extension to cotton-growing and live-stock regions, which had been overlooked in the draft, as well as for the surrender to the Kolkhozy of animals, including milch-cows and poultry, which the draft had proposed to leave in the possession of the individual peasant. The draft was revised in the light of these observations, and the revised text adopted by the party central committee on January 5, 1930.

The resolution of January 5, 1930 was the key decision in the process of collectivization. It proclaimed "the *replacement* of large *kulak* production by *large* Kolkhoz production", and "the liquidation of the *kulaks* as a class". Collectivization of the principal grain-growing regions—the Lower and Middle Volga and the North Caucasus—was "perhaps in the main" to be completed by the autumn of 1930 or the spring of 1931, and of the other grain-growing regions in the autumn of 1931 or the spring of 1932. The supply of tractors and machines was to be expedited, but this was not to be treated as a condition of collectivization. An awkwardly worded paragraph provided that, in the transitional period, "the *fundamental* means of production (animals and implements, farm buildings, live-stock reared for sale)" should be vested in agricultural cooperatives within the Kolkhoz. The fate of the *kulaks*—evidently still a controversial issue—was not yet settled. A further commission was set up under Molotov to deal with it, and on January 30, 1930, the Politburo adopted a resolution. Its text has never been published, but its substance was sufficiently indicated by its title "On Measures to Eliminate *Kulak* Households in Districts of Total Collectivization".

What happened in the countryside in the winter of

1929–1930 was determined not so much by the texts of resolutions as by the character of the operation which was mounted to carry them out. During the winter 25,000 industrial workers (said to have been selected from 70,000 volunteers) were assigned to permanent work in rural areas. These were merely the nucleus of a large army of party activists, officials, agricultural experts, tractor mechanics and Red Army men, dispersed over the countryside to shepherd the peasant into the new Kolkhozy. Considerable attention was paid to organization; military terms like "brigade", "headquarters" and "staff" were in use. All concerned received elaborate briefings. In some places courses of instruction were set up for peasants. But few of those responsible had any experience of the countryside, or of peasant life and mentality. The instructions themselves were confused and contradictory; and excess of zeal in interpreting them seemed a venial fault. The proclaimed intention not to apply compulsion to middle or poor peasants was soon frustrated. Since no mercy could be shown to the *kulak*, who was treated as an enemy of the régime, any peasant resisting collectivization was liable to be branded as a *kulak*, or, as being hand-in-glove with the *kulaks*, subjected to the same penalties. Tens of thousands of *kulaks* were evicted from their holdings and dwellings, and turned adrift to fend for themselves or deported to remote regions; their animals, machines and implements were turned over to the Kolkhoz. Few peasants of any category entered the Kolkhoz voluntarily. What the peasants most resented was the demand to surrender their animals. Many chose to slaughter these rather than hand them over. Throughout the campaign the line between persuasion and compulsion was thinly drawn.

A feature of the operation was the demand for larger and larger Kolkhozy—an extension of the "gigantomania" which had begun with the Sovkhozy. Giant Kolkhozy were formed in the principal grain-growing regions, of which the largest covered 80,000 hectares. But the main purpose of the Kolkhozy distinguished them from the Sovkhozy, being not so much to bring virgin lands into cultivation as to combine existing small Kolkhozy and peasant holdings into large units. These Kolkhozy, which might include several villages and several thousand peasant households, were steps, consciously taken, on the road to collectivization, meaning that the whole of the land in a given area was included in one or more comprehensive Kolkhozy; such localities were described as "areas of total collectivization". Much publicity was given to a petition from the Khoper district in the Lower Volga region to become an area of total collectivization, the process to be completed within the period of the first five-year plan. This was hailed as a model. But two major obstacles impeded the expansion of the Kolkhozy—their unpopularity among the majority of the peasants, who clung tenaciously to the possession of their own plots of land and animals, and the inadequate supply of tractors and other machines, which alone gave meaning and purpose to the policy of collectivization. A further grave handicap was a deficiency of personnel—both of party members and Soviet officials having any contact with the countryside or knowledge of its problems, and of the agronomists, veterinary workers and skilled mechanics essential to the working of so vast a transformation.

The widespread confusion resulting from these proceedings, and sporadic disorders among the peasantry, threatened the spring sowings and frightened the authorities. An article by Stalin, published on March 2, 1930, under the title "Dizzy from Success", called a halt to further collectivization. Pressure was relaxed; and during the spring many peasants who had been pressed into the Kolkhozy were allowed to leave them. The retention of small individual holdings and of some animals was now again tolerated. The retreat seems to have been signalled in time to allow sowings to proceed more or less normally. This fortunate step, combined with exceptionally favourable weather, accounted for the record grain harvest of 1930, the largest since the revolution. But a sharp decline in the number of animals was ominous for the future; and the respite was short. The hammer-blows of the first months of the year had broken the back of peasant resistance, and shattered beyond repair the old peasant order. The *kulak* had been expelled or crushed. In areas of total collectivization, the *mir* was formally abolished by a decree of July 30, 1930. When the collectivization drive was resumed at the end of the year, it encountered less active opposition, and proceeded more rapidly. By the middle of 1931 two-thirds of all holdings in the main grain-growing regions had been incorporated in the Kolkhozy, and the rest followed during the next few years.

The full costs of the transformation were, however, not long delayed. Production had been disorganized. The most efficient producers had been thrown out. Though the supply of tractors and machinery slowly increased, the Kolkhozy were not yet equipped to fill the gap. What were more efficient were the grain collections; a higher proportion of the harvest was extracted from the Kolkhozy than had been obtained from individual peasants. The peasant went hungry. More and more animals were slaughtered because they could no longer be fed. Bad harvests both in 1931 and in 1932 crowned the calamity. Grain was still remorselessly collected even from the worst-hit areas; and in the ensuing winter what had been the richest grain-growing regions were prey to a famine which was worse than anything experienced eleven years earlier after the civil war (see p. 36 above). The number of those who died of hunger cannot be computed. Estimates have varied from one to five million.

Collectivization completed the agrarian revolution which had begun in 1917 with the seizure of landlords' estates by the peasants, but which had left unchanged the ancient methods of cultivation and peasant ways of life. The final stage, unlike the first, owed nothing to spontaneous peasant revolt; Stalin aptly called it "revolution from above", but wrongly added that it had been "supported from below". In the past twelve years agriculture had remained a quasi-independent enclave in the economy, functioning on its own lines, and resisting any attempt from without to alter them. This was the essence of NEP. It was an uneasy compromise which did not last. Once a powerful central authority in Moscow had taken in hand the planning and reorganization of the economy, and embarked on the path of industrialization, and once the failure of agriculture under the existing system to supply the needs of a rapidly expanding urban and factory population became evident, the break logically followed. The battle was joined, and was fought out with great tenacity and bitterness on both sides.

The ambition of the planners was to apply to agriculture the two great principles of industrialization and modernization. The Sovkhozy were conceived as mechanized grain factories. The mass of peasants were to be organized in Kolkhozy constituted on the same model. But extravagant hopes of ensuring a supply of tractors and other machines sufficient to make such a project viable in practical terms were disappointed. The party had never had any firm foothold in the countryside. Neither the leaders who took the decisions in Moscow, nor the army of party members and supporters who descended on the countryside to enforce them, had any understanding of peasant mentality, or any sympathy for the ancient traditions and ancient superstitions which were the core of peasant resistance. Mutual incomprehension was complete. The peasant saw the emissaries from Moscow as invaders who had come, not only to destroy his cherished way of life, but to reconstitute the conditions of slavery from which the first stage of the revolution had freed him. Force was on the side of the authorities, and was brutally and ruthlessly applied. The peasant—and not only the *kulak*—was the victim of what looked like naked aggression. What was planned as a great achievement ended in one of the great tragedies that left a stain on Soviet history. The tiller of the soil had been collectivized. But it took Soviet agriculture many years to recover from the disaster which accompanied the process. It was not till the later nineteen-thirties that the production of grain returned to the levels achieved before forced collectivization began; and the loss in the number of animals persisted still longer.

# 17  Patterns of Dictatorship

THE defeat and expulsion of the united opposition at the party congress of December 1927 removed the last formidable obstacle in the way of Stalin's progress towards absolute power. Rifts soon appeared in the opposition itself. The attitude of Kamenev at the congress already smacked of surrender. A month later Zinoviev and Kamenev issued a statement that they had "parted company" with Trotsky's group, that they rejected its policies, and that their motto now was: "Back into the party, back into Comintern". Other defections followed, including some of Trotsky's own followers. The process was hastened when the new turn in official policy became apparent. Trotsky had confidently predicted that the victory of Stalin and Bukharin would presage a sharp reaction to the Right. What happened was exactly the contrary. The grain collections of the first months of 1928 proved that Stalin had abandoned the appeasement of the peasant which the opposition had condemned. Stalin scarcely waited to expel Trotsky from the party and from Moscow before embarking on a policy of forced industrialization at a pace, and at a cost for other sectors of the economy, far beyond anything hitherto contemplated by Trotsky or by anyone else. The exiles languishing in Siberia could now persuade themselves that Stalin had adopted the policies of the opposition, and that their rôle was to help and support those engaged on the work. This at any rate provided an honourable ground for surrender. Inducements as well as threats were offered to defectors. In June 1928 Zinoviev and Kamenev with some forty other penitents were re-admitted to the party.

Throughout the year Trotsky in Alma-Ata kept up a long-distance correspondence with exiles all over Siberia, and strove, with diminishing success, to strengthen their resistance. He was particularly hurt when Preobrazhensky and Radek, whom he had hitherto counted among his firmest adherents, announced their disagreement with him, and made overtures to the authorities in Moscow. Of the prominent former opposition leaders, only Rakovsky still shared Trotsky's view that Stalin's personal dictatorship and the degeneration of the party were key issues on which no compromise was permissible. Trotsky himself was indefatigable. In the summer of 1928 he sent to the Comintern secretariat a long *Critique* of the draft programme of Comintern submitted to the congress, which could not be concealed from foreign delegates. It constituted a biting attack on the doctrine of socialism in one country, which was held responsible for all the disasters of Comintern policy. For Stalin, Trotsky, even isolated in a remote corner of the USSR, still represented a focus of dissent, an organized challenge to his authority; and he decided to be rid of him. To hold one of the heroes of the revolution behind bars would at this time have been inconceivable—a measure of the distance which still separated this period from that of the great purges. The problem was to find a destination to which he could be sent. Neither Germany nor any other European country would admit the notorious revolutionary. Turkey, however, proved willing; and in January 1929 Trotsky was conveyed to Odessa and put on board a ship bound for Istanbul. For nearly four years he found refuge on the island of Prinkipo.

Whether or not Stalin under-estimated the damaging effects of Trotsky's indomitable campaign against him in the outside world, it was true that within the USSR he had divested himself of his last serious rival. The groups in the party which thereafter contested his authority offered no threat to his monopoly of power. They did not organize their sympathizers, and, like the united opposition, found it difficult to present any positive alternative programme. Both the united opposition and the later dissidents used traditional language in condemning the evils of bureaucracy and the repression of independent opinion. "Our disagreements with Stalin", Bukharin told Kamenev in June 1928, "are far more serious than those we had with you". But this was not strictly true. There was an important difference between them, resulting in part from the shift in Stalin's own attitude after his victory at the end of 1927. Trotsky, Zinoviev and Kamenev had criticized Stalin for betraying the aims of the revolution, and compromising with *kulaks* at home and nationalists and social-democrats abroad; this was an attack from the Left. Bukharin, Rykov and Tomsky blamed the haste and ruthlessness with which Stalin pursued the aims of the revolution, and sought to moderate the pace and the intensity of the pursuit; these were attacks, in the terminology of the period, from the Right. Nor did the later dissidents, like the earlier opposition, automatically exclude themselves from the framework of the party. They were commonly described as guilty, not of opposition, but of "deviation".

The new group of Right "deviators" began to form within a few weeks of the downfall of the united opposition, and well before Trotsky's final banishment from the USSR. Rykov, who had long stood on the party Right, openly expressed his dislike, which was shared by many party members, of the forcible grain collections of January–February 1928. Bukharin was slower to declare himself. He had worked hand-in-glove with Stalin in the campaign against Trotsky. But, once the opposition was defeated, he became expendable, and Stalin soon set to work to undermine his influence. Already at the party congress which expelled the opposition in December, Bukharin incurred sly taunts of neglecting what was called "the Right danger". These referred specifically to the affairs of Comintern, but had wider implications. In May 1928, Stalin addressed the Institute of Red Professors, of which Bukharin was the director, deprecating proposals to slow down the progress of industrialization, and speaking of the need to strengthen the Kolkhozy and Sovkhozy, and to improve the grain collections. Though Bukharin's name was not mentioned, the challenge to his views was unmistakable. About the same time Bukharin addressed two memoranda to the Politburo calling in question the pace of industrialization, the pressure which it imposed on the peasant, and the practicability of collective agriculture; and Tomsky became uneasy about the repercussions of industrialization on the workers and on his rôle in the trade unions. Bukharin, among his other functions, was the editor of the party newspaper, *Pravda*, and a member of the editorial board of the party journal,

*Bol'shevik.* New appointments were made to the boards of both organs with the evident motive of curbing Bukharin's authority. At the crucial meeting of the party central committee in July, Rykov, Bukharin and Tomsky, all members of the Politburo, appeared as a minority of three to contest current policies. Bukharin, in virtue of his reputation as the leading party theorist and of his skill in debate, emerged as leader of the group.

The moment was not yet ripe for an open break. The proceedings ended in an empty compromise, and the show of unanimity in the Politburo was maintained. But Bukharin had now read the signals. While the session was in progress, with the knowledge of Rykov and Tomsky, he secretly visited Kamenev, and offered him a coalition with the remnants of the old opposition against Stalin. Stalin he described as "a Genghis Khan", who "will wait for us to start a discussion and then cut our throats". It was a belated and futile gesture. The united opposition had been shattered and dispersed; and Kamenev was a broken reed. Bukharin was no tactician. But, when Stalin learned of the *démarche* some time later, it must have confirmed his determination to crush and humiliate Bukharin. Later in July, Bukharin presided at the sixth congress of Comintern. But Stalin publicly snubbed him by insisting on amendments to the theses which he had drawn up for the congress; and many of the delegates knew that his star was waning. At the end of September he launched his economic broadside "Notes of an Economist", and departed on holiday. But he did nothing to organize his supporters, and left the field open for an intensive propaganda campaign against his opinions, though none of the major dissidents were as yet mentioned by name. The session of the party central committee in November once more resulted ostensibly in a compromise (see p. 140 above). But this time it was plainly Bukharin who had executed a retreat to preserve formal unity, and had suffered a crushing defeat.

Tomsky proved less pliable, and was the first of the trio to incur public disgrace. He opened the trade union congress of December 1928, a month after the defeat in the party central committee, without attempting to canvass contentious questions. But his reluctance, and that of the other trade union leaders, to face the issue of industrialization, was clear.

*Pravda* accused the trade unions of taking an "a-political" line, i.e. of concentrating on the day-to-day interests of the workers, and neglecting "the new tasks of the reconstruction period". The Politburo showed its determination to bring Tomsky to heel by appointing Kaganovich, one of Stalin's most militant henchmen, as delegate of the party central committee to the trade union central council. Tomsky indulged in the bold, but empty, gesture—for which he was sharply censured—of resigning his post as president of the trade union central council, and absenting himself from the final session of the congress. Though he retained his membership of the central council for three months longer, he never again appeared on a trade union platform.

Bukharin did not long survive him. In January 1929, reduced to desperation, he had two more fruitless meetings with Kamenev; Kamenev's record of the earlier meeting was now being circulated in inner party circles. The break could no longer be avoided. It came at a joint session of the Politburo with the party control commission at the end of January. The three dissidents tendered their resignations; and Bukharin made a direct attack, though not by name, on Stalin, protesting against the oppressive régime in the party and "against the decisions of the party leadership being taken by a single person". Stalin retorted with a vituperative analysis of the zigzags of Bukharin's record, and of his early disputes with Lenin, and denounced "the Right opportunist, capitulationist platform" of the dissidents. The resolution adopted at the end of the session on February 9 rehearsed the catalogue of Bukharin's errors, and convicted him of disloyalty to the party. But it was neither published nor officially communicated to the party central committee, so that Bukharin's status was still formally intact. It was not till April that the central committee met, and, having listened to a further sweeping indictment by Stalin of Bukharin's record, confirmed the resolution of February 9, and removed Bukharin from further work in *Pravda* and in Comintern, and Tomsky from the trade union central council. But this merely provided formal endorsement of situations which already existed. After the meeting of the central committee, the decisions were communicated by Molotov to the large party conference which had been summoned to approve the first five-year plan. But neither

Molotov's report nor the resolution approving the decisions was published. No word of Bukharin's downfall had yet appeared in the press, or percolated to the world at large.

This extreme caution was characteristic of Stalin, who did not rate Bukharin as a dangerous opponent, and saw no reason to force this issue. But it was also a tribute to Bukharin's popularity among rank-and-file party members, many of whom, especially in the countryside, shared his moderate inclinations. The issue next arose when IKKI met in July 1929. At first nobody mentioned Bukharin's absence. But half-way through the session Molotov arrived to deliver a frank denunciation of the three dissidents, and in particular of Bukharin, who had engaged in "a Right deviation" and attacked "our socialist economy". After this, many delegates, Soviet and foreign, joined in the chorus; and a resolution was passed at the end of the session condemning Bukharin, and approving the decision of the party central committee to debar him from further participation in Comintern and its organs. But once more this resolution was not published with the rest, and appeared in *Pravda* only some weeks later. Now, however, a thorough-going campaign of denunciation was launched in the press. The climax was reached at a session of the party central committee in November. The three dissidents were induced to sign a somewhat half-hearted recantation of their views, which was published in *Pravda*. Bukharin was removed from the Politburo, Tomsky and Rykov merely censured and warned not to offend again. By slow process of attrition the dissidents had been discredited, and rendered helpless and harmless.

A month later, on December 21, 1929, Stalin celebrated his fiftieth birthday. The occasion epitomized tendencies which had grown up insensibly out of his struggles against rivals and his ascent to supreme power. Ever since his appointment, in the last year of Lenin's active life, as general secretary of the party, his strength had lain in his rigid and meticulous management of the party machine, which controlled appointments to key posts in party and state. His approval was a sure avenue to advancement. He had gathered round him a body of faithful henchmen—mostly, party leaders of the second rank—whose political fortunes were linked with his, and who owed him unquestioning personal allegiance. A policy of recruitment inaugurated by the Lenin enrolment of 1924 had built up a rank-and-file membership of reliable workers known for their ready submission to the party line. In the less congenial field of party doctrine Stalin took pains to present himself, not as an innovator, but as the devoted disciple of Lenin and the custodian of party orthodoxy; the spurious attempt to attribute the theory of socialism in one country to Lenin was an example of his eagerness to ground his authority in that of the master. The parallel was consciously cultivated by his entourage. Stalin's words, like those of Lenin, were constantly quoted in the press and in the speeches of his followers, and treated as authoritative. His portrait appeared everywhere in public places, often side by side with that of Lenin. These practices reached their apogee in the birthday tributes, which were marked by a hitherto unprecedented display of personal adulation.

Many traits, however, distinguished the character of Stalin's rule from anything that could have been imagined under Lenin. Stalin had a form of vanity totally alien to Lenin, which demanded, not indeed the holding or the trappings of office, but absolute obedience and the recognition of his infallibility. No overt criticism, no expression of dissent, appeared any longer in the party press, or even in specialist journals. Such discussions of current questions as could still be found were marked by tasteless and uniform tributes to the leader, and by the celebration of often mythical achievements. Stalin became a remote, isolated figure, exalted far above ordinary mortals, and indeed above his closest colleagues. He seems to have lacked any warmth of feeling for his fellow-men; he was cruel and vindictive to those who thwarted his will, or excited his resentment or his antipathy. His commitment to Marxism and socialism was only skin-deep. Socialism was not something that grew out of the objective economic situation and out of the revolt of class-conscious workers against the oppressive domination of capitalism; it was something to be imposed from above, arbitrarily and by force. Stalin's attitude to the masses was contemptuous; he was indifferent to liberty and to equality; he was scornful of the prospects of revolution in any country outside the USSR. He was

the only member of the party central committee who as
early as January 1918 had maintained, in opposition to Lenin,
that "there is no revolutionary movement in the West".

The commitment to socialism in one country, though the
attitudes which crystallized into the new doctrine were not
exclusively of Stalin's making, perfectly fitted the man. It
enabled him to match professions of socialism with Russian
nationalism, the only political creed which moved him at
all deeply. In Stalin's treatment of national minorities or
of the smaller nations, nationalism easily degenerated into
chauvinism. Notes of the old Russian anti-Semitism, sternly
denounced by Lenin and the early Bolsheviks, were heard;
and official condemnations of it, though persistent, began
to sound less decisive. In art and literature, the eager experi-
mentalism of the first years of the revolution was abandoned
in favour of a return to traditional Russian models, enforced
by an increasingly strict censorship. Marxist schools of history
and law passed under a cloud; to seek continuity with the
Russian past was no longer a cause for reproach. Socialism
in one country pointed back to an old Russian national
exclusiveness, rejected by Marx as well as by Lenin. It was
not altogether incongruous to place Stalin's régime in the
context of Russian history.

This constriction of the revolution within a narrow nationalist
strait-jacket had its reverse side. It would be unfair to depict
Stalin as a man moved exclusively by the lust for personal
power. He dedicated his indefatigable energy to the transformation of primitive peasant Russia into a modern industrial
Power, capable of facing the major capitalist Powers on equal
terms. The need to "catch up with" or "overtake" the
capitalist countries was an obsessive theme, and inspired most
of the rare purple passages in Stalin's drab prose. It provided
the peroration of his anniversary article of November 1929
on "The Year of the Great Break-Through":

> We are going full steam along the road of industrialization
> to socialism, leaving behind our age-long "Russian" back-
> wardness.
> We are becoming a country of metal, a country of the
> automobile, a country of the tractor.
> And when we have seated the USSR in an automobile,

and the peasant on a tractor, then let the honourable capitalists, who plume themselves on their "civilization", try to catch us up. We shall see which countries can then be counted as backward and which as advanced.

And later, rather more soberly, he conjured up a picture of Russia through the ages, "beaten for her backwardness" by a succession of foreign invaders, from "Mongol khans" to "Anglo-French capitalists" and "Japanese barons", and concluded:

> We have lagged 50 or 100 years behind the advanced countries. We must close this gap in ten years. Either we shall do it, or they will crush us.

This extraordinary combination of a commitment to the industrialization and modernization of the economy, which appealed to convinced Marxists as a vital step on the road to socialism, and a commitment to a revival of the power and prestige of the Russian nation, which appealed to the army, to the bureaucratic and technological élites, to all survivors of the old régime who had entered the service of the new, gave Stalin his unbreakable hold over the party, the government and the administration. To attribute this simply to Stalin's political astuteness, or to the efficiency of the machine, or to the severity of measures taken to suppress dissent, would be a mistake. It was not only defectors from the opposition in 1928 and 1929 who felt that Stalin's unflinching determination in the pursuit of long-desired ends outweighed the harsh methods used to enforce his policies. Some people argued that without these methods the ends could not be attained, others that they could not be attained without Stalin's forceful leadership, and that it was therefore necessary to tolerate his unwelcome idiosyncracies. The fact that this was a revolution from above, and that it placed the heaviest burdens on the very classes which were its declared beneficiaries, did not seriously disturb the picture. Enthusiasm for the great leap forward engulfed many party members and others engaged, in one capacity or another, in forwarding the grand design, and left them indifferent to other considerations. It was a society well accustomed to associate government with oppression, and to treat it as an inescapable evil.

Stalin on his fiftieth birthday stood at the summit of his ambition. Enough had indeed occurred to lend weight to Lenin's apprehensions of his rough and arbitrary use of power. He had already displayed an extraordinary ruthlessness in enforcing his will and in crushing all opposition to it. But the full revelation of the quality of his dictatorship still lay ahead. The horrors of the process of collectivization, of the concentration camps, of the great show trials, and of the indiscriminate killing, with or without trial, not only of those who had opposed him in the past, but of many who had assisted his rise to power, accompanied by the imposition of a rigid and uniform orthodoxy on the press, on art and literature, on history and on science, and by the suppression of every critical opinion, left a blot which could not be erased by victory in the war or by the sequel. The fluctuations in Stalin's reputation since his death in the eyes of his compatriots seem to reflect confused and conflicting emotions of admiration and shame. This ambivalence may persist for a long time. The precedent of Peter the Great has often been invoked, and is astonishingly apposite. Peter too was a man of formidable energy and extreme ferocity. He revived and outdid the worst brutalities of earlier Tsars; and his record excited revulsion in later generations of historians. Yet his achievement in borrowing from the west, in forcing on primitive Russia the material foundations of modern civilization, and in giving Russia a place among the European Powers, obliged them to concede, however reluctantly, his title to greatness. Stalin was the most ruthless despot Russia had known since Peter, and also a great westernizer.

# 18   The USSR and the World (1927-1929)

FOR nearly two years after the break with Britain in May 1927, and the collapse of the Chinese revolutionary movement and of the Soviet involvement in China, Soviet foreign relations were in the doldrums. Successive approaches from Moscow were ignominiously rebuffed by the British Government. Negotiations with France on debts and credits broke down; and the French Government, though it did not sever diplomatic relations, found a pretext for demanding the recall of Rakovsky, the Soviet Ambassador. Relations with Germany had been temporarily disturbed by her signature of the Locarno treaty and entry into the League of Nations; angry interludes from time to time marked their uneven flow. But, resting on the firm foundation of the secret military agreements, of Germany's desire to avoid an exclusively western orientation, and of common hostility to Poland, they remained closer and more fruitful than Soviet relations with any other country. Relations with Poland had further deteriorated since Pilsudski's *coup* of May 1926, being embittered by fear that Pilsudski would serve as a willing instrument of the anti-Soviet designs of the western Powers, and later by a persistent, though unsuccessful, Polish attempt to organize the other western neighbours of the USSR—Finland, the Baltic States and Rumania—in a pact or alliance under Polish leadership. Relations with Japan were rendered uneasy by ambiguous Japanese policies in China, and by Japan's jealous control over Manchuria, exercised through her *protégé*, the Chinese warlord Chang Tso-lin.

Paradoxically, the one important initiative undertaken at this time by Soviet diplomacy was participation in international activities at Geneva. Hitherto Soviet cooperation with the

League of Nations had been confined to a tenuous link with its health organization. The League had always been denounced in Moscow as an integral part of the oppressive Versailles peace settlement of 1919, and a hypocritical cloak for Allied military preparations. This ban still remained. But, now that Germany had entered the League, absence from the scene of action increased the sense of isolation. In May 1927 a large Soviet delegation arrived for the first time in Geneva to attend the World Economic Conference. Soviet delegates made their mark both in plenary sessions and in the commissions set up by the conference, castigating capitalist procedures and defending the monopoly of foreign trade, but calling for "peaceful co-existence of the two economic systems". The absence of concrete results did not remove the impression on both sides that contacts had been established which were susceptible of further development.

More sensational was the appearance in Geneva, six months later, of a Soviet delegation headed by Litvinov, the deputy Commissar for Foreign Affairs, at the session of the Preparatory Commission for Disarmament. Litvinov stole the limelight by putting forward a proposal for the total abolition of all military, naval and air armaments. It was a sensational and embarrassing gesture. The commission hastily adjourned the discussion till its next session in March 1928. On this occasion the indefatigable Litvinov submitted a revised plan for total disarmament by stages. When this, too, was shelved, he substituted an alternative draft for a limitation of armaments, which, though less Utopian than its two predecessors, went far beyond anything contemplated by the western Powers. It was greeted with some sympathy only by Germany, whose armaments had been rigidly restricted by the Versailles treaty, and Turkey, a new member of the commission. These proceedings continued to embarrass a majority of the delegates, who found no other resource but a further adjournment, and won for Litvinov and the USSR much favourable publicity in radical circles in the western countries interested in disarmament, which were already impatient at the slow progress made by the commission.

A further significant step in Soviet relations with the west was taken in the summer of 1928. Kellogg, the American Secretary of State, proposed the signature of an international pact to renounce war "as an instrument of national policy". The USSR was not among the fifteen countries originally invited to participate. But, when on the day of the signature, August 27, 1928, an invitation was sent to the USSR, as well as to all other non-signatory countries, to accede to the pact, it was promptly and warmly accepted. Moreover, when ratification of the pact by the western Powers was delayed, the Soviet Government proposed to its immediate neighbours to conclude a pact to bring the provisions of the Kellogg pact immediately into force between themselves. This subsidiary pact was signed in Moscow on February 9, 1929, amid a blaze of publicity, by the USSR, Poland, Latvia, Estonia and Rumania; Lithuania, Turkey and Persia acceded later.

In these manoeuvres the hand of Litvinov was clearly visible. Litvinov had now virtually supplanted Chicherin as People's Commissar for Foreign Affairs, though he did not formally succeed to the title till 1930. Chicherin, the eccentric scion of an ancient family who had joined the party, won Lenin's confidence. But strong mutual antipathies divided him from Stalin, who preferred Litvinov's cruder, brusquer style. In 1928, Chicherin, now a sick man, withdrew from active life. The significance of the change was that while Chicherin mistrusted the western countries, especially Britain, from which he had been ignominiously deported in 1918, and felt at home only in Germany, Litvinov had spent many years in Britain, spoke fluent English and had an English wife. For some years Litvinov worked not unsuccessfully, within the limits of Soviet policy, for a *rapprochement* between the USSR and the western world.

Ever since the general strike of 1926, the speeches of prominent British politicians had helped to build up the image of Britain prevalent in Moscow as the most implacable enemy of the USSR. The attitude of the Conservative government during this period was inspired by deep mistrust of the USSR and desire to have as few dealings as possible with Moscow. But by the end of 1928 the policy of the cold shoulder had yielded no results, and a milder climate set in. At a time when the Americans and the Germans were beginning to outstrip the British in modern industrial technology, the loss of British markets in the USSR was alarming; and this was attributed to the rupture of relations between the two countries. At the end of March 1929 a party of British businessmen, eighty strong, set out on a visit to the USSR, was enthusiastically received, and collected some orders. A general election in Britain was now imminent. Both the Labour and Liberal Parties inscribed a resumption of relations with the USSR in their platforms. The Labour Party emerged as the strongest of the three parties, and formed a government which carried out its pledge. Full relations were once more established, after some delay, towards the end of the year. But the reconciliation was no more than skin-deep, and did not break the underlying tension between the USSR and the western world.

Relations with the United States were ambivalent, and had a special character of their own. The Soviet leaders recognized that Britain was being rapidly eclipsed by the United States as the major capitalist Power; some expected this to result in acute animosity between the two English-speaking countries. But, in spite of the uniform hostility towards the USSR displayed by the American Government, by the American Federation of Labour, and by the American press, the reaction in Moscow was surprisingly mild, and was tinged with admiration and envy of the accomplishments of American industry. The United States was the most advanced country in the world in industrial technology, in mass production and in standardization; organization in large units of production brought it nearer than any other country to Soviet conditions and requirements. Reliance on American machinery and equipment was an important factor in Soviet industrialization policy; from 1927 onwards the United States began to challenge Germany as the principal supplier of industrial products to the USSR.

Still more significant was the extensive employment of American engineers. The staffing of Soviet factories and mines with qualified engineers and technicians had from the first presented a problem. Many who had worked in this capacity before the revolution had disappeared: the loyalty of others was suspect. There were few facilities for training a new generation to take their place. Many German engineers worked in Soviet industry in the early years. But, with the introduction of the first five-year plan and the rapid expansion of Soviet industry, the demand for expertise at the highest levels grew; and it was for the most part American engineers who filled the gap. Dneprostroi was only the first of several major construction projects planned and directed by American chief engineers who brought their staffs with them. The Soviet authorities protected them against outbursts of jealousy on the part of their Russian colleagues, and put more trust both in the efficiency and in the loyalty of American, than of old-style Russian, engineers. By 1929 several hundred highly qualified American engineers were working in the USSR. The number was said to be "utterly insufficient", and was soon to be further increased. While the hostility of official circles in the United States to Moscow remained obdurate, a break-through had been effected on the industrial and commercial front.

The activities of Comintern, being governed in all major questions by the same party leaders who directed Soviet policy as a whole, reflected the uneasiness and ambiguity of Soviet foreign relations in this period. In 1927 the "united front", meaning the cooperation of communists with other Left parties or groups in capitalist countries for defined objectives, still figured prominently in the directives of Comintern. But in that year the two most widely publicized experiments in united front tactics, the alliance of the Chinese Communist Party with Kuomintang and the Anglo-Russian trade union committee, both came to grief in conditions of some ignominy (see pp. 93, 102–103 above). The partners with whom cooperation had been sought in these enterprises were denounced as traitors; and the united front in the sense hitherto given to the term was tacitly abandoned. The rift occurred at the moment of a sharp turn for the worse in Soviet relations with the western Powers, when fear of war obsessed the Soviet leaders; and a turn to the Left in Comintern seemed a natural result of the breakdown of conciliatory tactics in Soviet diplomacy, as well as in the relations of communist parties to other Left parties in capitalist countries. That Stalin, having defeated the united opposition, was now moving to the Left in domestic policy, and preparing to confront Bukharin and the Right deviation, was a coincidence which fitted into the same picture.

From 1928 onwards the new line dominated the proceedings of Comintern. Recognition that the capitalist countries had achieved a phase of "stabilization", however "temporary", "relative" and "unstable", was rarer and more grudging. Class antagonisms were becoming more acute; "class against class" was a slogan of the new period. The united front was interpreted as a "united front from below", meaning cooperation with the rank and file of socialist and social-democratic parties to overthrow their corrupt and traitorous leaders. The sixth congress of Comintern meeting in July 1928—its first for four years, and its longest ever—recorded three periods in its history. The first covered the acute revolutionary ferment of 1917–1921, the second the recovery of capitalism from 1921 to 1927. The third period inaugurated by the congress was one in which the ever-growing contradictions of capitalism heralded its imminent decay, and opened fresh prospects of revolution. The worst enemies of communism were now the temporizing social-democrats. The German delegate bluntly called them "social-Fascists". The resolution of the congress admitted that they had some points of contact with the ideology of Fascism; and the new programme of Comintern adopted by the congress bracketed social-democracy and Fascism as twin agents of the bourgeoisie. While the congress was in session, Litvinov was cautiously steering the Soviet Government towards accession to the Kellogg pact, which was announced before the congress ended. No delegate of the Russian party at the congress mentioned the pact. But it was attacked by several delegates of other parties, and in the communist press of western countries, as a hypocritical mask for imperialist aggression; and a resolution of the congress, without mentioning the pact, contained an ironical reference to "abolition of war" (in inverted commas) as an example of the "official pacifism by which capitalist governments mask their manoeuvres". Any apparent discrepancy between governmental and Comintern policy was probably explained by uncertainties, or unresolved differences of opinion, among Soviet leaders. But in the event the two lines were pursued side by side, and Narkomindel and Comintern went their respective ways without any sense of incompatibility between them.

Bukharin's downfall was an incidental factor in the proclamation of the "third period" in 1928. His quarrel with Stalin turned primarily on economic affairs. But his tenure of office in Comintern had been associated with the conciliatory policies of the united front; and after his disgrace the line swung all the more violently in the opposite direction. An "objectively revolutionary situation" was diagnosed in the principal capitalist countries, even before the onset of the world economic crisis lent some slight plausibility to the claim. Revolutionary class war was the primary duty of all communist parties. The term "social-Fascist", invented in Germany, was now applied to all "reformist" parties of the Left; to seek or tolerate any compromise with them was to be guilty of "opportunism" and a "Right deviation". These injunctions embarrassed the communist parties of western Europe. In Britain and France they did not prevent some covert communist support for Labour and Socialist candidates in elections. It was in Germany that they were applied with the greatest rigour and with the most disastrous results. The support given by German social-democrats to the Locarno treaty and to the western orientation in German policy earned them the implacable hostility of the Soviet Government and of Comintern. The rift between the German Communist and Social-Democratic Parties persisted, and later proved too deep to be healed even by the imminent danger of Hitler's take-over.

The breach with other Left parties dealt a fatal blow at the practice of organizing international "fronts", in which non-communists of the Left were invited to cooperate with communists in support of causes of common concern (see p. 90 above). Münzenberg, the assiduous and versatile German communist who promoted and directed these joint undertakings, found it necessary, at the sixth congress of Comintern, to plead that such activities had "nothing in common with an 'opportunist policy' or a 'Right' deviation". But they were difficult to reconcile with the uninhibited abuse of social-democrats which was now the rule in communist parties. Nothing short of rigid adherence to the Comintern line was acceptable. Even the once spectacularly successful League against Imperialism wilted in the new climate; and it proved impossible to revive the spontaneous enthusiasm generated at its founding congress in 1927. When a second—and last—congress of the League met two years later in Frankfurt, it was entirely dominated by a Soviet delegation, and the non-communist sympathizers failed to appear, or drifted away. The international society of Friends of the Soviet Union, founded at the tenth anniversary celebrations of the revolution in Moscow in November 1927, was equally short-lived, surviving longer in Britain than elsewhere. The last of these ostensibly non-party demonstrations under Comintern auspices was an Anti-Facist Congress held in Berlin in March 1929.

A corollary of the new hard line in Comintern was the enforcement of stricter discipline on communist parties. Ever since 1924, when the Bolshevization of foreign parties was proclaimed as a goal, Comintern had sought from time to time to influence the selection of leaders of these parties. After 1928 such intervention became direct and constant. In the autumn of that year, the central committee of the German party, following a financial scandal, decided to remove its leader, Thälmann, who had owed his rise largely to support from Moscow. The Comintern authorities vetoed the decision and secured its reversal. Early in 1929, Comintern settled a long-standing split in the Polish party by installing in the leadership the group most obedient to its behests; and the existing leaders of the American party were abruptly expelled after a personal intervention by Stalin. Similar changes were rather more cautiously effected in the French and British parties. A feature of most of these changes was a new emphasis in the choice of leaders of unimpeachably working-class origin—Thälmann in Germany, Thorez in France, Pollitt in Britain—which seemed to accord with the Left inclination now prevailing in Comintern, and was a reaction against the trouble caused in the past by dissident intellectuals. Workers generally proved in this respect more malleable. While the new leaders were regularly hailed as Leftists, and those whom they replaced denounced as Rightists, the essential touchstone of the new appointments was prompt and unfailing submission to directives from Moscow.

This, however, created another dilemma. The decisions of Comintern were effectively the decisions of the Russian party. They could be, and were, imposed on the foreign parties, but at the cost of alienating a larger and larger number of workers in the countries concerned, who failed to respond to what seemed the wilful and sometimes plainly inappropriate dictates of a remote and alien power. At the end of the nineteen-twenties the communist movement in western countries was declining in numbers and influence, and attracting fewer sympathizers. The British and American parties had no mass following. In Germany, France and Czechoslovakia mass communist parties had split the workers' movement, but never succeeded in dominating it. Everywhere the strengthening of the links that bound the party leaders to Moscow weakened their hold on the rank and file of the workers. It was only when policies in Moscow were radically altered in the middle nineteen-thirties that these losses were retrieved.

The most important event in Soviet foreign relations in the latter half of 1929 occurred in the Far East. For two years after the debacle of 1927 the Soviet Government was excluded from any participation in Chinese affairs; and the Chinese Communist Party was reduced to scattered underground groups in a few principal cities. In December 1927 the rump of the party, prompted from Moscow, desperately attempted a military *coup* in Canton. It was a dismal failure, and led to a further massacre of communists and their supporters. About this time the communist peasant leader, Mao Tse-tung, and a communist general, Chu Teh, collected a small force of fugitives and landless peasants, a few thousand strong, in a remote and inaccessible mountain area of southwestern China; and a year later they began to establish their authority over the neighbouring countryside, setting up peasant Soviets. Mao professed formal loyalty to the party and to Comintern. But he went his own way, and had few communications with the party leaders, who mistrusted a movement which pinned its hopes of revolution on peasants in the country and not on workers in the town. Meanwhile Chiang Kai-shek, who had abated nothing of his hostility to Chinese communists and to the USSR, extended the authority of the nationalist government in Nanking over the greater part of China. Chang Tso-lin, the warlord of Manchuria, was killed in the summer of 1928; and at the end of that year Chiang made an agreement with Chang's son and successor for the reunification of China under the Kuomintang flag, while preserving the autonomy of the northern provinces. The northern provinces abutting on Soviet territory had

long been a source of anxiety in Moscow. Here the Chinese
Eastern Railway (CER), built and owned by the pre-revolutionary Russian Government on Chinese territory, had long
constituted a bone of contention between the two countries
(see p. 99 above). Diplomatic agreements for Chinese representation on its board did not prevent a succession of crises
over the control of the railway. But relative calm had prevailed for three years when, in the spring of 1929, the
Chinese authorities launched a number of minor attacks on
the line. On May 27 they raided the Soviet consulate in
Harbin, the headquarters of the CER, arresting officials and
seizing papers—a small-scale replica of the raid on the Soviet
Embassy in Peking two years earlier. Pronouncements from
Nanking left little doubt that the attacks had been inspired
by Chiang Kai-shek, and were a first step towards the taking
over of the railway. Finally on July 10 the Chinese authorities
seized railway installations, closed the Soviet trade delegation
and other Soviet establishments in Manchuria, arrested the
Soviet general manager of the railway, and expelled him,
together with 60 other Soviet officials, from Chinese territory.
The Soviet Government, having protested in vain against
these high-handed measures, withdrew its staff from the CER,
suspended railway communications with China, and demanded
the recall of all Chinese officials from the USSR.

Chiang Kai-shek had assumed that, as happened in 1927,
the Soviet Government would protest loudly, but would and
could do nothing. This was a grave miscalculation. Soviet
interests in central China had never been substantial, and
nothing could be done to defend them; the defeat of 1927
was humiliating, but not materially disastrous. But to forfeit
Russia's historical position in Manchuria, and to abandon
the railway which had been built with Russian capital by
Russian engineers, and which was the direct link with Vladivostok, the one Soviet Pacific port, would have been a staggering
blow. Moreover, the Red Army had now been built up
into an effective fighting force. It was not equipped for a
major war. But, once Japan had signified her neutrality in
the present quarrel, it was more than a match for the ill-found,
ill-disciplined Chinese levies which had fought one another
on Chinese soil. Chiang appears also to have assumed that
the western Powers would be as favourable in 1929 to his

moves against the USSR as they had been two years earlier. This was another miscalculation. Fears of communism had abated, and the British Labour government was just about to resume relations with the USSR. Chiang's aggressiveness looked like another case of something with which the western Powers were all too familiar—the violation by Chinese warlords of foreign treaty rights; and for the first time western sympathies veered to the Soviet side.

The Soviet Government steadily refused to negotiate on any basis other than the total withdrawal of the measures taken on July 10 and the restoration of Soviet rights over the CER. In August, Blyukher was appointed commander of a reinforced eastern army. Sporadic raids across the frontier marked growing Soviet impatience; and in November, when these pin-pricks failed to impress the Chinese authorities, the Red Army launched an extensive incursion into Chinese territory, dispersing local Chinese forces and capturing two small towns. This time the warning was heeded, and negotiations began in earnest. On December 22, a protocol was signed reinstating the Soviet general manager of the CER and other Soviet officials, restoring the *status quo ante*, and reserving disputed questions for a future conference. The Red Army had shown up the impotence of the Chinese warlords. The USSR had emerged as a military and diplomatic force in the Far East, and had forged links of common concern with the western Powers. It was a turning-point in Soviet external relations.

The dispersed, persecuted and dispirited Chinese Communist Party played no part in these events. Instructed by Comintern, its central committee put out the slogan "Defence of the Soviet Union", and stepped up its denunciations of the Nanking government. What, however, was seen in Moscow as a flagrant threat to Soviet security appeared to some patriotic Chinese as a move to liberate Chinese territory from foreign, i.e. Soviet, control. Ch'en Tu-hsiu, who had been deposed from the party leadership after the disasters of 1927, was now expelled from the party for voicing these embarrassments, and subsequently proclaimed himself a follower of Trotsky. Here as elsewhere, Comintern could impose discipline, but could not breathe life into the enfeebled party ranks, whose impotence in the urban centres could no longer be disguised.

Only Mao Tse-tung's peasant levies and the local Soviets sponsored by them could boast of some successful revolutionary activity. But these exploits were confined to a remote corner of China, and their leaders paid at best hypocritical lip-service to the rulings of the party and of Comintern. Much as the Chinese communist movement owed to Russian inspiration and example, it survived, and would ultimately triumph, in forms unplanned and mistrusted by Moscow.

# 19   The Revolution in Perspective

WHEN Lenin in the April theses proclaimed that the revolution of February 1917 was not simply a bourgeois revolution, but marked a transition, led by workers and poor peasants, to the desired socialist revolution of the future, he made a sensitive response to the tumultuous conditions prevailing on his return to Petrograd. The Russian bourgeoisie, weak and backward in comparison with its western counterparts, possessed neither the economic strength nor the political maturity, neither the independence nor the inner coherence, necessary to wield power. On the other hand, the conception of an alliance between the proletariat and the bourgeoisie to complete the bourgeois revolution was pure myth. The proletariat, once it became an effective force, could not instal in power a bourgeois régime, whose function would be to exploit its labour. The bourgeoisie could not brook the alliance of a proletariat, whose eventual function would be to destroy it. When Lenin attempted to escape from this impasse by placing on the proletariat, supported by the poor peasants, the onus both of completing the bourgeois revolution and of starting the socialist revolution, he no doubt believed, not that he was abandoning the Marxist scheme of two separate and successive revolutions, but that he was adapting it to special conditions. But this solution, which became the programme of the October revolution, had its Achilles' heel. Marx had envisaged a socialist revolution developing on a foundation of capitalism and bourgeois democracy established by a previous bourgeois revolution. In Russia this foundation was rudimentary or non-existent. Lenin looked forward to the building of socialism in an economically and politically backward country. The dilemma could be avoided only so long as it was assumed that the revolution was about to become international, that the European proletariat would also rise in revolt against its capitalist masters, and provide the conditions for an advance into socialism which Russia in isolation lacked. Socialism installed by revolution in a country where the proletariat itself was economically backward and numerically weak was not, and could not be, the socialism predicated by Marx and Lenin as the outcome of a revolution of the united proletariat of economically advanced countries.

From the first, therefore, the Russian revolution had a hybrid and ambiguous character. Marx noted that the embryo of bourgeois society had been formed within the matrix of the feudal order, and was already mature when bourgeois revolution installed it in the seats of power. It was assumed that something analogous would happen to socialist society before the victory of the socialist revolution. In one—but only one—respect this expectation was vindicated. Industrialization and technological modernization, which ranked high among the achievements of capitalist society, were also important pre-requisites of socialism. Long before 1914 the capitalist economies of the western world had begun to transcend the limits of small-scale production by individual *entrepreneurs*, and to substitute production by large-scale units which dominated the economic scene, and became involved willy-nilly in the exercise of political power. Capitalism itself was already blurring the line which separated economics from politics, paving the way for some form of centralized control and laying the foundations on which a socialist society could be built.

These processes reached a climax in the first world war. Study of the German war economy inspired Lenin's remark in the summer of 1917 that "state monopoly capitalism is the fullest *material* preparation for socialism"; and a few weeks later he added, a little whimsically, that "the material, economic half" of socialism had been realized in Germany "in the form of state monopoly capitalism". The contradictions of capitalism had already produced, within the capitalist order, the embryo of the planned economy of the USSR. This fact has led some critics to describe what was achieved under Soviet planning as "state capitalism". Such a view seems untenable. Capitalism without *entrepreneurs*, without unemploy-

ment and without a free market, where no class appropriates
the surplus value produced by the worker, and profits play
a purely ancillary role, where prices and wages are not subject
to the law of supply and demand, is no longer capitalism
in any meaningful sense. Soviet planned economy was recognized everywhere as a challenge to capitalism. It was "the
material, economic half" of socialism, and was a major outcome of the revolution.

If, however, it would be foolish to deny the title "socialist"
to this achievement, it would be equally misguided to pretend
that it constituted a realization of Marx's "free association
of producers", or of the dictatorship of the proletariat, or
of Lenin's transitional "democratic dictatorship of workers
and peasants". Nor did it satisfy Marx's requirement that
"the emancipation of the workers must be the task of the
workers themselves". The Soviet industrial and agrarian revolutions plainly fell into a category of "revolution from above",
imposed by the joint authority of party and state. The limitations of "socialism in one country" were plainly revealed.
The vision of a trained and educated proletariat growing
up within bourgeois society, like the bourgeoisie within feudal
society, had not been realized—and, least of all, in backward
Russia, where the working class was small, down-trodden,
and unorganized, and had assimilated none even of the condi-
tional freedoms of bourgeois democracy. The tiny core of
class-conscious workers played a major part in the victory
of the revolution. But the task of ordering and administering
the broad territories incorporated in the Soviet republic called
for a more complex and more sophisticated form of organization. The party of Stalin, a disciplined corps led by a small
and devoted band of revolutionary intellectuals, stepped into
the vacant place, and directed the policy of the régime by
methods which, after Lenin's death, became more and more
openly dictatorial, and less and less dependent on its proletarian
base. Devices, first sparingly used amid the passions and
atrocities of the civil war, were gradually elaborated into
a vast system of purges and concentration camps. If the
goals could be described as socialist, the means used to attain
them were often the very negation of socialism.

This does not mean that no advance at all had been
made towards the most exalted ideal of socialism—the libe-

ration of the workers from the oppressions of the past, and
the recognition of their equal rôle in a new kind of society.
But progress was halting, and was broken by a series of
set-backs and calamities, avoidable and unavoidable. After
the ravages and shortages of the civil war, a brief respite
ensued in which the standard of living of both workers and
peasants slowly rose somewhat above the miserable levels
of Tsarist Russia. During the decade which began in 1928,
these standards once more contracted under the intense pressures of industrialization; and the peasant passed through
the horrors of forced collectivization. Scarcely had recovery
once more set in when the country was exposed to the cataclysm
of a world war, in which the USSR was the target of Germany's
most sustained and most devastating offensive on the continent
of Europe. These terrifying experiences left their mark, material
and moral, on Soviet life and on the minds of the Soviet
leaders and the Soviet people. Not all the sufferings of the
first half century of the revolution can be attributed to internal
causes or to the iron hand of Stalin's dictatorship.

Yet, by the nineteen-fifties and nineteen-sixties, the fruits
of industrialization, mechanization and long-term planning
began to mature. Much remained primitive and backward
by any western measurement. But standards of living substantially improved. Social services, including health services and
primary, secondary and higher education, became more effective, and spread from the cities over most parts of the country.
Stalin's most notorious instruments of oppression were disman-
tled. The pattern of life of ordinary people changed for the
better. When the fiftieth anniversary of the revolution was
celebrated in 1967, account could be taken of the magnitude
of the advance. During the half century, the population of
the USSR had increased from 145 millions to more than
250 millions; the proportion of town-dwellers had risen from
less than 20 to more than 50 per cent. This was an immense
increase in the urban population, most of the newcomers
being children of peasants, and grandchildren or great-grand-
children of serfs. The Soviet worker, and even the Soviet
peasant, of 1967 was a very different person from his father
or grandfather in 1917. He could hardly fail to be conscious
of what the revolution had done for him; and this out-weighed
the absence of freedoms which he had never enjoyed or

dreamed of. The harshness and cruelty of the régime were real. But so also were its achievements.

Abroad, the immediate effect of the Russian revolution had been a sharp polarization of western attitudes between Right and Left. The revolution was a bugbear to conservatives, and a beacon of hope to radicals. Belief in this fundamental dichotomy inspired the foundation of Comintern. But, in the international revolution conceived by Marx and Lenin as a mass movement of the united European proletariat, no Marxist would have claimed a predominant rôle for the weak Russian contingent. When the European revolution failed to materialize, and when socialism in one country became the official ideology of the Russian party, the increasingly assertive demand to treat the USSR as the exemplar of socialist achievement, and Comintern as the repository of socialist orthodoxy, led to a new polarization between east and west within the Left. Communists and western social-democrats or socialists confronted one another, first as mistrustful allies, then as open enemies—a state of affairs misleadingly attributed in Moscow to the treachery of renegade leaders. It was a symptom of the rift that no common language could be found. International revolution as conceived in Moscow from 1924 onwards was a movement directed "from above" by an institution claiming to act in the name of the only proletariat which had made a victorious revolution in its own country; and the corollary of this re-orientation was the assumption, not only that the Russian leaders possessed a monopoly of knowledge and experience about the way in which a revolution could be made, but that the first and over-riding interest of international revolution was the defence of the one country where revolution had been effectively achieved. Both these assumptions, and the policies and procedures dictated by them, proved totally unacceptable to a majority of the workers of western Europe, who believed themselves far more advanced, economically, culturally and politically, than their backward Russian counterparts, and could not close their eyes to the negative aspects of Soviet society. Persistence in these policies merely brought discredit, in the eyes of western workers, on the authorities in Moscow, on the national communist parties subservient to them, and eventually on the revolution itself.

Relations with the backward non-capitalist countries turned out quite differently. Lenin was the first to discover a link between the revolutionary movement for the liberation of the workers from capitalist domination in the advanced countries and the liberation of backward and subject nations from the rule of the imperialists. The identification of capitalism with imperialism was the fruitful theme of Soviet propaganda and policy almost everywhere in Asia, and enjoyed its most dramatic success in stimulating the Chinese national revolution in the middle nineteen-twenties. As the USSR consolidated its position, its prestige as the patron and leader of "colonial" peoples increased rapidly. It had achieved, through the process of revolution and industrialization, a spectacular accretion of economic independence and political power—an achievement worthy of envy and emulation. Outside Europe, even the exaggerated claims of Comintern made sense. The defence of the USSR, far from seeming an embarrassing excrescence on the programme of revolution, meant the defence of the most powerful ally of the backward countries in their struggle against the advanced imperialist countries.

Nor did the methods which aroused revulsion in countries where the bourgeois revolution was a matter of history, and where strong workers' movements had grown up within the elastic framework of liberal democracy, prove seriously repugnant in countries where the bourgeois revolution was still on the agenda, where bourgeois democracy was an unsubstantial vision, and where no sizable proletariat yet existed. Where hungry and illiterate masses had not yet reached the stage of revolutionary consciousness, revolution from above was better than no revolution at all. While in the advanced capitalist world the ferment generated by the Russian revolution remained primarily destructive, and provided no constructive model for revolutionary action, in the backward non-capitalist countries it proved more pervasive and more productive. The prestige of a revolutionary régime which, largely through its own unaided efforts, had raised itself to the status of a major industrial Power, made it the natural leader of a revolt of the backward countries against the world-wide domination of western capitalism, which before 1914 had been virtually uncontested; and in this context the blots which tarnished its credentials in western eyes seemed irrelevant. Through the revolt of the backward non-capitalist world, the revolution presented a renewed challenge to the capitalist Powers, the potency of which is not yet exhausted. The Russian revolution of 1917 fell far short of the aims which it set for itself, and of the hopes which it generated. Its record was flawed and ambiguous. But it has been the source of more profound and more lasting repercussions throughout the world than any other historical event of modern times.

# Index

Agriculture: and socialization of land, 21,
161; early failures, 22–3; and NEP,
30–1, 36, 59, 107, 139, 161; and
famines, 36, 50; prices, 53, 56, 58, 77,
79, 127; and industry, 76, 123, 139;
taxation, 78–9, 151; and planning,
107–9; crisis in, 115; cooperatives, 123,
129; and collectivization, 124, 129–30,
154–62; methods, 128–9, 161;
mechanization, 130, 146–7, 149, 154,
161; and Five-Year Plan, 148–9, 156;
shortage of skilled personnel in, 160;
see also Grain; Kolkhozy; Peasants;
Sovkhozy
All-Russian Association of Proletarian
Writers (VAPP), 120
All-Russian Central Executive Committee
(VTsIK), 38–9
All-Russian Congress of Soviets (of
Workers' and Soldiers' Deputies), 4–6,
8–9, 35, 38
All-Russian Congress of Trade Unions, 26
All-Russian Cooperative Society (Arcos),
43, 93–4, 103
All-Union Communist League of Youth
(Komsomol), 67
All-Union Communist Party (Bolsheviks):
named, 14; and Comintern, 15, 88;
organization, discipline and authority,
34, 39, 41–2, 61, 119–20; Left
opposition in, 34–5; purge, 61; workers'
representation, 68; membership, 68–70,
169; Right opposition in, 127, 165

Central Committee: October 1917
meeting, 5; and Brest-Litovsk, 10;
expulsions from, 34, 118; authority
and organization, 41–2, 61–3; and
economic policy, 57; Lenin on, 62;
conflict with Trotsky, 65–7, 73, 75;
industrial policy, 78, 140; supports
planning principle, 110; and united
opposition, 115–17; Trotsky and
Zinoviev removed from, 118; and
discipline, 119; and writers, 120;
peasant policy, 124–5; and grain
crisis, 127; and Five-Year Plan, 144;
and Sovkhozy, 154; and
collectivization, 156, 158; and Right
opposition, 166–8
Central Control Commission, 117
Orgburo, 42
Politburo: formed, 42; and unions, 53,
137; and scissors committee, 58;
Trotsky and, 66, 72, 116, 118; and
socialism in one country, 75; and
united opposition, 118; and wage
agreements, 134; doubts on
industrialization, 139, 165; and
Five-Year Plan, 144–5;
collectivization commission, 157–8;
on elimination of *kulaks*, 158; and
Right opposition, 166–8
Secretariat, 42, 61
Conferences: 1921, 56; 1924, 108; 1925,
75, 78–9; 1926, 116, 119, 123, 141;
1929, 141, 145

Congresses: 7th (1918), 14, 25; 8th
(1919), 42; 9th (1920), 27; 10th
(1921), 28, 32–4, 37, 43, 50, 53, 61,
65, 116, 119; 11th (1922), 61, 70;
12th (1923), 55–6, 63–5; 13th (1924),
59, 71–2; 14th (1925), 82–3, 109,
111, 115, 131, 141; 15th (1927), 115,
117–18, 124, 143–4, 162
American Communist Party, 47, 180–1
American Federation of Labour, 176
American Relief Administration, 36
Amtorg, 94
Andreev, A., 53
Anglo-Russian Trade Union Committee,
92–3, 177
Anglo-Soviet Trade Agreement (1921),
43–4, 47, 84–5
Anti-Fascist Congress (Berlin, 1929), 180
Armenian Soviet Republic, 14, 39–40
Averbakh, L., 120
Azerbaijan Soviet Republic, 39–40

Baldwin, Stanley, 93
Baltic republics, 14, 173
Belorussian Soviet Republic, 14, 39–40
Bismarck, O. von, 87
"Bloody Sunday" (1905), 2
Blyukher, V. (*alias* Galin), 100, 183
Bokhara, 41
Bolshevik Party, 2–9, 20, 26, 34–6; *see
also* All-Union Communist Party
(Bolsheviks)
*Bol'shevik* (journal), 80, 117, 166
Borodin, M., 97–8, 100–3
Brandler, H., 84
Brest-Litovsk treaty (1918), 10–11, 16, 20,
25, 31, 35, 42–3
Briand, A., 87
Bukharin, N.: on Provisional
Government, 7; and revolutionary war,
10; leads left opposition, 25; on
industrial decline, 29; and role of
unions, 33; Lenin on, 62; opposes
Trotsky, 67, 74; on socialism in one
country, 75; and peasant policy, 77–8,
81–2, 113, 115, 125–6, 129; conflict
with Zinoviev, 81–3; opposes
industrialization, 112, 139–40, 143–4,
165; on literary schools, 120; "Notes of
an Economist", 139, 144, 166; leads
Right opposition, 164–7, 179; downfall
167–8, 178; and foreign affairs, 179

Canton, 98–101, 181

Central Executive Committee (TsIK),
40–1
Central Institute of Labour (TsIT), 33, 133
Chamberlain, Austen, 86–7
Chang Hsüeh-liang, 181
Chang Tso-lin, 99–100, 103, 173, 181
Changsha, 103
Cheka *see* Extraordinary Commission
Ch'en Tu-hsiu, 183
Chiang Kai-shek, 97–8, 100–3, 116, 181–3
Chicherin, G., 46, 49, 96, 175
China, Soviet relations with, 96–9, 116–17,
173, 181–4, 190; nationalist movements,
96–101, 190; internal conflicts, 99–103;
peasants in, 102; at 1924 Pacific
Workers Conference, 104
Chinese Communist Party, 98, 102–3, 177,
181, 183–4
Chinese Eastern Railway (CER), 99–100,
104, 182–3
Chu Teh, 181
Churchill, Winston, 16
Comintern *see under* Internationals
Communist Party of Great Britain, and
Labour Party, 16–17, 91–2, 98, 179;
formed, 17, 90; exhorted by Comintern,
47; and Trotsky, 80; and "Zinoviev
letter", 85; membership, 90, 181;
leadership changes, 180
Communist Saturdays, 27, 133
Congress of Peoples of the East, 95–6
Congresses of Soviets of the USSR, 40, 68,
119, 140, 144
Constituent Assembly, 6–7, 34
Cooper, H., 145–6
Cooperatives, 24, 52, 123, 129
Council of Nationalities, 41
Council of People's Commissars
(Sovnarkom): of RSFSR, 39; of USSR,
6, 40
Council of the Union, 41
Councils of National Economy
(Sovnarkhozy), 51
Currency, 55–6, 59, 124, 149–51
Curzon, Lord, 49, 84
Czechoslovakia, 11, 91, 181

Dawes Plan (1924), 86
Declaration of Rights of the Toiling and
Exploited People, 9, 38
"Declaration of the 83", 116
Denikin, A., 13, 27
Disarmament, 174
Dnepropetrovsk, 146

Dneprostroi dam, 112, 145–6, 148, 177
Dzerzhinsky, F., 59, 63, 112

Eastman, M., 80
Egypt, 105
Enver Pasha, 96
Estonia, 43, 175
Extraordinary Commission (Cheka), 20,
    27, 40, 121–2; *see also* Unified State
    Political Organization (OGPU)

Feng Yü-hsiang, 99–100, 103
Finland, 173
Fischer, Ruth, 89
Five-Year Plan, formulated, 110, 131,
    138, 140–2; drafts, 142–4; adopted,
    145, 152; industrial effects, 145–8; and
    agriculture, 148–9; and productivity,
    151; as model, 152
Ford Motor Co., 146
Formosa, 104
France, and First World War, 6, 10;
    1918 military intervention, 11–12;
    opposes 1922 Genoa conference, 46;
    occupies Ruhr, 84; recognizes USSR,
    85–6, 173; trade unions in, 91; at
    Pacific Workers' Conference, 104
French Communist Party (PCF), 18,
    180–1
French Socialist Party, 16, 18
Friends of the Soviet Union, 90, 180
Frunze, M., 73

Georgian Soviet Republic, 14, 39–40, 63
German Communist Party (KPD), and
    creation of Comintern, 14; at 2nd
    Comintern congress, 16; and SPD, 18,
    179; "March action" (1921), 44, 47;
    1923 *coup* planned, 84; at 5th
    Comintern congress, 88; leadership
    changes, 89; and trade unions, 91, 101;
    internal dissent, 180
German Independent Social-Democratic
    Party (USPD), 16, 18
German Social Democratic Party (SPD),
    16, 18, 87, 179
Germany, and First World War, 6–7, 10;
    and Brest-Litovsk, 10–11; defeat,
    12–13; 1921 "March action", 19, 44,
    47, 84; Soviet relations with, 44–5,
    85–8, 173; military collaboration with,
    45, 87, 147; 1922 Rapallo treaty, 46;
    and French occupation of Ruhr, 84;
    Dawes plan on reparations, 86; and

Locarno treaty, 86, 88, 173; admitted
    to League of Nations, 86, 173; 1925
    trade agreement with, 87; 1927 treaty
    with, 87; unions in, 91; and dis-
    armament, 174; industrial exports to
    USSR, 176; Lenin on State capitalism
    in, 186
*Glavki*, 23, 51, 54
Grain: production and supply, 23, 31, 76,
    79, 149, 153, 160–2; surpluses, 36, 79,
    123; collection and marketing, 79, 81,
    93, 109, 123–7, 129, 131, 149, 153, 161,
    165; peasant holdings of, 123–5;
    imported, 125; prices, 127, 137; quotas,
    153; and forced collectivization, 156
Great Britain: and First World War, 6,
    10; 1918 military intervention, 11–12,
    16; 1921 trade agreement with, 43–4,
    47, 84–5; and Soviet debts, 46;
    intervention in Turkey, 48; 1923
    government change, 84; relations with
    USSR, 85, 87, 93, 175; trade unions in,
    90–3; communist MPs elected, 91–2;
    1926 general strike, 92–3, 175; severs
    relations with USSR, 93, 173;
    imperialism, 95–7; and China, 97–8,
    102; at Pacific Workers' Conference,
    104; and India, 105; Litvinov and, 175;
    trade with USSR, 175–6; 1929 Labour
    government, 176; resumes relations with
    USSR, 176; *see also* Communist Party
    of Great Britain; Labour Party
Groman, V., 142

Hankow *see* Wuhan
Harriman Manganese Co., 94
Henderson, A., 16, 91
Herriot, E., 85
Herzen, A., 129
Hitler, A., 179
Hungary, 12, 14

IKKI *see under* Internationals
India, 84, 104–5, 179
Indonesia, 104–5, 179
Industry: nationalization of, 21, 29, 50–1;
    and war communism, 23–5, 29;
    production, 29, 53, 58, 78, 108, 111, 113,
    141–2, 144–5, 150–1; centralization
    policy, 30; and NEP, 32, 36–7, 50–1,
    55; Lenin on, 33, 51; control of, 51;
    prices, 53, 56, 58, 137–9; management,
    54, 113, 132; investment, 59, 78–9, 111,

140, 142, 145–6, 148, 150; and foreign trade, 59; and socialism in one country, 76; growth of, 78–9; Bukharin on, 82, 126; and planning, 106–12, 114–15, 123, 126, 134–5, 138, 141; rationaliza-tion, 113, 133; and peasants, 131–2, 138–9; forced development, 131–3, 139; and Five-Year Plan, 141–50; location of, 147–8; credit and profits, 150–1; *see also* Labour
Institute of Red Professors, 165
International Class War Prisoners' Aid, 90
International Federation of Trade Unions (IFTU; Amsterdam International), 91–2
International Workers' Aid, 90
Internationals
  Second (Social Democratic), 13–15
  Third, Communist (Comintern): formed, 13–15, 95, 189; and foreign parties, 15–18, 47, 88, 180, 189; incompatibility with Narkomindel, 44, 88; supports KPD rising, 44; supports united front, 90–1; and colonialism, 95; and China, 98, 183–4; and Pacific workers, 104; Trotsky criticizes, 164; turns to Left, 177–8, 180;
    Congresses: 1st (1919), 14, 95; 2nd (1920), 16–17, 46–7, 91, 95; 3rd (1921), 46–8; 4th (1922), 14; 5th (1924), 88–9; 6th (1928), 89, 164, 166, 178
    Executive Committee (IKKI), 14, 47, 67, 89, 116, 118, 168
Italian Communist Party (PCI), 18
Italian Socialist Party, 16, 18
Italy, 12, 85

Japan, 12, 96–7, 104–5, 173
Japanese Communist Party, 104–5
Joffe, A., 97

Kadet Party, 1–2, 35
Kaganovich, L., 167
Kalinin, M., 83
Kamenev, L.: and Provisional Govern-ment, 3; and October revolution, 5, 73; proposes Sovnarkom, 6; and internal trade, 59; Lenin on, 62; opposes Trotsky, 64–7, 72–3, 115; on Lenin, 71; and socialism in one country, 75; peasant policy, 81; in struggle with

Stalin, 82–3, 109; supports industrial-ization, 115; in united opposition, 115–16, 165; dropped from central committee, 118; banishment, 119; recantation, 163; and Bukharin, 164, 166–7
Karakhan, L., 99
Kellogg pact, 174–5, 178
Kemal Ataturk, 48
Kerensky, A., 5
Khorezm, 41
*Khozraschet*, 51, 55
Kirov, S., 83
Kolarov, V., 88
Kolchak, A., 13, 27
Kolkhoztsentr, 130
Kolkhozy (collective farms): formed, 22–3, 129–30, 165; harvests, 153; and Sovkhozy, 154–5; and grain collection, 156; and collectivization, 156–161; large, 158–160; *see also* Sovkhozy
Kollontai, A., 31
Komsomol *see* All-Union Communist League of Youth
Kopp, V., 45
Korea, 104
Kornilov, L., 5
Krasin, L., 43, 45–6, 52, 59
Kronstadt, 32, 44, 70
Krupskaya, N., 63, 72, 83
Krzhizhanovsky, G., 145
Kuibyshev, V., 62, 112, 118, 126, 140, 142, 145
*Kulaks*: expropriated, 21; classification of, 22; dominance, 36, 60; indulgence towards, 59, 78, 116; profits, 77; denounced, 81–2, 124, 157–8; and grain hoarding, 125, 153–4; conservatism, 130; and forced collectivization, 155–7; offensive against, 158–60; *see also* Peasants
Kuomintang, 97–9, 101–2, 104, 177, 181

Labour: and productivity, 26, 113, 133–5, 142, 151; compulsory drafting of, 27, 29, 53, 135; Trotsky on, 27–8, 33, 53, 67; NEP and, 33; unemployment, 53, 55, 108, 152; and scissors crisis, 58; supply, 108; training, 133; incentives and system, 133–4; peasant recruits, 136; industrial numbers, 142; *see also* Trade unions, Wages
Labour Party (British), 16–17, 85, 90–2, 98, 176, 183

Latin America, 179
Latvia, 175
Law, 121–2
League against Imperialism, 90, 179
League of Nations, 86, 173–4
Lenin, V. I.: and Social-Democratic
Workers' Party, 2; 1917 arrival in
Petrograd, 3, 73, 185; 1917 "April
theses", 4, 73–4, 185; on state, 4–5, 69;
*State and Revolution*, 4–5, 69; and 1917
October revolution, 6–7, 73, 185–7;
and peace with Germany, 10; founds
Comintern, 13–14; 4th Comintern
congress, 14; at 2nd Comintern
congress, 16, 91; *The Infantile Disease
of "Leftism" in Communism*, 16–17;
assassination attempts on, 20, 35; and
peasants, 22–3; and supply shortages,
25; and labour, 27–8; introduces NEP
at 10th Party congress, 32–3, 37, 43, 50,
52; on industry, 33, 51; on party
discipline, 34, 61; on dictatorship of
party, 34; as decision-maker, 42; on
foreign relations, 43; on relations with
Germany, 44; on 1922 Genoa
conference, 45; at 3rd Comintern
congress, 47–8; health, 48, 61–2; on
freedom of trade, 52; death, 58, 67–8,
71; "testament", 61–3, 71–3, 80, 116;
and Stalin, 62–3, 172; on Party
machinery, 62–3; on Georgian question,
63; and Party enrolment, 68–71, 169;
Stalin extols, 71, 76, 169; Trotsky on,
72–3; disagreements with Trotsky,
74–5, 81, 116; denounces *kulaks*, 81; on
imperialism, 95, 190; on China, 96; on
monopoly capitalism, 106, 186; on
electrification, 107, 145; on tractors,
130; denounces anti-semitism, 170; and
Chicherin, 175; on democratic
dictatorship, 187; on international
revolution, 189–90
Leningrad (Petrograd; St Petersburg), 20,
24, 68, 82–3, 121, 127; *see also*
Petersburg Soviet
*Leningradskaya Pravda*, 82–3, 117
Lithuania, 175
Litvinov, M., 43, 46, 174–5, 178
Lloyd George, D., 16, 45–6, 84
Locarno treaty (1925), 86, 88, 179
Lozovsky, A., 104

Magnitogorsk, 148
Manchuria, 99, 104, 173, 182

Mao Tse-tung, 102, 181, 184
Martov, Yu., 2
Marx, K., historical scheme, 2; Lenin
expounds, 4–5; on revolution, 75,
185–7, 189; on capitalist accumulation,
77; and East, 95; and planned economy,
106; on peasant *mirs*, 129; on capitalist
collapse, 152; rejects nationalism, 170
Maslow, A., 89
Menshevik Party, 2, 4, 14, 20, 26, 34–6,
39, 116, 132
Mikoyan, A., 83
Molotov, V., 62, 70, 83, 124, 126, 156–8,
167–8
Mongolian People's Republic, 97, 99
Moscow: 1917 Soviet, 5; as capital, 11;
unrest in, 20; population losses, 24; 1918
disorders, 35; trading in, 52; and
leadership struggle, 82; bread supply,
127
Münzenberg, W., 179
Mussolini, B., 85

*Narodnik* movement, 1
National Minority Movement (NMM),
91–2
National Unemployed Workers
Movement (NUWM), 91–2
Negroes, 90
Nepmen, 52, 57, 60, 138
New Economic Policy (NEP): introduced,
19, 28–9, 32–5, 43; and foreign policy,
19, 47, 84; rejects war communism,
30–1, 37; and centralization, 38; Lenin
explains, 47; and link with peasants, 47,
50, 56, 77, 79, 81, 109, 139, 152, 161;
and freedom of trade, 52–3, 112, 128;
and management, 54; and unemployment, 55; success of, 59–60; Trotsky
criticizes, 66; and socialism in one
country, 76; Zinoviev on, 81;
commitment to, 107; and planning, 108,
111, 114; and civil law, 121; and food
supplies, 128; and labour, 135–6
*New York Times*, 116

Ordzhonikidze, S., 63
Outer Mongolia, 97, 99

Pacific Transport Workers' Conference
(1924), 104
*Pacific Worker*, 104

Palestine, 105
Pan-Pacific Seccetariat, 104
Peasants: and Social-Revolutionary Party,
1; in 1905 revolution, 2; and 1917 land
decree, 6; and All-Russian Congress of
Soviets, 8; disturbances (1920–21), 19,
31; take over land, 21–2; committees of
poor peasants, 21–2; classification of,
22, 116; and shortages, 23, 25;
opposition from, 28; and war
communism, 30–1; and NEP, 32, 36–7,
47, 50, 55, 58, 77, 79, 109, 139, 152;
and grain supply, 76–7, 79, 123–5, 129,
131, 153–4; changing policies towards,
77–8, 81, 162; and planning, 113, 131,
149, 161–2; extraordinary measures
against, 125–6, 144; land holdings and
farming methods, 128–9, 160;
conservatism, 130; and industrialization,
131–2, 136–7, 139; and Five-Year Plan,
143, 149, 152; and collectivization,
154–5, 158–62, 188; and 1917
revolution, 185, 188; *see also Kulaks*
People's Commissariat of Agriculture
(Narkomzem), 108–9, 113, 132, 142
People's Commissariat of Finance
(Narkomfin), 108, 113, 132, 142, 149–51
People's Commissariat of Foreign Affairs
(Narkomindel), 44, 88, 178
People's Commissariat of Internal Trade
(Narkomtorg), 59
People's Commissariat of Justice
(Narkomyust), 121
People's Commissariat of Labour
(Narkomtrud), 26, 137
People's Commissariat of Supply
(Narkomprod), 21–2, 24
Persia, 47–8, 84, 105, 175
Peter the Great, 172
Petersburg Soviet of Workers' Deputies,
2–3, 5–8; *see also* Leningrad
Petrograd *see* Leningrad
Philippines, 104
Pilsudski, J., 16–18, 93, 173
"Platform of the 46", 57, 65
Plekhanov, G., 2
Poincaré, R., 84
Poland, 16–19, 28, 43–4, 87, 93, 173, 175
Polish Communist Party, 180
Pollitt, H., 180
*Pravda*, 57, 65–7, 82, 117, 139, 156, 165,
167–8
Preobrazhensky, E., 62, 66, 77–8, 164
Prices, 52–3, 55–9, 77, 79, 108, 137–8,
142, 151

Provisional Government (1917), 2–8, 20
Pyatakov, Yu., 67, 150

Radek, K., 14, 17, 25, 66–7, 164
Rakovsky, Kh., 118, 164, 173
Rapallo treaty (1922), 46, 86–7
Rathenau, W., 46
Red Army: formed, 11; in civil war, 13,
18; invades Poland, 16–19; and supply
shortages, 24–5; and Kronstadt revolt,
32; and German military collaboration,
45; officers, 54; party members in, 69;
strengthened, 74; and peasants, 125;
rearmament, 147; and China, 182–3
Red Guard, 5, 8, 11
Red International of Trade Unions
(Profintern; RILU), 91, 104
Revolutions: 1905, 2; Feb. 1917, 2–3;
Oct. 1917, 1, 5–8, 185–91; 10th
anniversary of, 90, 118, 122, 133, 180;
50th anniversary, 188
Right opposition ("deviation"), 127, 145,
165–7, 177, 179
Rumania, 173, 175
Russian Communist Party *see* All-Union
Communist Party (Bolsheviks)
Russian Socialist Federal Soviet Republic
(RSFSR), 38–41, 121
Rykov, A., 83, 125, 139, 145, 165–6, 168
Ryskulov, T., 158

Seeckt, H. von, 45, 85
Shevchenko Sovkhoz, 154
Shlyapnikov, A., 31
Siberia, 12–13, 112, 147–8, 155
Snowden, P., 16
Social-Democratic Workers' Party
(Russian), 2, 14
Social-Revolutionary (SR) Party,
1–2, 4, 6–7, 34–6, 132
"Social-Fascism," 178–9
Socialism in one country, 74–6, 81, 89,
116, 164, 170, 189
Sokolnikov, G., 109
South Manchurian Railway, 104
Soviets, 3–5, 7–8, 20, 26
Sovkhozy, 23, 129–30, 153–6, 159, 161,
165; *see also* Kolkhozy
Soyuzkhleb, 126
Stalin, I. V., and Provisional Government,
3; opposes Pilsudski, 17; and party
machinery, 42; appointed general
secretary of party, 62, 68, 168; Lenin
on, 62–3, 172; opposes Trotsky, 62–7;

and Georgian dissidents, 63; and Lenin succession, 64, 68, 71; and party membership, 69–70; extols Lenin, 71, 76; opposes Trotsky's expulsion, 72–3; and socialism in one country, 74–6, 170; rise to power, 76, 79–80, 83, 115, 163, 168; and peasant policy, 77–8, 82, 124, 126, 163; Zinoviev attacks, 81–2; at 14th party congress, 82–3, 115; attends 5th Comintern congress, 89; favoured in the west, 90; attacks Sokolnikov on agrarian policy, 109; on industrialization, 112, 126, 140, 163; united opposition attacks, 115–18, 163–4; and literary controls, 120; and grain stocks, 125; and Five-Year Plan, 144; on Sovkhozy, 154; on collectivization, 156, 160–1; attacks *kulaks*, 158; dominance, 164–5, 168–9, 171–2; defeats Bukharin and Right opposition, 166–8, 177; 50th birthday, 168–70, 172; character, régime and doctrines, 169–71, 187–8; prefers Litvinov to Chicherin, 175; and American CP leadership, 180
State Bank (Gosbank), 56, 150–1
State Commission for the Electrification of Russia (GOELRO), 107, 145
State Planning Commission (Gosplan), 58, 66, 107–11, 132, 141–4, 150
State Political Administration (GPU), 40, 121; *see also* Unified State Political Administration (OGPU)
State Universal Store (GUM), 52
Stolypin, P., 21, 78
Stresemann, G., 85, 87
Strumilin, S., 142
Sun Ch'uan-fang, 102
Sun Yat-sen, 96–8
*Sunday Worker*, 80
Supreme Council of National Economy (Vesenkha): and nationalization, 21; and state farms, 23; and "war communism", 23; and productivity, 26; control of industry, 51; and GUM, 52; Dzerzhinsky as president of, 59; and industrial growth, 79, 140, 150; and planning policy, 108, 110, 112; and wage agreements, 134–5; and Five-Year Plan, 142–4; and financial control, 150
Supreme Court of USSR, 121
Sverdlovsk, 148

Taxation, 78–9, 151

"Taylorism", 25, 133
Thälmann, E., 180
Thorez, M., 180
Tomsky, M.: as trade union president, 53–4, 136; and Zinoviev, 83; attends British TUC, 92; and peasants and industrial policy, 125, 139, 166; in Right opposition to Stalin, 165–6; disgraced, 166–8
Tractors, 130, 146, 149, 154–5, 158, 160–2
Trade union congresses (USSR), 54, 92, 166
Trade unions: Menshevik control of, 20, 26; relation to state, 26–8, 33, 53–4, 135–6; Trotsky on, 27–8, 33, 53; at 10th party congress, 53; foreign, 91; and wages, 134–5; and productivity, 135–6; rôle and responsibilities, 135–7; and industrialization, 166–7; *see also* Labour; Wages; *also* names of individual countries
Trades Union Congress (British), 92–3
Traktortsentr, 154
Transcaucasian Socialist Federal Republic, 40
Trans-Siberian Railway, 182
Trotsky, L. D.: in October revolution, 5; on world revolution, 9, 47; and German peace treaty, 10; organizes Red Army, 11; at 1st Comintern congress, 14; opposes Pilsudski, 17; on labour and unions, 27–8, 33, 53, 67; favours agreement with Germany, 44; on scissors crisis, 56–8, 65; Lenin on relations with Stalin, 62–3; status, 64; in leadership crisis, 64–7; ill-health, 65–7, 73; 1924 open letter, 66–8; denounced, 67, 72–3, 80, 83, 143; at 13th Party congress, 72; on Lenin, 72–4; demotion, 73, 80; on permanent revolution, 74–5; and Eastman, 80; KPD Rightists support, 89; attends 5th Comintern congress, 89; and foreign parties, 90; on planning, 107; favours industrialization, 112, 139, 143; attacks on Stalin, 115, 118, 163–5; dismissed from Politburo, 116; expelled from Party, 117–18, 163; removed from posts, 118, 143; exile and deportation, 119; sent to Turkey, 164; final banishment, 165; Ch'en supports, 183
Tukhachevsky, M., 17
Turkey, 47–9, 85, 87, 105, 164, 174–5
Turkish Communist Party, 48

Turkmen Socialist Soviet Republic, 41
Turksib railway, 112, 147

*Udarniki* (shock workers), 27
Ukraine, 10–11, 13–14, 16, 39, 148
Unified State Political Administration
(OGPU), 40, 117, 121; *see also* State
Political Administration
Union of Soviet Socialist Republics, 40
United front, 47, 90–1, 97, 117, 177–9
United opposition, 115–19, 123, 131,
137–8, 142–4, 163–4, 166
United States of America: and Brest
Litovsk Treaty, 10; 1918 military
intervention, 11–12; famine aid from,
36; and Dawes plan, 86; investment in
Europe, 89; refuses recognition to
USSR, 93–4; trade with, 94;
imperialism opposed, 97; at Pacific
Workers' Conference, 104; supplies
tractors, 130; technical aid from, 146,
176–7; competition with Britain,
175–6; relations with, 176–7; negroes
in, 90; *see also* American Communist
Party
Ustryalov, N., 81
Uzbek Socialist Soviet Republic, 41

Versailles treaty, 44–5, 86, 174
Voroshilov, K., 83

Wages, 53, 55–6, 58, 112, 133–5
Wang Ching-wei, 98

War communism, 21, 23–5, 27–8, 30–1,
36–7, 42, 50, 52–3, 125–6
Witte, S., 106
Workers' and Peasants' Government
(1917–18), 6–9, 12, 20
Workers' Group, 55
Workers' Opposition, 31–4, 61, 88
World Economic Conference (Geneva,
1927), 174
Wrangel, P., 18
Wu Pei-fu, 99–101
Wuhan (*formerly* Hankow), 101–3

Yudenich, N., 13

Zaporozhie, 146, 148
Zetkin, K., 88
Zinoviev, G., and 1917 revolution, 5, 73;
elected IKKI president, 14; on trade
unions' role, 26; supports KPD rising,
44; on heavy industry, 59, 112; Lenin
on, 62; opposes Trotsky, 64–7, 115;
and Lenin succession, 68; on Lenin,
71; at 13th Party congress, 72; and
socialism in one country, 75, 81;
peasant policy, 77, 81; conflict with
Stalin, 81–2; attacked and demoted,
83, 109; on Bolshevization of foreign
parties, 89–90; supports industrialization policy, 115; in united opposition,
115–16, 165; expelled from Party,
117–18; removed from central
committee, 118, 143; banishment, 119;
recantation, 163
"Zinoviev letter", 85, 92